POLITICS in
NEW YORK STATE 1800-1830

Alvin Kass

How DID "Jacksonian Democracy" develop in New York in the early decades of the nineteenth century? Did it evolve from a tug of war between conservatives and liberals? On the contrary, Mr. Kass maintains in this fresh analysis of the period, expediency determined New York's politics, and the democratic reforms popularly credited to Jackson had been achieved before he came to power.

Through a case study of Martin Van Buren the author illustrates the conflict between principles and opportunism in politics, revaluating the importance of economics and ideology, considered paramount by earlier historians such as Dixon Ryan Fox. He develops the idea that power is more appealing to most men than wealth or ideas. Party lines in Van Buren's day were indistinct and politicians opportunistic; to further their own careers they would even switch from one faction to another overnight — anything to win!

After presenting a brief history of the Empire State, the author explores "how politics works." He examines the nature, functions, and interrelationships of political parties within early nineteenth-century New York and analyzes the idea of party membership. He also discusses the emergence of political machines during this period when New York became a virtually complete equal-rights democracy, achieving wider suffrage, more frequent elections, and greater popular control than enjoyed earlier.

Unlike other studies of this period, which by and large direct attention to the national scene, the focus of this volume is local. The author contends, and ably demonstrates throughout the book, that local interests rather than national or international events shaped politics. Mr. Kass briefly compares New York's experience with that of other states, relating his findings to his central thesis about the evolu

Among the more important collections the author has consulted are the De Witt Clinton Papers, the Martin Van Buren Papers, the Stephen Van Rensselaer Papers, and the Azariah C. Flagg Papers. He provides ample notes, a bibliographic essay, a glossary, and an index.

ALVIN KASS, a teacher and rabbi, received his education at Columbia University and the Jewish Theological Seminary and has taught history at both institutions. He holds the rank of Captain in the United States Air Force Reserve. A member of Phi Beta Kappa, the author was a Woodrow Wilson Fellow and has received many other academic awards.

POLITICS IN
NEW YORK STATE, 1800–1830

CE

Politics in
New York State
1800-1830

☆

ALVIN KASS

SYRACUSE UNIVERSITY PRESS 1965

497695

This work has been published
with the assistance of a Ford Foundation grant.

Manufactured in the United States of America

for

Mother and Father

CONTENTS

PREFACE

The present volume is an analytical study of politics in the state of New York between 1800 and 1830. This period, which stretches from the age of Jefferson to the ascendancy of Andrew Jackson, is one of the most neglected in American history. Moreover, what little has been written concerning this so-called Era of Good Feelings has taken the national government as its principal focus. The crucial events of the time, however, were occurring on the local and state scene. Hence, the most significant findings can be uncovered from a study of the individual states. My examination of the structure of political life in the Empire State during its crucial and formative stages is intended to fill partially this gap in our knowledge of the past.

It begins with a brief background of New York state history and a statement of my basic assumptions about how politics works, assumptions that unquestionably influence judgments throughout the volume. An attempt is then made to examine the nature, functions, and interrelationships of political parties within the Empire State, along with an analysis of the concept of party membership. Among the important developments of the time was the emergence of political machines which evolved effective techniques designed to control the behavior of party members and the public life of the state.

A federalist system of government such as exists in the United States implies the existence of multiple centers of political power. Although the national government is the preeminent focus of politics in the twentieth century, this study attempts to show that the direction of events a hundred and fifty years ago came, not from the administration in Washington, but from the local potentates, the masterminds of political strategy and intrigue within the states. The populace also was more profoundly concerned with the maneuvers of state rather than national politics. State politicians, moreover, created institutional mechanisms to maintain contact with and occasionally domination over local and national governmental organs.

One of the most significant phenomena during the interim between Jefferson and Jackson was the evolution of democracy. Democracy, of course, is a relative term. There are different degrees of democracy, ranging from the almost literal rule of the people in a tiny Swiss canton to the more common representative democracy that is found in larger political units such as the state or nation. Within the classification of "representative democracies," there can and does exist a tremendous variety of qualifications for both the people who choose their leaders and the leaders themselves. Whatever laws or institutions increase the control of the people over the government should be regarded as democratic changes. From this point of view, New York became a virtually complete equal-rights democracy during this period. Among the most significant democratic innovations of this era were almost total manhood suffrage, more frequent elections, greater popular control of the executive and judiciary; in addition, the election of many officials was taken from the assemblies or special councils and put into the hands of the people.

In his classic study, *The Decline of Aristocracy in the Politics of New York* (New York: Columbia University Press, 1919), Dixon Ryan Fox conceives of the development of New York democracy as the outcome of a persistent struggle between conservative or aristocratic forces on the one hand, and liberal or democratic groups on the other. The conservative tradition, Fox believed, was upheld first by the Federalists, then the Clintonians, and finally the Whigs. The equalitarian side was defended initially by the Jeffersonian Republicans and then the Jacksonian Democrats. Although the time span covered by this work is not as extensive as Fox's book, my findings require a serious modification of his essential thesis. Moreover, Lee Benson's volume, *The Concept of Jacksonian Democ-*

racy, New York as a Test Case (Princeton: Princeton University Press, 1961), which concentrates on politics in the Empire State during the 1830's and 1840's, largely confirms my own criticism of Fox's position. For the enactment of democratic reforms in New York was the result of the support of politicians of different parties at different times rather than the victory of a consistently democratic group against an equally consistent conservative group. The two political factions that dominated New York politics during this period, the Clintonians and the Bucktail Republicans, were to be found on one side of the ideological fence virtually as often as on the other.

The development of an equal-rights democracy in this country during the early part of the nineteenth century is most often connected with the rise to power of Andrew Jackson; indeed, the whole phenomenon is popularly referred to as "Jacksonian Democracy."[1] In order to ascertain whether a connection actually exists between these two events in New York, an effort is made in this volume to trace Jackson's ascent to a position of political influence in the Empire State. The evidence indicates that the democratization of the government had taken place *before* Jackson became a figure of political importance to New York. Moreover, his own supporters in the state saw little connection between the Tennessean and the movement for increased popular control of public affairs.

Politics does not operate within a vacuum but is part of the daily, ongoing life of the people. Karl Marx may not have been correct in positing economic factors as the fundamental determinant of social institutions, but they certainly do exert an important influence on the life of the people. Consequently, an effort is made in this book to examine the way economic interests expressed themselves in New York's political life. My estimate of the role of economics in determining the political processes of the Empire State differs quite sharply from that of Dixon Ryan Fox. My evaluation of the extent to which ideology and philosophic commitment affected the reaching of political decisions in New York also diverges from that of Fox and other scholars of the period. A case study of Martin Van Buren is provided in order to demonstrate the conflict between principles and opportunism operating on the political calculations of the important personalities of the era. The study of New York concludes with an examination of the part politics played in the general life of the community.

The developments in the Empire State, important in themselves, take on even deeper significance when viewed within the context of the rest of the Union. Consequently, I have undertaken to compare the major events in New York during this era with what was going on in the other states. Unfortunately, the paucity of state studies on this period poses a grave handicap to any comprehensive attempt at comparative analysis. Nevertheless, even on the basis of the limited materials available, it is possible to make some notable observations about political life, in general, and the evolution of democracy, in particular, in the United States during the eventful years between the presidencies of Thomas Jefferson and Andrew Jackson.

I am grateful for the boundless courtesies extended to me by the Columbia University Library, the New York Public Library, the New York Historical Society, and the Library of Congress during my many visits to these institutions. To my wife, Miryom Arnold Kass, I am deeply indebted not only for her aid in typing the manuscript and in offering helpful criticism, but for the understanding and encouragement that are prerequisites to extended research. I, however, must bear the sole responsibility for any errors in the work.

ALVIN KASS

Rantoul, Illinois
June, 1964

I
INTRODUCTION

New York politics between 1800 and 1830, which helped to create a genuine political democracy in the Empire State, brought to a climax a process that dates back to the earliest days of New York's history as a province of the English king. Since the initial grant of Charles II to his brother, James, the Duke of York, contained no provision for a representative government, many struggles were required to establish the basic institutions of democratic government. Despite a slow start, New York had managed to secure a representative assembly by the end of the seventeenth century. Constant bickering marked relations between the Assembly and Parliament during the eighteenth century, but through control of the province's finances the Assembly managed by 1740 to acquire a position of supremacy in the government of the colony. Soon after the outbreak of the American Revolution, New York adopted a constitution, conservative in nature and rooted in colonial precedents, that served as the fundamental law of the colony for forty-four years. Although the document was far from democratic in many respects, it provided the basic elements of representative government, and was an indispensable prerequisite to the political forays in New York state that bridged the era between Jefferson and Jackson.

An understanding of politics in the Empire State during the early nineteenth century necessitates a clarification of the concept "political democracy." Webster's Dictionary explains "political" as relating to the "science of dealing with the regulation and control of men."[1] According to John

Franklin Carter, that which is political pertains to "the struggle to gain or to hold power."[2] V. O. Key has caught the essence of these definitions in his succinct but revealing explanation of "Politics as Power."[3] The operation of power involves a reciprocal relation between the ruler and his subjects, where the leader is dominant and his followers are subordinate. "Democracy" is a form of power structure that in its most extreme form makes the ruler and the ruled one and the same. Such complete self-government, however, is rarely found; most often, the people select their leaders in a democracy. Although the governing officials may compel the people to obey their decisions, the ultimate source of authority still lies in the people, who can remove overbearing and otherwise undesirable leaders through legally constituted electoral procedures.

Even within the limited category of "political democracy" there are varying degrees of popular participation in the governing process as well as a large variety of structures. Despite the regular appearance of such institutions as political parties, elective representative bodies, publicly chosen leaders, electoral procedures, and nonparty associations and groups[4] there is a multitude of possible variations. Indeed, the state political systems within the United States alone reveal many patterns of action, some of which fit neither the biparty nor the multiparty model. Sometimes, for example, despite the existence of more than one party in the state, the government is dominated by a single political organization that is rarely ousted from office and within whose ranks most of the political competition takes place. There is a wide spectrum of possibilities that separates an uncompromisingly one-party system from genuine bilateral competitiveness.[5]

Realization of the many different degrees of political democracy helps to place in proper perspective the changes that took place in New York between 1800 and 1830. For the state experienced at that time, not a revolution that destroyed all that came before it, but an extension and refinement of institutions that were imbedded in the past. The Constitution of 1777, in complete accordance with the situation prior to the Revolution, gave the state a governor, lieutenant-governor, and popular assembly. It substituted a senate and two new councils known as the Council of Appointment and the Council of Revision respectively for the old colonial councils. Almost no changes were introduced into the state's judicial structure or into the operation of local government. The suffrage requirements under the constitution permitted freeholders or, in effect, 65 to 70 per cent of the men to vote for members of the Assembly, although two-thirds of this group did not fulfill the more stringent demands made on those who wished to cast ballots for the governor and the senators.[6] Most of the reform efforts in the early nineteenth century centered around attempts to enlarge the suffrage as well as make the government more responsive to the people through such measures as reduction of the governor's term, abolition of the Council of Revision, and modification of the appointing system.

The limited and essentially conservative nature of the reform endeavor in the Empire State is also evident from Marvin Meyer's study entitled *The Jacksonian Persuasion* (Stanford: Stanford University Press, 1957). Martin Van Buren's rhetoric echoed constantly the belief that his activities involved no innovations but were designed to achieve a "general resuscitation" for the "old democratic Party."[7] One of his political lieutenants in the Empire State accused James Monroe of "herecy" to the ideals of Jefferson.[8] The ruling coterie of Bucktail politicians over which Van Buren presided required that the "politics of this state" be "governed by Old Party Feelings."[9] De Witt Clinton and his followers also justified their undertakings as faithful attempts to realize the venerable democratic ideals of Thomas Jefferson.[10] And if Leonard W. Levy is right in *Jefferson and Civil Liberties,* (Cambridge: Belknap Press, 1963), Jefferson's ideals were not always the most liberal.

The early history of New York state also helps to illustrate some of the possible variations in democratic political structure. Active biparty competition dominated the political scene in the quarter-century prior to Jefferson's election to the presidency in 1800 as a result of concrete differences over public policy that arose after the ratification of the state constitution of 1777. The story of New York politics at this time is largely a tale of conflict between the two self-conscious groups that emerged, the Federalists and the Antifederalists. After Jefferson's presidential triumph, however, squabbling within the ranks of the Antifederalists soon overshadowed in importance interparty fights, although the Federalists remained a substantial electoral threat to their opponents until 1820. Factions constantly formed and re-formed within the Antifederalist Party throughout this era with seeming caprice and startling rapidity.

Dixon Ryan Fox[11] has explained the political factionalism of this period in terms of a conflict between different economic groups in society, each one of which articulated a point of view consistent with its material well-being. This economic interpretation of New York politics, which follows the general Beard-Hacker approach to the study of American history, seems completely untenable in the light of my findings as well as those of Lee Benson in *The Concept of Jacksonian Democracy*.[12] But, if economics is not necessarily the mainspring of politics, what is? Why do people seek political power? Almost every psychologist will agree that fundamentally every act of human behavior is motivated by the desire to satisfy a biologically determined drive such as hunger, thirst, or sex. Although an individual never loses or outgrows these unlearned needs, the process of adjusting to his environment leads him to reshape them in several ways. One of the most significant of these is the emergence of intermediate goals or means to an end. In our society, for example, the way to satisfy hunger is to acquire money which will buy food. Consequently, the pursuit of money becomes a dominant concern since it is a necessary means to an indispensable end. However, the effort to reach the intermediate goal may become so absorbing that the ultimate goal is temporarily forgotten. Thus, the means to an end becomes an end in itself. Money is only a means to some further end, but the desire for money itself is very strong in many people.

This general explanation of human conduct is also applicable to man's aspirations for political power. Initially, the desire to attain a position of influence may be motivated by the realization that such a position helps satisfy the primary needs of life. However, with the passing of time, a man can become so involved with the pleasures of exercising power that he pursues political activity as an end in itself. Hence, it should not be incomprehensible that a prominent New York leader like De Witt Clinton should have pursued a vigorous career in public life with so little concern for his material well-being that in 1815, after fifteen years in politics, he faced imminent bankruptcy.[13] In order to understand politics, therefore, it is not necessary to attribute conflicting economic aspirations or ideological differences to the opposing factions competing for public office. Men often play the game of politics solely for its own sake without consciously trying to achieve any other objectives.

If it is true that political leaders can be motivated to participate in public life on grounds other than the satisfaction of one of their fundamental biological needs, it is also true that the populace can make its electoral decisions for a number of noneconomic reasons. Again, this is not to deny that voting, initially, like any other human response, must be reinforced by the satisfaction of a basic drive; but after awhile the response can become sufficiently strong to occur even when the specific reinforcement is not forthcoming. For example, an unemployed mechanic might have voted for the Democrats in 1932 with the hope that their economic policies would enable him to earn enough to sustain himself and his hungry family. Now the response of voting Democratic, if carried on for awhile, might become so firmly established that it is made even when no economic benefit follows it. Thus, Lee Benson has shown that ethnic and religious considerations were much more important than economic benefits in determining how New Yorkers voted in the 1830's and the 1840's.[14] Moreover, in the absence of serious divisive issues, subjective whim and apparently irrational caprice can be decisive in determining how a voter casts his ballot. Although Angus Campbell's study of motivational factors in voting and nonvoting indicates that concern about issues can bear significantly on voting, it also shows that purely subjective considerations like a sense of civic duty, habitual party attachment, exposure to political discussion, and group affiliation also affect voting behavior in a crucial way.[15]

Even when a voter is concerned with using politics for economic gain, this may not lead him to follow any single party with consistent loyalty. This was true in nineteenth-century New York, and is very common in our own time as well, since the two major parties differ ever so slightly on many pressing public issues and completely evade certain others. Consequently, a particular candidate, regardless of his party label, may be chosen by a voter because he forthrightly defends a cause which his party either ignores or opposes. As a result, legislative bills on fundamental public issues are rarely passed on strict party lines but through interparty coalitions of like-minded men.

Although political parties in the early history of New York did not represent different social classes or embody a consistent ideological position, they did perform a significant role which they have continued to perform to the present day. They organized the many disparate groups in society into broad coalitions that enabled the people periodically to choose their leaders from a few candidates. The absence of clearly articulated ideological programs, moreover, did not prevent the processes of party competition from advancing important causes such as the development of democracy. For party leaders, in a desire to strengthen their positions, voiced support for ideas that would increase their attractiveness to the voters. Hence, the necessity of appealing to the public for its ballot kept what were essentially opportunistic conglomerations of political leaders responsive to the will of the people. This kind of political structure has been criticized in many quarters for denying to the voter the ability to make a realistic choice at the polls between clearly defined alternatives, as would be the case where parties represented specific social and economic groups. To a large extent this criticism is valid; but it is more than offset by the ability of such inclusive parties to blunt the differences that separate various social groups, forging a more cohesive community. The legitimate problems of small groups that demand political action are then left to solution in the legislature through formation of interparty alliances that fight for the passage of necessary laws.

The political party also served as the chief link between the state and national governments. Indeed, the national party was essentially a collection of state parties. As a result, the vagueness and ambiguity of state party positions were more sharply magnified in the national party which had to contain an even larger number of conflicting elements. This problem is quite evident in the difficulties that confronted Martin Van Buren over the tariff in 1827-28 when he was trying to forge a national organization in support of Andrew Jackson's aspirations for the presidency. To obtain southern backing he had to create an image of himself and Jackson as free traders; on the other hand, Van Buren's constituents at home strongly favored tariff protection. Evasion, inconsistency, and ambiguity were the primary means he employed to keep the party united. His skill in this area is reflected in the observation one listener made on a speech given by Van Buren at a tariff convention in Albany during 1827: "That was a very able speech. . . . On which side of the tariff question was it?"[16] Although this kind of party finds it difficult to take a strong stand on a highly controversial question, it does help to hold people together when antagonisms run high. Indeed, the Democratic Party during the antebellum period was one of the most important unifying forces in the country. Roy Nichols has shown that when the party split in 1860, civil war became almost inevitable.[17]

The student of American political history of the late eighteenth and early nineteenth century quickly learns to turn to the state rather than the national scene for the most significant developments. Living in an age that has curtailed state sovereignty, that has deified nationalism, and in which the national government has such a direct impact on the totality of our lives through numerous institutions from the draft to the income tax, we must be careful not to impose our perspective on the American of the nineteenth century. This early American also lacked the telegraph, the telephone, the radio, and television whereby he could keep in direct and continuous contact with what was transpiring in Washington. Consequently, it was at the local and state level that affairs of government impinged most upon his consciousness. He was, for example, much more concerned about the building of a new road than the promulgation of the Monroe Doctrine. Although New Yorkers during the era between Jefferson and Jackson may have known that they were part of something much larger than their state, it was New York that interested them most, and it was there that most young men who desired a career in public life would have preferred to serve.

Between 1800 and 1830, New York state was a society in flux. Swarms of people moved westward, conquering the problem of inland communication by improved roads, steamboats, canals, and railroads. Towns expanded at a spectacular pace; indeed, New York City became the largest city in the nation by 1815, with a population of 150,000, while Albany's rate of growth after the War of 1812 exceeded that of all other American cities. The emergence of larger centers of population made possible an increase in specialized callings, a more complex economic organization, and the development of industry. These changes, in turn, contributed to severe economic dislocations as manifested in the Panic of 1819. In addition, the increasing popularity of democratic ideology in philosophical thinking, and the evangelical approach to religious attitudes brought about important modifications in the intellectual life of the state. There was also during this period a deepening moral sensitivity that manifested itself in numerous efforts at humanitarian and social reform. All of these occurrences, finally, had far-reaching implications for the political development of the Empire State.

II

THE NEW YORK POLITICAL SYSTEM

"An opposition to a candidate which is abstractly right may be politically wrong. We had better support a man that we believe to be unsound than to oppose him if by so doing we insure success to others equally unsound and at the same time hazard the election of political friends who are worthy of our confidence and whose success is necessary to the triumph of our cause."[1] These comments, made by William L. Marcy, the state adjutant-general in the 1820's and one of the foremost leaders of the Bucktails, reflect the fact that New York's political parties during the pre-Jacksonian era were simply organizations for the nomination of candidates and for the conquest of administrative and political offices. Founded on no ideological or social basis and including heterogeneous doctrines and elements, the parties were held together by the drive for electoral victory. Indeed, the winning of seats in political assemblies was the essence of the party's activity, the very reason of its existence, and the supreme purpose of its life. To insure the continued success of the party at the polls, practical considerations, uncontaminated by principle, almost always determined what sides would be taken on a particular issue. Hence, the Bucktails' opposition in 1824 to the popular choice of presidential electors was fired, not by the abstract principle, but rather by the inexpediency of immediate change. As Edwin Croswell, the crafty editor of the Bucktail paper, the *Albany Argus,* put it: "The danger to the rep[ublican] party lies in the repeal and not in the refusal."[2]

Since the party's efforts were directed almost exclusively toward elections and legislative alliances, it possessed a somewhat seasonal character. For example, a political group known as the Quids came into existence in 1804 to elect Morgan Lewis as governor; after the balloting, however, its name is not mentioned in the newspapers again until 1807 when Lewis was up for re-election. Soon, thereafter, the party disappeared.[3] In similar fashion, the factions that were organized to elect De Witt Clinton as governor in 1817, 1820, and 1824 were completely inactive and ineffective during the periods between the electoral contests. As an election approached, there was a sharp acceleration in the activity of the political organizations and their adjunct, the party press. Thus, in 1825, the *Albany Argus* was completely reticent on the subject of presidential politics; in 1826, while still maintaining a noncommittal posture, it occasionally threw jibes at the Adams administration; in 1827, its attacks became more frequent and acrid, until by the beginning of 1828 it had taken a frank stand in behalf of Andrew Jackson.[4]

Martin Van Buren felt that between elections it was essential to future success that the party exercise extreme caution in its pronouncements. Two years before the federal election of 1824 when agitation regarding that event was beginning to take shape, he advised Charles E. Dudley, the mayor of New York City, that the state ought "to pause before mingling in the fray." He felt that Adams, Crawford, and Calhoun, who were already competing for the nomination, would, if studiously ignored, "sooner or later . . . come to us bearing gifts and promises. With firmness at Albany and prudence at Washington, New York can be placed on higher ground."[5] Rudolph Bunner, one of the authors of the *Bucktail Bards* and a member of congress, knew that despite the Little Magician's reticence, he was "unwilling to let the President be made without having his oar in so goodly a boat."[6] New Hampshire's William Plumer, Jr., speculated that the Bucktails "had come on, in a body, to make their fortunes by joining the strongest party, and that for the present they declared for no one in particular but were waiting and watching the progress of events."[7] Van Buren was convinced that the Empire State would play a significant role in the contest providing that she avoided premature committals and "kept out of the contest as long as that can be done without exposing herself to the danger of distraction at home or subjecting ourselves to the imputation of being governed by selfish motives."[8] Despite the Bucktail decision in behalf of William Crawford's candidacy by the middle of 1823, the *Albany Argus* did not openly support the Georgian until 1824.[9] Clearly, the pace of party activity was regulated by the rhythm of the elections.

In addition to nominating and electing candidates, the party also performed a number of subsidiary functions. The most important of these was to provide unity in a government where so many offices were elective and authority was divided. Perhaps the most noteworthy example of the party maintaining unity is seen in the Bucktail opposition to a bill for the popular choice of presidential electors that came before the state Senate in 1824. Because of strong popular sentiment in behalf of the bill most Bucktail politicians were hesitant about accepting the Regency position against electoral reform. William L. Marcy indicated to Van Buren that many party members in the Senate were troubled by the problem and had "serious apprehensions of its consequences." Indeed, they contended that "there is a demand for it by the great body of the people and that a refusal to yield . . . exposes the party to an overthrow." Moreover, the senators were embarrassed by "indiscreet pledges given before the election" and apprehensive that a failure to comply with their promises would result in De Witt Clinton's restoration to political power.[10] Nevertheless, the leadership of the Bucktail party under Martin Van Buren's tutelage maintained that the success of its presidential candidate, William Crawford, militated against any bill that would empower the people to choose their presidential electors. Consequently, the Regency first induced Governor Yates to speak against any proposed change in the electoral law in his opening address to the legislature on January 6, 1824.[11] On account of the strong public sentiment in behalf of reform the governor could not express open opposition to it, but he achieved the same goal by asking the legislature to withhold action pending the enactment of an amendment to the federal constitution.[12] The proponents of electoral reform, however, were not so easily quieted. A savage debate in the Assembly evoked concrete plans for reform that attracted widespread backing. In an effort to defeat one of the proposals that was passed in the Assembly, the Regency leadership secured the support of most of the Bucktail senators behind a motion of Edward R. Livingston that all action on the Assembly bill be postponed until the first Monday in November. The resolution passed by the count of 17 to 14. The reaction to the resolution was immediate. The seventeen senators who voted for it were denounced as "infamous"; they were hanged or burned in effigy and threatened with defeat at the next election.[13] But to the Albany Regency the behavior of the seventeen senators revealed the organization's success in maintaining unity in its ranks. That all of these men were willing to hazard their own careers for the good of the organization at large is amazing and clear testimony to the party's ability to insure that its adherents behaved in a uniform and unified way on crucial questions.

The skill of the Bucktail organization in controlling the conduct of its officials is also revealed in the behavior of the party during a special session of the legislature in the summer of 1824. The meeting, called by the friends of electoral reform as a final bid to have their proposals enacted into law, elicited the Regency's stout opposition. Immediately after the opening of the session, Azariah Flagg arose to assert his position that nothing had changed since the spring to require this special meeting; consequently, the legislature should adjourn. James Tallmadge and Henry Wheaton proceeded to argue against Flagg's motion, but they were overruled after the Regency-dominated Senate informed the Assembly that the calling of the special session was unconstitutional. After four days of unproductive wrangling, the legislature adjourned on August 6. The behavior of the Bucktails at the extra session makes abundantly evident the Regency's skill in uniting the politicians behind the organization's predetermined course of action.

Another important function of New York's political parties during the early nineteenth century was to superintend the perpetual succession of administrations. Before the Constitutional Convention of 1821, the Council of Appointment played a crucial role in this area of the party's activity. The Council consisted of the governor and one senator chosen annually by the Assembly from each of the four senatorial districts. Since the Constitution of 1777 provided for the appointment of sheriffs, mayors of cities, district attornies, coroners, county treasurers, and all other officers of the state save the governor, lieutenant governor, state treasurer, and town officers, control of this Council represented an inestimable source of power in controlling the political life of the state.

Article XXIII of the constitution directed the governor to be president of the Council and to "have a casting vote, but no other vote; and with the advice and consent of the Council shall appoint all of the said officers." The framers intended that the governor should nominate and the Council confirm, and in the event of a tie the governor should have the casting vote.[14] In practice, however, the governor was subordinated to the Council whenever a majority of that body was politically opposed to him, and the annual election of the Council increased the likelihood of such opposition. In 1795 the Council successfully established the claim that the power of appointment was vested concurrently in the governor and each of the four senators, thus practically stripping the executive of power. The recurrence of this question in 1801 led to a constitutional convention that passed an amendment to the Constitution of 1777, recognizing each senator in the Council as having equal voice with the governor in appointments.[15] This move transformed the Council into a political tool of supreme significance. Under the amendment, all that was required to control all the appointments in the state was to elect a majority of the legislature; conversely, if one controlled all the appointments, he was frequently in a position to elect a majority of the Assembly. Thus, a vicious circle was created, and the Council, which controlled over fifteen thousand appointments by 1821, became a center of corruption. It probably would have been better if the governor himself had borne the responsibility for the appointments.

The operation of the Council of Appointment during the early nineteenth century indicates clearly how the parties and factions that attained political power completely altered the administrative personnel of the state. When the Republicans regained political dominance in New York in 1801, the Federalists found themselves politically proscribed. "In this state, all power and all the offices are also engrossed by the Democrats."[16] Incidentally, De Witt Clinton's Council of Appointment in 1801 did not invent the Spoils System; indeed, they had inherited the practice from the Jay administration which six years before had cleansed the government of all who stood with George Clinton, the Republican governor.[17] Throughout the opening decades of the nineteenth century when the reins of political power passed rapidly from one Republican faction to another, each change resulted in the wholesale removal of old appointees and the subsequent choice of the politically faithful to fill the vacancies. The most extreme instance of this was the behavior of the Bucktail-dominated Council of Appointment of 1820 which was determined to "turn out the whole" of the Clintonians from office.[18] However, they not only ousted their political opponents ruthlessly, but also turned out loyal public servants without any regard for previous achievements. Gideon Hawley, the nonpartisan superintendent of the Common Schools, who had held his post for ten years and was widely recognized as an excellent administrator, was dismissed. Archibald MacIntyre, who had made such a sensation as a trusted and competent comptroller that the "waves of factional and party strife had broken at his feet" for fifteen years, likewise lost his job.[19] Oakley, the gifted attorney-general; Jay, the able recorder for the City of New York; Colden, the popular mayor of that metropolis; all vanished within a day. "Skinner's Council" pursued the military arm of the government as vigorously as the civil. Solomon Van Rensselaer was removed as adjutant-general and numerous commandants were replaced. When the Bucktails had finished, only one Clintonian, Simon De Witt, the state's surveyor general for over forty years, was left in office. Jabez D. Hammond, who witnessed the upheaval, reported that the Council appeared in "every county and removed all or nearly all the sheriffs, clerks, surrogates, judges of the courts of common pleas, and justices of the peace, who were known or suspected to be politically opposed to them."[20] Thousands were hurled into political oblivion from which most of them never returned.

After the Convention of 1821 abolished the Council of Appointment, it became somewhat more difficult for a single political party to control the administrative apparatus of the state. Under the revised constitution, all militia officers with the exception of major generals and adjutant-generals were elected by persons performing military duty; state officers such as the attorney general, the secretary of state, the comptroller, and the surveyor general were appointed by the two houses of the legislature; the adjutant-general and the major generals were chosen by the governor; most other officers, except some in the cities, were decided upon by the governor and the Senate.[21] In addition, the electors of each county chose their own sheriffs and county clerks, although the governor selected the justices of the peace until 1825.[22]

Another important function of New York's political parties was to energize the mass of citizens into political activities. Note, for example, all the arts of the politician that were used in 1828 to sway men's minds and wills. The widely differing backgrounds, sentiments, and points of view of New York's populace necessitated a variety of approaches to win its support. First of all, it was important to stress themes that would win a sympathetic audience. For the most part, the Empire State's numerous mechanics, artisans, and farmers responded warmly to the emphasis on Andrew Jackson's military career and his alleged identification with the causes of democracy, the common man, and reform. The *Albany Argus* hailed Jackson in every issue as the "Soldier Boy of the First War of Independence, The Hero of the Second. He saved the Country. Let the cry be Jackson, Van Buren, and Liberty."[23] In order to attract the Irish vote and that of other immigrant groups the Jacksonians firmly condemned all nativist sentiments. At the heading of a quote from an opposition newspaper which downgraded the Irish contribution to the American character, the *Albany Argus* composed the following caption: "Irishmen, Sons of Erin. Look at what follows, and if you have a drop of true Irish blood in you, let it boil as you read; and remember what you have read when you go to vote."[24] The political managers also used religious arguments to promote their goals. The Jacksonians condemned Adams for his disbelief in the Trinity and Incarnation, and characterized his traveling through New England on the Sabbath as "a shameful violation of the religious feelings and usages of the nation."[25] In regard to Andrew Jackson, Martin Van Buren advised James A. Hamilton, one of his chief lieutenants in New York: "Does the old gentleman have prayers in his own house? If so mention it modestly."[26] Other appeals employed by the New York Jacksonians included the "corrupt bargain" cry; the president's patronage policies; the squandering of public money; and the undemocratic nature of the Panama Mission, the American system, and the subsidizing of the press.[27]

There were other significant techniques employed to attract the political loyalties of the people. Public pronouncements were "coaxed" from some of New York's best-known men of letters.[28] The professional politicians, moreover, used such other accoutrements of their trade as campaign chests, flamboyant oratory, parades, newspapers, and especially designed clothing like hats, buttons, and vests, with Jackson's name or features stamped upon them. Clearly, the political parties of New York in the pre-Jacksonian era performed essential functions in providing unity in the government, supervising the succession of administrations, and exciting the political emotions of the masses.

One of the most striking characteristics of the party and factional organizations that arose in New York is that they were highly personal machines, as had been those of the De Lancy and Livingston factions before the Revolution. The

Yankee Federalist, Theodore Sedgwick, was quite correct when he wrote to Rufus King that the "line of division" by which the parties were separated elsewhere was "more obscurely marked" in New York, and that the people "were more under the domination of personal influence."[29] All of the numerous factions in the Empire State in the pre-Jacksonian period were grouped about notables like George Clinton, Aaron Burr, Morgan Lewis, Daniel D. Tompkins, De Witt Clinton, and Martin Van Buren. Of course, during most of the momentous period of the democratization of New York's political institutions, De Witt Clinton and Martin Van Buren dominated the scene. Clinton and Van Buren provided an interesting contrast in personality and physique. The former was physically impressive, being six feet tall and of such massive dimensions that he acquired the sobriquet of "Magnus Apollo"; the latter, however, was slight in stature, standing only five feet six inches tall, though he walked in erect, soldierly posture and dressed immaculately. In addition, Clinton had an overbearing and tactless manner that diverged sharply from Van Buren's amiable and diplomatic disposition. Yet each had qualities that made him a great leader. Clinton was a man of broad learning, humane ideals, and administrative ability, while Van Buren was a brilliant tactician, keen in his power of analysis and shrewd in his understanding of men. The association of the party organizations with such personalities as these rather than institutions or principles, which are more durable, helps to explain the impermanence of the political factions during this era. For the factions rarely survived the demise of their leaders. Indeed, personality factors influenced the situation so completely that "Clintonianism" or the "Magnus Apollo" himself often became a political issue.

The parties and factions in New York during the early nineteenth century were constantly forming and re-forming; and leadership in state-wide politics tended to be ephemeral. As a result, new factions and leaders continually emerged, rose to power, and disappeared as others took their places. Voters, too, grouped themselves first in one faction, then in another, in confusing fashion. Thus, in 1800, the Clintonian and Livingstonian branches of the Republican Party combined to oust the Burrites from a position of dominance. Five years later, the Livingstons turned on their former allies while the majority of the remaining Burrites rejoined the Clintonians, except for a few disgruntled followers of Burr who sided with the Livingstons. In 1807, Morgan Lewis created a new faction called the Quids, which drew into its ranks discontented Clintonians and Livingstons. In order to destroy the Lewis machine, a group of Republicans under the leadership of Daniel D. Tompkins united with the Clintonians to capture control of the state government. Tompkins' pleasant and congenial manner, combined with his deep concern for the problems of others, made him a popular favorite. For many years he was described fondly as the "farmer's boy." The conflicting ambitions of Tompkins and Clinton, however, led to a break between them in 1812. The next few years saw an additional rupture within the Clintonian ranks when competing aspirations caused the alienation of Martin Van Buren and the formation of the Bucktails. Moreover, during the course of all these maneuvers the Federalists complicated the situation further by their continuous movement in and out of the various factions of the Republican Party in accordance with the dictates of opportunism.[30]

The continual formation, dissolution, and re-formation of parties suggest the connection of a politics without clearly defined issues to the nature of factional organization. When only prestige and patronage are the prizes, political leaders are obstructed by no principle in changing alliances. The mutable politics of New York may also be the consequence in part of the fact that a large percentage of the state's population during the pre-Jacksonian era had been there only a short time, having been transplanted either from New England or the Old World. When New York had ratified her first constitution in 1777 her population was estimated at a little over 190,000.[31] By 1790, the population had increased to 340,000.[32] From 1790 to 1820, however, New York's population rose from 340,000 to 1,300,000, the settlement sweeping to the farthest limits of the state.[33] As a result of this fourfold growth of population within a period of thirty years, individual status was less fixed by family connections and by community accordance than in an old society that projects its structure through generation after generation. In politics, similarly, loyalties had not been built up; nor had traditional habits of action with respect to local personages, leaders, parties, and issues been acquired. As a result, flux, fluidity, and uncertainty in political behavior were the rule.

The conduct of John Syndam, an "able" and "distinguished" member of the New York Senate exemplifies the frequent, rapid, and unpredictable changes in political loyalty that characterized this period. One evening, at a late hour, late in 1820, Syndam visited Jabez D. Hammond, revealing that he had just left a caucus of the Federalist Party at which the main topic of discussion was which gubernatorial candidate the Federalists as a group ought to support at the coming election. Syndam spoke glowingly of De Witt Clinton and expressed his deep hopes that the Magnus Apollo would achieve victory in the balloting. While they were talking, a stagecoach arrived to transport Syndam to Kingston; and in less than a week afterwards, Hammond received a paper in the mail which carried a speech given by Syndam within forty-eight hours after he had left Hammond in which he denounced Clinton in the most strident tones. Hammond goes out of his way, moreover, to stress the fact that Syndam was a man of "unimpeachable integrity and altogether incapable of dissimulation."[34] This is but one dramatic illustration of many tales which indicate the suddenness with which men of standing and character at that time would alter their political allegiances.

The growth of factions within the Republican Party of New York during the opening decades of the nineteenth century illustrates how under an essentially one-party system strong political leadership compels competing groups to organize as an opposition faction. Vigorous administration, whether it is personal or organized, appears to produce counterorganization.[35] Thus, the stalwart generalship of the Republican Party engaged in by Daniel D. Tompkins compelled rival elements under the guidance of De Witt Clinton to organize themselves as a distinct faction. Their differences began in 1807 over the question of Jefferson's embargo policy.[36] Although Clinton managed to remove this disagreement by reversing himself and endorsing Tompkins' defense of the embargo, a more serious difference developed the following year when Tompkins refused to support De Witt Clinton's efforts to persuade the New York legislature to choose electors who would support George Clinton for the presidency. Dissension was further exacerbated in 1810 when Tompkins tried, unsuccessfully, to prevent Clinton's election as lieutenant governor.[37] Clinton saw this honor as a steppingstone to the presidency since up to that point he had held no elective state-wide position. The clashing ambitions of Clinton and Tompkins reached a climax in 1812 when Clinton decided to run for the presidency. Since Clinton's decision interfered with Tompkins' aspirations to be the first New Yorker to hold the highest office in the land, it met his unrelenting opposition. The ensuing conflict initiated a series of events which finally divided the Republican Party, in which the embers of factionalism had been smoldering for so long, into two separate parts. In similar fashion, the subsequent dominance of De Witt Clinton brought about the organization of the Bucktails, while the authoritarian control of the Bucktails under Martin Van Buren produced the People's Party.

To be sure, in a state with a well-grounded political establishment, aspiring politicians find the safest path to political advancement via the organization. For unified political forces with more durable power usually consist of the followings of an individual leader. But the foundation of the faction is loyalty to an individual. Consequently, there is no place in the party for an individual who wants to rise to the summit, for the summit place is occupied, and when it becomes empty, with rare exception, the faction itself breaks up, as did the Clintonians after the demise of their leader in 1828. Therefore, the professional who aspires to the highest post in the party must oppose the regular organization and become an "anti." Unity and leadership, however, are often difficult to achieve in the opposition faction since it consists primarily of members who are disgruntled for various and sometimes contradictory reasons. Witness, for example, the perennial feuding that split the People's Party and affected adversely its attempts to subdue the Bucktails after 1824.

The electoral conflict between the factions of New York during the pre-Jacksonian era was almost totally divorced from principles. The parties were rival teams, one occupying office, the other seeking it. It was primarily a struggle between the "ins" and the "outs," which lessened the significance of the opposition as a group with distinct ideas of its own, diminishing its role in the state and decreasing democracy by giving the electorate little real choice. The elections reflected public opinion very poorly because the very machinery of party conflict prevented opinion from forming itself clearly and adopting an attitude on the major problems which overshadowed the existence and future of the Empire State. An individual politician's momentary position on a public question was dictated by self-interest, and might, therefore, be completely different the following week. Having adopted a particular position, the politicians then employed their logic to defend the view they felt impelled to take; their action, consequently, was the result of circumstances operating upon their endowment of character and thought. Personal relation to the events of the time had much more to do with shaping a politician's point of view than any abstract theory of government they might have professed.

It is noteworthy, nevertheless, that some of the greatest changes in New York's government, some of the most radical principles of reform, were introduced by opportunistic parties acting from new considerations of self-interest on special occasion. The movement to replace the caucus with the nominating convention, for example, was usually led by the political opposition, especially new political groups whose influence had yet to be strengthened in the ranks of the legislature. Their desires ran counter to the legislative caucus where entrenched political interests had developed. Hence, the New York Federalists in 1812 tried to win popular favor by holding a nominating convention and attempting to establish a regular convention system; in the following year Tammany Hall made identical proposals in an endeavor to break De Witt Clinton's control over the counsels of the Republican Party; finally, the Antimasonic party, which sprang up in 1826, was similarly driven to the expedient of holding conventions of its own.[38]

The forms and modes of operation of a political system are the product of many factors. The noted political scientist, Maurice Duverger, summarizes these into four categories: tradition and history; social and economic structure; ideology; and technical matters such as the electoral regime.[39] The political system of New York during the nineteenth century was, as noted in the Introduction, deeply rooted in British and colonial precedent. Indeed, the rapid growth of political democracy in the state during the decade or so before 1828 was not the beginning but the acceleration and climax of a process which goes back to New York's early experiences as a province of the English sovereign. Most of the essential underpinnings of representative government were established by New York in the course of its history prior to the turn of the nineteenth century.

New York had a sluggish beginning in developing the institutions of a democratic political system. Charles II's grant to his brother, James, the Duke of York, in March, 1664, was unique among all the colonial charters in its failure to contain any provision for a representative assembly. Due to popular insistence, however, the Duke of York authorized the calling of a representative assembly in 1683. The members enjoyed the privileges of free discussion and of considering bills, but measures they approved were subject to vetoes by the governor and the proprietor. This first assembly enacted fifteen laws, the most important being a charter of liberties and privileges which lodged the legislative power with the governor, council, and assembly, extended the ballot to all freeholders and freemen, provided for elections by the "free choice and vote of the majority, and set up a proportional scheme of representation by counties. Other sections of the charter outlined the principles of land tenure, inheritance, and judicial procedure, and guaranteed freedom of worship and trial by jury."[40] After the Duke ascended to the throne in 1685, however, he changed his mind and ordered abolition of the assembly and its laws. It was not until 1691 that the assembly was restored in the form that lasted, essentially unchanged, until the American Revolution. Although only 8 or 10 per cent of all the inhabitants could vote, the organization of this assembly marked the most important advance in the development of New York's political institutions during the seventeenth century.[41]

The Empire State's political and constitutional evolution throughout the eighteenth century signalized an increasingly important role for the assembly in governing the state. This expansion in the powers of the assembly was the outcome of a perennial conflict between the principles of prerogative and popular control. An election law in 1699 greatly reduced the opportunities of the governor to exert illegitimate pressures on the choice of representatives since it referred all cases of disputed elections and questions concerning the qualifications of members to the assembly. The assembly, in turn, proceeded to establish precedents, leaving itself in full control of the subject. New York was also the scene during these years of the famous Zenger Trial (1735) which is rightly celebrated as an epic of American liberty. The case struck a powerful note for freedom of the press by asserting that the truth of a statement can be used as a defense in a case of libel. But, most importantly, the assembly achieved complete control over its revenue expenditures during this era. The climax of this development occurred in 1739 when the assembly passed a law manifesting meticulous solicitude for possible holes in the spending procedure. Attempts by the British to reassert their full authority over New York in the decades immediately preceding the American Revolution were stubbornly resisted by the assembly which was adamant about holding on to what it had achieved. And the consequence of the grave predicaments posed by the French and Indian War was to enable the leaders of colonial New York to hold on to their pre-eminent position in running the government. In the experiences of the eighteenth century, then, one finds not only the background of the American Revolution but also the soil in which New York politics was to grow during the state's career as a member of the Union.[42]

As far as the influence of the social and economic structure upon the political system is concerned, it will be clearly indicated in subsequent chapters that the parties in New York did not correspond to definite classes, and no party was completely homogeneous in social composition. This fact reflects a fluid society which lacked precise class distinctions and which was characterized by a high measure of social mobility. Although the Empire State had both its venerable aristocrats and its impoverished degenerates, the vast majority of the population, in the city and country alike, belonged to the "middling sort." Moreover, passage up the social ladder of distinction was easily achieved by the able and enterprising regardless of origins. As a result, there was little opportunity for class hatred to implant itself and become the basis for political division. For similar reasons, ideology never played an important role in the conflict between political factions. Most New Yorkers agreed on the basic questions of government and society. Hence, political conflict cut across most groups and was concerned with more mundane matters related to strategy for party victory. Membership in a party was generally based upon self-interest or habit; and doctrine or ideological pronouncements, except for campaign rhetoric, played a very small part in the life of New York's political factions.

Technical matters such as the electoral machinery also affected the evolution of New York's political activity in important ways. For example, the presence, for the most part, of the simple majority, single ballot system encouraged the development of a two-party system with alternation of power between the major groupings. In truth, despite the constantly shifting factionalism that characterized New York politics, there were usually not more than two significant factions competing for electoral victory at any one time. The conflict during most of the pre-Jacksonian era was between the Bucktails and the Clintonians. Moreover, the relatively small constituencies increased the natural tendencies for parties to play

only an insignificant role in determining an individual's political decisions. Since the small constituencies made it possible
for the electors to have individual knowledge of the candidates,
the campaigns became principally a clash of personalities, so
that the elector made his choice because of the candidate's
personal qualities rather than his party allegiance. Thus,
numerous factors helped to shape the nature and functions of
political parties in New York.

The vague and transient character of parties under New
York's political system during the pre-Jacksonian era was
paralleled by a nebulous and indefinite concept of party membership. Admission to the party was accompanied by no official
ceremonies such as the signing of a promise to support the
party in all its political endeavors, and occasional donations
took the place of annual subscriptions. As a result of the absence of precise criteria of membership, only the member's
activity could determine the degree of his involvement. Within this context, essentially three concentric circles of involvement can be indicated. The largest comprises the voters who
cast ballots for the party nominees at the various elections.
The second circle contains the "backers," an unclear word for
an unclear idea equivalent nevertheless to a real thing. The
backer was a voter, but his involvement was greater than a
voter's: he admitted that he supported the organization, he
fought for it and occasionally contributed money to it. He
even joined organizations indirectly related to the party. The
bulk of the Bucktail members in the Tammany Society and
the Federalists of the Washington Benevolent Society, both of
which organizations were fraternal orders with strongly political overtones, are examples of the "backers" in New York.
Finally, the last and innermost circle was composed of "zealots." They regarded themselves as the leaders of the party, the
supervising members of the party hierarchy; they saw to its
arrangement and functioning; they designed its propaganda
and strategy. Those who participated in the party caucuses belonged to the group of zealots.

The inmost circle of members, in animating and guiding

the outer circles, generally reflected the views of the latter in order to retain their backing. Thus, the oligarchic nature of the arrangement is more apparent than real. Three talents in particular were desired in the ranks of the zealots for the successful conduct of the election campaigns. In the first place, revered personages were required whose reputation, status, or relationships would attract votes for the candidate; in the second place, skilled leaders who knew the psychology of the electorate and how to secure its backing; last of all, men of wealth who would contribute the means of putting the party strategy into action. The most important element was quality: status, know-how, and money. Hence, the opposing sides tried to capture the active allegiance of famous families such as the Hamiltons, the Jays, and the Kings for the sake of electoral gain. Moreover, the aid of a rising new breed of professional politicians such as Martin Van Buren, Silas Wright, and Thurlow Weed was being increasingly considered as indispensable with the growing size of the electorate. Finally, the need for funds to meet the expenses of electioneering compelled the recruitment as zealots of large landowners like Stephen Van Rensselaer, prominent manufacturers like Benjamin Knower, and influential merchants like James Emott. It was natural for such "capitalist financing" of elections to evolve in a system based on property suffrage. But it worked out so effectively that it survived the property qualification, and even today, despite universal suffrage, it is our primary method of covering campaign costs.

What was the background of the people who became members of the Empire State's political parties in the early nineteenth century? The time-honored interpretation of Dixon Ryan Fox pits Federalist merchants and landlords against Republican farmers and artisans.[43] Further, after the War of 1812, according to Fox, the Clintonians absorbed the Federalists, and the Republicans were called Bucktails. Throughout this volume, we will attempt to show the inaccuracy of this position. First of all, although some Federalists did join the Clintonians, many others became Bucktails. Similarly, just as many Bucktails were farmers and artisans, so a substantial number of Clintonians followed these callings particularly on the frontier and in the large cities. Conversely, landlords, merchants, and manufacturers felt as at home among the Bucktails as they were among the Clintonians. In short, it is a mistake to explain political alignments in New York during the 1820's in terms of social and economic origins. Party positions on basic political, economic, and social issues were not consistent or unanimous. There were members in all parties who stood on both sides of most of the great questions of the time. For the most part, lines of party cleavage were drawn by opportunistic considerations which offered the best chances for electoral victory.

Professionally, most of the party leaders were lawyers. One is reminded of Tocqueville's persuasive suggestion that the lawyers, who dominated party affairs, were the supple, colorless, and odorless political aristocracy of democratic America.[44] When the wealthy, aristocratic, and capable lost touch with their community, the eloquent, nimble, self-educated, upright party lawyers, with the help of the local newspaper editor and some influential merchants and farmers, accepted the responsibility for directing the political life of the people. They may not have been Jefferson's natural aristocrats, but Martin Van Buren, Morgan Lewis, Silas Wright, Benjamin Butler, Ambrose Spencer, Daniel Tompkins, James Tallmadge, James Kent, and De Witt Clinton, to mention only a few, did well enough within their limits.

III

THE STRUCTURE OF THE POLITICAL MACHINE

"Unity among Republicans must be preserved . . . and to effect this I would support any candidate."[1] This expression of deep loyalty to the party was a product of the highly developed political machines that emerged in New York state during the early nineteenth century. Although not every party machine functioned with equal efficiency, each attempted to impose discipline upon its membership through the distribution of patronage. The machine was aided in its operations by the use of such associated appendages as the party press, fellowship societies, and governmental institutions like the Council of Revision, the Council of Appointment, the congressional caucus, and the indirect choice of presidential electors by the state legislature. Many of the political techniques which evolved during this era have persisted until today as standard weapons in the battle for control of the government.

In order for the party to operate effectively it was necessary to maintain strict discipline. The Bucktails, under the guidance of Martin Van Buren and such faithful cohorts as Silas Wright and Azariah C. Flagg, were particularly successful in setting up the party as an end in itself that demanded the unflinching obedience of the members to its dicta. Considerations of party welfare were the predominant determinants of what sides of an issue the organization would take in an election. After the dominant clique of the party arrived at a decision, the information was immediately transmitted to the legislators, newspapers, and politicians. Rallies and public meetings were sponsored to popularize the policy. Once the party line had been determined, irresoluteness and irregularity were forbidden. Hence, although Silas Wright in 1823 would have preferred John Quincy Adams for the presidency, while Flagg preferred Clay or possibly Calhoun, they both became ardent Crawford men when their colleagues had arrived at a joint decision.[2] Similarly, three years later, Michael Hoffman, who did not care for Jackson, suppressed his prejudices in deference to the general party will. He declared: "I don't like the Jackson frolic very well, but I suppose we must have him."[3] Indeed, the Bucktails seemed to assert an absolutist, almost mystical conception of the rights of the party, so important and so precious as to be beyond the laws of private ethics. "Don't be too fastidious," wrote Marcy, "when party is strong almost anything that is done is right. I have not time to carry out fully my ideas on this subject, but a hint is enough to such a wise and experienced body as the Albany Regency."[4]

The primary force available to secure internal party regularity was the power to fill and vacate offices. While the conclusion of the campaign was the end of the season for the voters, it was just the beginning for the politicians. During this period, the spoils system—the idea that offices exist not as a necessary means of administering government but for the support of party leaders at public expense—became deeply rooted in New York. To be sure, there were instances of it much earlier. The New York Federalists in 1792, for example, exploited to the full their control of the Council of Appointment. The Council claimed that with the governor it had the concurrent right of nomination, that it could enlarge at will the number of public officials not limited by law, and that it could replace every holder of public office after his commission had expired if it was renewable annually. As a result, with the exception of the governor, the lieutenant governor, the members of the state legislature, and the aldermen, all public officers required the approval of the Council in order to continue in office. Commenting on the foregoing state of affairs, the historian, De Alva Stanwood Alexander, wrote:

"This arbitrary proceeding led to twenty years of corrupt methods and political scandals."[5]

In 1801, De Witt Clinton's Council of Appointment offered posts to Clintonians and Livingstons only. Edward Livingston, whose Louisiana code was soon to evoke widespread admiration for its humaneness, was appointed mayor of New York City; Thomas T. Tillotson, a brother-in-law of Chancellor Robert R. Livingston, was called to serve as Secretary of State in New York; Brockholst Livingston was named a judge of the state supreme court; Smith Thompson, who had married a daughter of Gilbert Livingston of Poughkeepsie, was also granted the post of a supreme court justice; Morgan Lewis, the brother-in-law of Edward and Chancellor Livingston, was offered the position of chief justice of the supreme court. As far as the Clintonians were concerned, William Stewart, a brother-in-law of Governor George Clinton, became district attorney of Tioga and other counties in the southern tier; Sylvanus Miller, a Clinton lieutenant in Kingston, was named surrogate of New York County; and De Witt Clinton himself served successively as United States senator from New York state and mayor of New York City when John Armstrong, a brother-in-law of Chancellor Livingston, and Edward Livingston resigned from these offices respectively.[6] After Morgan Lewis was elected governor in 1804 he tendered state offices to his followers only.[7] When the Republicans regained control of the state legislature in 1815, Federalists were removed in large numbers from public office. The *New York Post* indicated in the spring of that year that such varied officials as the recorder in New York City, the warden of the state prison, health officers, and the post wardens were exclusively Republican.

The effect of the spoils system doctrine in New York was to awaken the cupidity of the idle and ambitious, to make useless every consideration of principle in the formation of party attachments, and to substitute for it blind devotion to powerful leaders. It held out the idea that all men were qualified for all offices, decried the value of experience, faithfulness, and skill, and invited the momentary incumbent to fraud and negligence. In spite of these serious shortcomings, the foremost hero of the system, Martin Van Buren, tried to defend party control of the patronage as a legitimate and necessary instrument of majority rule. He asserted that the evils of patronage were not so obvious as men seemed to think. Moreover, the New York senator would "go as far as any man, in endeavoring to curtail dangerous patronage in distinct bodies of men—but . . . not so far as to cut every cord that binds together the people to the government."[8] The sway wielded by the state-wide majority, honestly obtained in free elections, need not be surrendered. The appointing power ought to be "put in the hands of the executive, not for himself, but to secure to the majority of the people that control and influence in every section of the state to which they are justly entitled."[9] Van Buren was attempting to win acceptance for the heretofore not wholly reputable contention that the voice of the people is heard through the pronouncements of the leadership of the dominant party. In short, patronage was something more than dirty politics.

Through its control of candidature, the party constituted a remarkable system for recruitment and advancement of political leaders from the ranks of the membership. Since state elective and appointive offices were prizes sought by men rising in the organization, the management of the party was extremely careful so that the claims of members were balanced by the allocation of rewards. On the other hand, individuals, who in the legislature or other lower offices demonstrated "unpredictable" qualities, i.e., failed to follow the organization line, found their way blocked to political preferment. In almost the manner of a churchly order, the machine, especially the Bucktail organization, which represented a much higher degree of development, tested the loyalties and abilities of its neophytes. Those with unquestioned faith in the organization and belief in its doctrine were advanced. Those found wanting, either in ability or doctrine, remained in a lowly status.

To be sure, where party welfare conflicted with individual well-being, the latter was often sacrificed in the name of the

former, as was the case when Governor Yates was denied re-
nomination in 1824 despite his faithful service. From the time
of his selection as governor in 1822, Yates had unflinchingly
obeyed the dictates of the Albany Regency. His opening
address to the state legislature in 1824, which advocated suspen-
sion of any action to give people the right to choose presidential electors directly, set the tone of the whole convocation in accordance with the wishes of the Bucktail leadership.
Nevertheless, sensitive to the fact that the Bucktail failure to
secure for the people the right to choose their presidential
electors directly had called down the public wrath upon the
party's head, the Regency decided to sacrifice Governor Yates.
The ruling clique felt that his dismissal would remove public
discontent, since Yates' part in preventing the proposed electoral change, though relatively small, was still remembered.
Men like Benjamin Butler believed that an individual's ambitions and aspirations must be ignored when they conflict with
the welfare of the party. He wrote to Van Buren in Washington that Yates could under no circumstances be renamed as
the party's candidate for governor in the approaching electoral
contest. To insure the "ultimate safety of the party," he said,
"some other man must be selected. In this way angry feelings
would be soothed and the individual electoral vote of New
York would go to Crawford. If you was here you would
acquiesce in the expediency and absolute necessity of this
course."[10] Other Regency leaders like Azariah C. Flagg and
Silas Wright, however, contended that the party must uphold
in all circumstances those who stood by it with unswerving
loyalty.[11] Nonetheless, it must be generally conceded that the
ideals of supreme loyalty to the party and rewarding supreme
loyalty to the party complemented each other, and Bucktail
political behavior most of the time reflects a strikingly consistent adherence to both.

The selection, advancement, and reward of only those party
members who conformed to the machine's will placed in positions of power people who almost instinctively acted according to the machine's unwritten code. This situation helps to
explain how and why those seventeen Bucktail senators jeopardized their careers in 1824 by voting to shelve considera-

tion of a measure that would grant to the people the right to choose presidential electors directly. They knew that although public opinion was overwhelmingly in favor of such a bill, their future advancement within the party depended upon their casting a negative ballot. If they momentarily lost public favor by their behavior, they depended on the wiles of party strategy and propaganda to alter popular opinion by the time the day of election had arrived.

When one grasps the Bucktail attitude toward the party, it is easier to understand why they were so insistent on preventing the people from choosing presidential electors directly. Such an innovation would reduce sharply the influence of the party hierarchy in determining the outcome of presidential elections. Martin Van Buren, the generally acknowledged head of the Albany Regency, contended that the party was an "all-hallowed" end in itself. He was persuaded that the objectives of freedom and democracy were best achieved through the machinery of the organization, which could shelter and care for as well as help and preserve the people of the United States.[12] He was encompassed, moreover, by a coterie of associates who possessed the same dedication to the organization, and a similarly realistic and pragmatic approach to politics. One of these, Silas Wright, was regarded by Garraty as a typical example of the new type of professional politician who was rising all over the country at that time.[13] Wright wrote to his co-worker, Azariah C. Flagg, "It is part of my political creed always to act with my political friends, and to let the majority dictate the course of action." On another occasion, Wright related to Flagg his deepseated conviction regarding the wisdom of the spoils system: "On the subject of these appointments, you know well my mind. Give them to true and useful friends who will enjoy the emolument if there is any, and who will use their influence to our benefit. . . . This is the long and short of the rule by which to act . . . and when our enemies accuse us of feeding our friends instead of them, never let them lie in telling the story."[14]

The actual control of the factions in New York was in the hands of a small group that made use of close personal solidarity as a means of establishing and retaining influence. It took the form of a clique grouped around an influential leader. This leader's retinue monopolized positions of leadership and took on the characteristics of oligarchy. The Albany Regency, gathered around Martin Van Buren, is a perfect exemplar of this type of group, but the coterie that surrounded De Witt Clinton represents the same tendency. This small group was able to impose its will upon the rank and file by a number of subtle, though effective, techniques. For example, since the leaders of the party were not elected directly by the members, except at the local level, but by delegates who were themselves elected, each additional state of delegation increased the gap between the will of the base and the decision of the apex, thereby decreasing the dependence of the latter upon the former. Moreover, since the central authority had to approve nominees for appointive or elective office on the local level, candidates were usually "given" to the members, rather than chosen by them. In addition, the party elite often called meetings without adequate notice so as to prevent hostile members from being notified in time, or meetings were fixed at awkward times and places so as to keep certain elements away. Finally, since members had to indicate their positions openly at party meetings and caucuses, opposition was reduced by the psychological manipulation of the participants. All these "tricks" hid a greater or lesser degree of autocratic control under a more or less democratic mask.

In order to insure the election victories that were essential for the functioning of the machine, the party found it necessary to employ certain techniques. Among the most important of these was control of the press. The use of public printing contracts, postmasterships, contributions, loans, and guaranteed subscription lists enabled the political parties to keep certain editors subservient to them. The anticipation of a substantial amount of job printing at election time in the form of issuing party handbills, circulars, tickets, and the like also enticed numerous editors to cast their lot with a particular political organization. A common way of evaluating the popularity of candidates and issues was to add up the publications backing them. The overwhelming majority of newspapers were subservient to the various political factions. Their main objective was not to give utterance to the truth, but to induce the voters to cast their ballots in a particular way. A man was identified by the publications he declined to read; an editor, by what he declined to print. It was irrefutable evidence of treachery to spot a politician subscribing to an enemy newspaper, and in an editor to discover him printing the political activities of the opposition.

The Bucktails, cognizant of the importance of having an organ of the press obedient to their will, took swift action during the campaign of 1824 when recalcitrance on the part of the editor of the *Albany Argus* was reported. William L. Marcy wrote to Senator Van Buren: "Your protogee [*sic*] Leake is and has been for some time hostile to us. He has mutilated many articles. . . . He is in favor of the electoral law, decidedly hostile to a caucus, has a great respect for the character of the opposition in the Legislature and has lately discovered that it is highly improper for the *State Paper* to be a party paper. . . . This conduct of Mr. L. is very vexatious to C[roswell]—and very embarrassing to us."[15] Members of the Albany Regency called in Leake in an unsuccessful effort to dissuade him from his policy of defiance. Van Buren then induced a close friend of both himself and Leake, Gorham A. Worth, to reason with the newspaper editor. The senator disclosed to Worth his disgust and revulsion at Leake's unanticipated treachery. The editor is "good for nothing under heaven except to excite prejudice agt. the establishment and to cause me plagues for my misplaced confidence and favor. It appears . . . that he has taken into his head to control Mr. Croswell in the conducting of the paper and make every difficulty in his power. I feel I confess great disgust and indignation at the pitiful conduct and will be obliged to you if you can open his eyes to the disgrace which will be brought down upon him."[16] As a result of these pressures the Regency succeeded in convincing Leake to resign during the summer of 1824. Thereafter, under the editorship of Edwin Croswell, the *Argus* followed religiously the Bucktail position on the basic issues of the day.

Another indispensable element in the structure of the political machine, particularly at election time, were the committees of correspondence. These committees, appointed by those who made the party nominations, consisted of a state or central committee, assisted by local committees in each county. The most reliable, enthusiastic, able, and ardent men of the party constituted these committees. They had the task of giving official replies to the libelous tales spread by the opposing factions, advising the party press what to publish, determining what public questions should be emphasized and which should be muffled, strengthening the organization's fortifications, publicizing party rallies and addresses, evaluating the results of certain appointments, preserving communications with representatives of the machine in the counties and towns as well as in other states, formulating political strategy, drawing up formal intraparty communications, and handling the numerous, unanticipated occurrences that were constantly arising to threaten the party's position. The significance of these committees can hardly be exaggerated. Their members were the backbone of the machine, their communications the sole method of circulating important facts to the party at large, their views provided whatever ideological agreement there was during the campaign, and their prophecies were the most dependable conjectures available.

The importance of the committee of correspondence can be readily ascertained from the role it played in the campaign of the People's Party for electoral victory in 1824. This committee succeeded in unifying the People's Party, which consisted of numerous dissident factions that hated one another, behind a single slate of candidates. It provided a method of organization essential to electoral victory. By means of a steady stream of pamphlets, moreover, the central corresponding committee together with its adjuncts throughout the state kept alive the antagonism aroused by the Bucktail stand on the revised electoral law. In addition, they served as the official respondents of the People's Party to the accusations of the Albany Regency. Finally, they decided the principal literary themes for the Clintonian campaign.

The success of the corresponding committee in recruiting support for the People's cause from anti-Bucktail ranks that were also opposed to De Witt Clinton is indicated by the stand of numerous men like James Finch. In a letter to the editor of the *Orange County Farmer,* Finch said that despite his personal dislike of Clinton, he would support the People's ticket because the former governor is "the candidate of those men who are in favor of the electoral bill." He maintained, further, that "unity of action is required; otherwise, the enemies to the bill will prevail, which would be of incalculably more evil than the election of Mr. Clinton. To support Colonel Young would be effectually supporting the men who made our dearest rights their sport."[17] Without the aid of the steady barrage of campaign oratory that the central committee published to stress the identity of democratic sentiments with the principles of the People's Party, it is unlikely that multitudes like James Finch would have overcome their deep-seated hostility toward Clinton and voted for the People's ticket.

The literature of the central committee, moreover, contended that the "lawless ambition" of the Bucktails had caused the "prostration" of the state.[18] The followers of Van Buren knew quite well that William H. Crawford was not the man of the people and that is why "they dare not trust his election to the democracy of this state where the voice of every citizen could be heard from the ballot box."[19] On the state level, Samuel Young, the Bucktail candidate for governor, was accused of the "most palpable mismanagement along the whole line of the Northern Canal, the construction of which was under his exclusive superintendence." It was also claimed that his "want of capacity or his *personal partialities* for certain men at Black Rock in a single case, have swept from the treasury of the state at least ONE MILLION DOLLARS!"[20] Thus, the literature of the campaign committees maligned their opponents for impure motives and a dearth of talent.

In contrast to his enemies who "disgraced, degraded, and betrayed" the state by rejecting the electoral law and supporting the nominating caucus, the People's campaign committee described Clinton as the "MAN OF THE PEOPLE," the one who can "redeem" and "restore" New York to its proper place in the Union.[21] The particular publication from which the above remarks were drawn, incidentally, was circulated by Charles G. Haines, chairman of the General Corresponding Committee for the City and County of New York, one of the most significant branches of the state corresponding committee. Haines claimed credit for the extremely effective organization that the People's movement exhibited in the southern district of the state. Other circular letters praised Clinton "as conspicuous in the history of the state by his sublime acts of public policy." He was hailed as favorable to the interests of agriculture and manufacturing, the "fast friend" of internal improvements, an economical spender of the public money, and a patron of science and letters.[22]

Another major task that faced the corresponding committee was to disprove the allegedly slanderous accusations published by the Bucktails against De Witt Clinton. An example of their execution of the obligation is the pamphlet entitled "Caucus Calumny Refuted," which was published by the Central Corresponding Committee whose chairman was Joseph D. Selden and whose secretary was Ebenezer Wilson, Jr. This circular attempted to refute a charge carried in the October 15, 1824, edition of the *Albany Argus* claiming that Clinton had opposed the Constitutional Convention of 1821. The People's Men contended that although Clinton had voted against the first convention bill in the Council of Revision, this action was prompted by his insistence that the people have the right to declare in the first instance whether they would or would not have a convention. Moreover, it was Clinton who first recommended the calling of such a convention, and his enemies concealed the fact that he did vote for the second bill under which the convention was called. The campaigning efforts of the corresponding committees were not restricted to expounding the virtues of their candidate for governor. James Tallmadge, the candidate for lieutenant governor, received his share of publicity. He was cited as a man "whose eloquence made a venal senate tremble," who nobly supported the rights of the people and the state, and who attempted to arrest the "progress of corruption which disfranchised 260,000 freemen."[23] Clearly, the corresponding committee performed essential tasks in helping to realize the party's bid for electoral victory.

For voters who did not buy newspapers, the corresponding committees made sure that pamphlets, handbills, and flyers were widely circulated. They were thrown on doorsteps, posted in taverns, tacked on fence rails, and on the backs of wagons. From the printshops also poured broadsides of every description and kind, ranging from the dignified announcements of candidates "respectfully submitting their names" to violent "tabloids."

One of the primary themes of the Bucktail handbills and pamphlets in 1824 was the alleged insincerity of the democratic professions of the leaders of the People's Party. An "aristocrat" was defined as a "noisy boisterous demagogue, vociferous for the interests of the 'people'—meaning his own."[24] They argued that Clinton, the standard-bearer of the opposition, "frowns upon the poor" and is the brother-in-law of Ambrose Spencer who at the Constitutional Convention of 1821 "would exclude the poor man from voting." "Remember that Spencer controls him, and if Clinton should be elected, Spencer will be governor." In addition to having the wrong brand of relatives, Clinton was charged with being the enemy of the wrong people. He was an alleged "traducer, persecutor, and opposer of the patriotic Tompkins, the poor man's friend, and emphatically the friend of the people." Further, the former governor and his associates presently oppose Samuel Young because he is supported by Tompkins and at the recent convention was in favor of extending the rights of the common man.[25]

In addition to exposing the "hypocrisy" of the democratic assertions of their opponents, the Bucktails tried to advertise themselves as the true friends of the people and espoused a program more radically equalitarian than that of the People's Party. "The Republican party is desirous to procure a uniform mode of election for president and vice president by the people which Clinton and the federal party oppose. Republicans, are you not as competent to vote for president as for governor? Will you acknowledge that you require thirty-six men scattered throughout the state, with whom you are unacquainted to vote for you? Away with such a doctrine—we are competent to vote for all our rulers. Now judge who are the friends of the people."[26] In this manner, the party that preferred the caucus method of nomination to more open and public procedures, and was afraid to permit the people to select presidential electors directly, had the audacity to say that they favored having the people choose the president without resorting to any intermediaries.

The gubernatorial candidate of the People's Party in 1824, De Witt Clinton, was a favorite target of the Regency handbills and was attacked on many grounds. He was, for example, condemned for an excessive propensity to increase the number of banks. Although Clinton declared upon his previous election as governor of the state that he would follow "the footsteps of Mr. Tompkins, in advising the legislature against the multiplication of banks, . . . immediately after his inaugural address in 1818 he gave his assent to the incorporation of three banks two of which stopped payment within three months." Of these banks, one was the Franklin Bank of New York "to the directors of which Mr. Clinton sold an old family mansion, called the Franklin House (where the bank is now kept) for an extravagant price. Mr. Oakley, the present attorney general, was then in the legislature and he voted for the Franklin Bank; and afterward, his brother, a young lawyer, was transplanted from Poughkeepsie to New York and made the attorney and public notary to that bank." Further, it was claimed by the Republicans that in the winter of 1812 when New York agents of the Bank of America were involved in some notorious scandals, Clinton, as lieutenant governor, was their "bosom friend."[27]

Not content with denouncing his political principles, the Bucktails proceeded to vilify the personal character of the former governor. He was accused of arrogance, ill temper, a want of integrity, hypocrisy, and a cynicism "always unenlivened by wit and often unchastized by decorum."[28] It was asserted, in addition, that his private morals were even worse than his public ones, and that the rubric of his face showed the nature of his religion and the deity he worshipped. Perhaps the capstone of all the variegated propaganda against Clinton was the attempt to devaluate his contributions to the development and maintenance of the Erie Canal, the most notable feats of his career. The Regency declared that Clinton's services to the Canal Commission were not gratuitous as generally believed. The *Albany Argus* contended that $164,600 was paid to De Witt Clinton "out of the pockets of the People of the State" in connection with the performance of his duties as canal commissioner, and it gave an itemized account of how it arrived at this sum.[29] Thus, character assassination and very free usage of the democratic slogans provided the major literary motifs of the Bucktails' pamphlets and handbills.

Printed "dram-shop dialogues" in which partially inebriated coachmen and saloon idlers engaged in farcical conversation about the campaign using the colloquialisms of the day (whose profanity was made less objectionable by an abundant scattering of dashes and asterisks) had wide public appeal as did campaign songs, ballads, and doggerel verse. A typical example of the "poetic talents" (and that term is used liberally) of the politicians is the following poem entitled *Political Hobbies,* which was a product of the People's Party:

Now the hobby Old Caucus is scouring the plain
Stiffneck'd and hard bitted and ugly as Cain
Bill Crawford is mounted unsafe on his back
With Albany Junto full speed in his track
Hold the hobby! Stop the hobby!
Catch the hobby. Gee up and Gee O.

New York lately found on the public highway
A hobby of worth that had wandered astray.
The monk she well knew—'twas the Electoral Bill:
So she mounted and rode with Republican skill
Freemen's hobby, etc.

Sam Young was a hobby that once had a trick
When the caucus drum sounded, to rear and to kick;
But by coaxing and patting, he soon loved the sound,
And neighed with delight while he marched o'er the ground.
Junto's hobby! etc.

The hobby of Root for a long time had been
The People. The People again, and again;
But high charged with brandy, he mounted to ride,
And buried his spur in the poor hobby's hide.
Down from his hobby! Down from his hobby!
Down from his hobby! he tumbled gee O!

The hobby that freemen behold with delight
Is Clinton, the courser, so powerful and bright;
He is the jay of the turn, which no jockey can ride;
He's the boast of the state, of the nation the pride.
Here's your hobby! Here's your hobby etc.

The corresponding committee clearly made an effort to use
all the "arts of speech" in performing its numerous tasks. If a
voter managed to evade the onslaught of printed materials
that deluged the state at election time, the machine probably would have succeeded in making contact with him at a
political rally. If not, the party organization also sponsored
parades, barbecues, poleraisings, and dinners in order to
attract the ballots of the citizenry. The attendance at these
affairs was frequently stressed. Indeed, the expertise of the
party editors in exaggerating the size of these affairs exceeded
every other subject. When a rally drew a couple of hundred
people, the press of the party backing him raised the number
to a thousand while the opposition newspapers reduced the
figure to a "pitiful turnout" or a "mere handfull." Normally,
the political rally began with a parade from the center of
town which grew progressively noisier as the throngs marched
to a place near the outskirts of the community where refresh-
ments had been set up. In the event that several political factions had arranged parades for the same day, extraordinary
efforts were undertaken to make sure that their respective
routes did not interfere with each other; for, if there were contact it would have required a junior army to prevent a major
war from erupting. At these gatherings an attempt was made
to give some speeches but much more popular were the consumption of barrels of beer, the devouring of oxen, the drinking of toasts, and the giving of cheers. When these functions

had concluded, those who were still capable of responding to discipline marched back to town.

Campaign ruse and deception, which played a part in every political contest, compelled the organization to appoint committees of vigilance. These crime detectors had the task of concealing their own party's political trickery while exposing the diabolical artifices of their opponents. Counterfeit printed tickets with the names of some of the regular nominees omitted were circulated. Occasionally, on the morning of the election, opposition newspapers would announce the demise of the enemy candidate. Voters were sometimes warned to stay away from the polls or threatened with violence if they voted. Attempts were made to rig the membership of the election board so that all the inspectors and judges were members of the same party. People who had no right to vote such as transients or citizens not on the tax list often cast ballots in an election. Waggoners, travelling from one place to another, often succeeded in voting several times on election day.

One of the most famous examples of electoral intrigue at this time occurred in 1792 when the Clintonians tried to deprive John Jay, the gubernatorial candidate of their Federalist opponents, of an electoral victory to which he was rightfully entitled. Jay had obtained a clear majority of the votes, but antifederalists on the board of election canvassers invalidated the ballots of Otsego, Tioga, and Clinton counties on the tenuous technicality of their having been improperly delivered to the secretary of state. Since there was no question of the regularity of the election, the identity of the ballot boxes, or their content, it is evident that the will of the people was ignored. At the time he was robbed of the governorship, Jay was holding a circuit court in Vermont, and an outraged public welcomed him back to the state with a triumphal procession at Lansingburg in the Hudson Valley. The *New York Daily Advertiser* wrote that Jay was escorted by a reception committee as far as Troy "where he crossed the river and was saluted on his landing with 15 discharges of a field piece, by attachment of the Albany Independent Artillery Company, and a volley by the troop of cavalrymen."[30] The public was in a rage, and many people called for an armed revolt. Only Jay's sober counsels retained the peace. His patience and dignity are revealed in a letter that he wrote to his wife about this incident: "The reflection that the majority of electors were for me is a pleasing one; that injustice has taken place does not surprise me, and I hope it will not affect you very sensibly. The intelligence found me perfectly prepared for it. A few years more will put us all in the dust, and it will then be of more importance to me to have governed myself than to have governed the state."[31]

In 1800, the Federalist victims of the "steal of 1792" tried their own hand at achieving by stealth what they could not accomplish honestly at the polls. In a desperate effort to prevent New York's electoral votes from going to Thomas Jefferson, Hamilton advised John Jay, who had been elected governor in 1795 and 1798, to call a special session of the old Federalist-controlled legislature in order to change the method of choosing presidential electors before the new Republican-dominated legislature took office. Hamilton wrote that the "scruples of delicacy and propriety . . . ought not to hinder the taking of a legal and constitutional step to prevent an atheist in religion and a fanatic in politics, from getting possession of the helm of the state."[32] General Schuyler also pressed the governor to comply with Hamilton's advice, comforting him with the thought that "your friends will justify it as the only way to save a nation from more disasters which it may and probably will experience from the misrule of a man who has given such strong evidence that he was opposed to the salutory measures of those who have been heretofore at the helm, and who is in fact, pervaded with the mad French philosophy."[33] Other Federalists such as John Marshall joined in this frantic counsel; but, fortunately, John Jay, with his traditional good sense, withstood the promptings of suspicion and wrath. He refused to be part of a conspiracy to frustrate the popular will for "party purposes which I think it would not become me to adopt."[34] Thus, members of both parties were involved in the devising of techniques to defeat the people's desires.

The political organization in New York was aided in its efforts to control public policy by a number of institutions. Among the most important of these until 1821 when it was abolished was the Council of Revision. Established by the Constitutional Convention of 1777, the Council limited considerably the legislature's power. It seems to have been suggested by the veto power possessed by the King's Privy Council in colonial times.[35] All bills passed by the legislature had to be submitted for approval to the Council which consisted of the governor, the chancellor, and the judges of the state supreme court. A law could get by without the Council's explicit approval only if the legislature repassed the bill by a two-thirds majority after the Council had disapproved it, or if the Council failed to act within ten days after possession of the bill.

The Council of Revision was subject to a number of objections. First of all, it deprived the governor of a veto, which in his hands alone would probably have proved beneficial. Similarly, the Council divided the responsibility for legislation. By giving legislative powers to the chancellor and the highest judges of the state, it involved them in politics. Likewise, it gave the veto power to judges who held office on good behavior and who were, therefore, not responsible to public opinion. However, the greatest source of public discontent arose from the Council's not infrequent flaunting disregard of the popular will. During the years of the first constitution, 1777 to 1821, the Council vetoed 169 bills, 51 of which were passed over its veto. But perhaps even more significant than the several score bills that actually encountered its veto was the restraining influence it exerted on the minds of legislators who knew that whatever they proposed would have to pass the critical eye of the Council before becoming law.[36]

The manner in which the Council of Revision could be used to frustrate the will of the people is illustrated by De Witt Clinton's action in voting against a bill, which had passed the legislature by an overwhelming majority, to convoke a constitutional convention. The bill had been reported to the legislature in November, 1820, by Michael Ulshoeffer, a Bucktail

Assemblyman; it provided for the election of delegates, gave the convention unlimited powers, and stipulated that the sections of the new constitution were to be voted upon by the people in gross rather than separately. The Council of Revision divided equally on the matter, giving De Witt Clinton as governor the power to make the final decision. The governor commented: "The Tammany Horse rides through the legislature like a wild ass's colt, but we will put a stop to it."[37] After Clinton had vetoed the bill it was sent back to the legislature on January 15, 1821, together with the Council's objections. The primary complaint of the Council was that the bill failed to offer the people the right to decide whether they wanted a revision of the constitution.[38] Clinton personally felt that there was not widespread sentiment favoring a convention in 1820.[39] Moreover, the legislature had no right to grant the convention unlimited powers or to stipulate that the amendments should be submitted to the people in gross rather than separately.[40] Clinton wrote to Henry Post: "I am in favor of a Convention properly and fairly called, but not for one got up precipitately for bad purposes, under bad auspices, and with a view to shake society to its foundations in order to sustain the predominance of bad men."[41]

According to Dixon Ryan Fox, Clinton's veto was dictated by purely partisan considerations. The governor knew that a convention of some kind would have to be held, but he wanted to wait until after the census of 1820 when the growth of the western part of the state where Clinton was strong would increase his power at the convention as a result of a reapportionment of delegates. Moreover, in the intervening time, the Clintonians might win back control of the legislature, redraw the convention bill, and thereby preserve those sections of the old constitution like the Council of Revision which served the purposes of the machine so well. "While Chancellor Kent, Chief Justice Ambrose Spencer, Jonas Platt, and William W. Van Ness, as a majority could veto any law, democracy might well complain."[42]

Although the Bucktails attacked the action of the Council, they decided to save time by revising the convention bill in order to meet the objections of the Council. The new bill granted the populace the privilege of deciding whether or not they wanted a convention, but gave all taxpayers and militiamen the right to vote. If the bill were adopted, an election of convention delegates would take place in June while the meeting would begin its deliberations in August. The convention would have unlimited power in suggesting amendments which were to be individually submitted to the people for their approval. The Council accepted the new version of the bill without delay.

The Council of Revision, whose abuses had become notorious, was the first relic to be abolished, without a single nay, at the Constitutional Convention of 1821. The opponents of the Council argued that it had acted *ultra vires* since it vetoed laws on the basis of expediency although it should have made its judgments on the ground of constitutionality alone. Despite the unanimous decision to abolish the Council, the attempt to find a substitute aroused considerable controversy. After lengthy debate, the convention accepted the proposal of the Committee on the Council of Revision, which advocated separating the judiciary from the other two branches of the government by vesting the veto power exclusively in the governor with a two-thirds majority of the legislature necessary to override it.[43]

Another important institution employed by the political machine until 1821 was the Council of Appointment. Its use as an instrument of government as well as its abolition is discussed in the previous chapter.[44]

One of the key elements in the party's organization of political life was the caucus—the congressional on the national level and the legislative on the state level. By determining important issues behind closed doors the caucus expedited the activities of the legislature and strengthened party regularity. The congressional caucus as an instrument for nominating candidates was established in 1800.[45] From that time until 1824, nominating caucuses drawn from party members in Congress were held regularly at four-year intervals to agree on candidates for president and vice president. The energetic effort of William Crawford to seize the nomination from James Monroe in 1816 became the first signal for intensified opposition to the caucus.[46] In 1824, the conviction on the part of Crawford's opponents that his nomination by a congressional caucus would be a foregone conclusion if his name were to be brought before that body, led them to renew the attack on the caucus as an undemocratic institution. The insistence by Crawford's backers, on the other hand, that the congressional caucus be kept, made this method of nominating candidates a subject of fierce debate and one of the hottest issues in the campaign of 1824.

The Bucktails, who fought for the preservation of this technique of party control, justified their defense of the congressional caucus on a number of grounds. Van Buren, for example, argued that while "a nomination by the Republican members of Congress is not entirely free from objections, yet that, assembled as they are from the different quarters of the nation . . . they bring into one body as perfect a representation as can be expected."[47] Besides maintaining that the congressional caucus was not as unrepresentative and undemocratic as was contended by the anti-Crawfordites, the Bucktails asserted its value as a promoter of the unity and welfare of the party. Benjamin F. Butler fought for the caucus on conservative grounds, on the "necessity of adhering to the old forms and established doctrines of the party."[48] Other Regency men feared that dangerous consequences would flow from the abolition of the caucus system. Marcy declared that to do away with the caucus would be to court disaster since "it is certain that our opponents will act against us in union and with vigour."[49] To Croswell's mind, "the change w'd threaten the prostration of the rep. party"; "worse, De Witt Clinton himself might try to run for the presidency."[50]

Despite these arguments there was a tremendous opposition to the caucus in 1824. Why should the caucus have been so unpopular? Why did the people refuse to listen to its defenders who quite rightly argued that the caucus concentrated the mass vote, prevented the people from being unduly swayed by local demagogues, and served to strengthen and unify the party? Moreover, the alleged prostitution of patronage, and the bargaining between the presidents and the members of Congress do not seem to have presented a grave aspect, however justifiable the apprehensions with regard to the future may have been. Further, although intrigues were not entirely absent from the proceedings of the caucus, they do not appear to have given rise to actually corrupt practices. The personages raised to the presidency by the caucus were not so much its creatures as men designated beforehand by public opinion or by a very considerable section of it, owing to their great services. In short, the caucus was by no means as bad as it was made out to be.

The reason for the public's passionate antagonism to the congressional caucus lies in the ardent democratic spirit of the times. The 1820's was a decade in which the American people felt a new self-confidence and pride. A sovereign people was replacing the rule of the Virginian aristocracy. The American succeeded by his own wits in business. In politics, too, he recognized no superior. As a result, the oligarchical nature of the congressional caucus made it intolerable. Furthermore, the aristocratic caucus no longer possessed the saving grace of being operated by the eminent men of the Revolution to whom public opinion had awarded a deep respect. It was this same enthusiasm for democratic reform which brought about the Constitution of 1821 and produced electoral victories, without exception, for the party and candidates who supported democratic reform. One of the few remaining vestiges of aristocratic authority in 1824 was the congressional caucus. Its annihilation symbolized the end of party control from above. Henceforth, for better or for worse, American politics would be directed from below.

The various presidential aspirants whose chances for election would be improved by the destruction of the congressional caucus exploited the democratic temper of the times by attacking the institution in an exaggerated and irrational fashion. The opportunistic nature of the candidates' stand on the caucus is indicated by the fact that Adams, Clay, Calhoun, and Jackson were as willing as Crawford to accept caucus nominations when they could get them. All of them had the blessing of state legislative caucuses. While Virginia, Georgia, New York, and North Carolina nominated Crawford, Kentucky, Missouri, Illinois, Ohio, and Louisiana supported Henry Clay. South Carolina put forth William Lowndes and, after his death, a second caucus nominated Calhoun. Most of the New England states nominated Adams. Furthermore, the vigorous resolutions of the Tennessee legislature opposing the holding of a congressional caucus must be interpreted in the light of the fact that this body had earlier nominated Jackson for the presidency. The conclusion seemed to be inescapable that men used the caucus when they could and called it evil when it blocked their path.

The nominating convention as a replacement for the caucus came into prominence in New York during 1824. The Utica Convention of the People's Party in that year helped to establish the nominating convention system in the state's politics. To be sure, there were earlier attempts to institute the convention system. For example, a movement was started by Tammany Hall in 1812 for a state convention, but it failed. In 1814, a convention was held, not for nominating candidates, but for determining party policy, and a mixed convention composed of both members of the legislature and delegates took place in 1817. But these efforts were sporadic. It was only after 1824 that the state convention became a fixed part of New York's nominating apparatus.

The numerous local meetings or "conventions" to select delegates for the state-wide convocation at Utica was an institutional innovation of the election of 1824. A typical example of these gatherings was the Troy convention that met on July 28. It consisted of delegates from most of the towns in Rensselaer County. The meeting was so crowded that "the stairs which led to the meeting room were thronged and many returned to their homes without being able to participate in the proceedings, regretting that the assemblage had not been convened at the park."[51] Resolutions were passed in support of a law restoring to the people the right of choosing presidential and vice-presidential electors. Moreover, the caucus was condemned and the meeting declared that henceforth backing would be withheld from anyone "who manifested a disposition to deprive the people of the exercise of their constitutional rights." A committee of one from each town represented in the convention was appointed to "nominate four persons to represent this county in the state convention to be holden on the 21st day of September."[52] This committee resolved to work for Clinton's nomination at the Utica convention. The procedural methods and substantive declarations of the Troy convention reflect quite accurately what transpired at other local convocations throughout the state.

For over thirty years, a basic element in the local organizations' influence on national politics was the right enjoyed by the members of the legislature in New York to choose the state's presidential electors. The legislature had granted itself this important privilege in 1792. According to the preamble of the law, the right to choose presidential electors had been assumed originally, not because the legislature indorsed the general idea, but because there was not sufficient time prior to the election of 1792 to make arrangements for a popular choice of electors. The power, nevertheless, was never surrendered and no widespread popular objection to the legislative choice of presidential electors seems to have appeared until 1823, when Calhoun's friends stimulated the movement for repeal in order to prevent the nomination of Crawford.

The People's Party, which led the movement for the reform of the electoral law in 1824, claimed that under the existing system the will of the people might be easily obstructed. For the members of the legislature, who selected the electors, were chosen an entire year before the presidential balloting occurred, and during that period they were "exposed to the arts of seduction and to the influence of unprincipled politicians."[53] Indeed, state senators were in some cases elected more than one year before the election of the chief executive. Clearly, the legislature might not under such circumstances truly represent popular sentiment on the presidential candidates. As for the charge of their opponents that the popular choice of presidential electors might result in a split of the state's electoral votes among the several aspirants, the promoters of reform claimed that this danger might be obviated by the use of a general ticket.[54]

The Bucktails, who conducted the fight to preserve the existing electoral system, also attempted to convince the public of the wisdom of their position. The *Albany Argus* was even bold enough to contend that "of the proposed change in the mode of choosing electors of the President in this state, there is not a solitary indication that the people demand it or are prepared for it."[55] They insisted that it was folly to change a law formulated by the "wise forefathers" of the state and "tested in many a Presidential Election."[56] The Regency men, in addition, asked those who were concerned about the well-being of the state to think about the upheaval that would unquestionably disrupt the campaign if the people were granted the right to vote directly for the presidential electors. If the law were altered apprehension would also persist that the ballot of New York might be distributed among the numerous nominees—on the needless assumption that the district method of voting would be used. Finally, the Bucktails managed to use their favorite argument that the movement for electoral change was just a ruse to get De Witt Clinton elected President.[57]

It is probable that the idea of the popular choice of presidential electors did not really disturb the Bucktails very much. More alarming than the abstract principle was the inexpediency of immediate change. As Edwin Croswell put it: "The danger to the rep[ublican] party lies in the repeal and not in the refusal."[58] Having alienated large numbers of people everywhere by their support of the congressional caucus, the Crawford forces felt that they could win only if the election reverted to the House of Representatives and New York could be held in the Crawford column. Congressman Plumer, Jr., declared that "Everything is here considered as depending upon New York."[59] Martin Van Buren expressed his point of view in a letter to Benjamin F. Butler: "From a greater variety of circumstances I am well satisfied that if New York does not repeal the electoral law and supports the caucus which has been held by her recommendation Mr. Clay will retire and his friends will support Mr. Crawford."[60] Thus, the Bucktails were convinced that their best chance for winning the state over to the Crawford side lay in opposing all change in the method of choosing presidential electors. The following year the Regency might sing an entirely different song.

The political parties were aided in their tasks by the use of ancillary organizations which were controlled by the leadership of the machine. The Republicans were served by the Tammany Society, while the Federalists found a haven in the Washington Benevolent Society. Ostensibly social and benevolent clubs, they performed important political functions. The Society of St. Tammany had been founded in 1789, and was named after an Indian chief who was famous for wisdom, kindness, and dedication to freedom. In opposition to organizations that grew up during the Revolution in support of the English cause and which were named St. George, St. Andrew, and St. David, Tammany was elevated to the stature of a saint as a gesture of ridicule and made the name-bearer of the new club by its patriotic founders.[61] As an effort to democratize American life the organization rejected traditional English forms and followed aboriginal usages and Indian titles for the society's officers. It was largely through the efforts of Aaron Burr that the Tammany Society became a political tool of the Republican Party. Pamphlets, speeches, and social pressures became the club's main techniques in promoting party solidarity.[62]

The success of the Tammany Society led a group of Federalist merchants under the guidance of Isaac Sebring, Gulian C. Verplanck, and Richard Varick to found the Washington Benevolent Society in 1808. The club, which attempted to make political capital for the Federalist Party from the use of George Washington's name, quickly established branches all over the state and infused the Federalists with new vigor and enthusiasm for awhile. The customs of the Tammany Society in holding its meetings behind closed doors, and in stimulating a sense of kinship among the organization's members were closely followed. An effort was made to provide financial assistance to those in dire need, particularly to veterans of the Revolution. The quaint, colorful, and mysterious practices of the group appealed to men of all walks of life, and served to increase popular appeal of Federalist principles.[63] The group lasted about a dozen years. Its last public celebration took place in 1817, although there are public records of its meetings as late as 1820.[64]

Clearly, New York's political parties had succeeded in constructing efficient and sophisticated machinery to achieve their goals by the end of the first quarter of the nineteenth century. Although the structures did not function equally well for all parties and the passing of time brought about inevitable changes, the basic modes and procedures of operation for American politics were established during this era.

IV

LOCAL, STATE, AND NATIONAL POLITICS

"I fear I may not see Mr. Van Buren and I regret much that I cannot but give my best respects and best wishes to him, and tell him if he gives his orders to the Senior member of the Regency at home I shall receive them regularly and give to them coming through that channel full faith and credit."[1] The importance of maintaining regular channels of communication between the national and state governments is evident in this attempt by Silas Wright to ensure Martin Van Buren, who was serving in Washington as Andrew Jackson's Secretary of State at the time, an effective liaison with party leaders in Albany. A study of the interrelationships of local, state, and national politics is essential for understanding the evolution of American democracy. Here one finds sharp differences from the situation of our time. For the political perspective of the average citizen of the nineteenth century varied widely from that of a contemporary American. The populace in the time of Jackson was much less concerned with national affairs than with local and state matters. Despite these narrower horizons, however, one can discern a movement in the direction of broader concern.

A thorough investigation of the connections between local, state, and national politics can uncover a wealth of information regarding the type of party organization and institutional apparatus that existed in New York in the first quarter of the nineteenth century. Effective political machines were being constructed on a "grass roots" level in almost every locality throughout the state, and party zealots made strenuous efforts to control the political behavior of the multitudes. The Albany Regency, of course, represents the most fully developed instance of this type of leadership. It could rapidly discern the direction of popular opinion, stimulate powerful emotions in behalf of the organization, and exert a potent influence over the people's thinking and behavior. An able and clever leadership, under the guidance of Martin Van Buren, formulated tactics and strategies that succeeded in regulating to a substantial degree the action of Bucktail outposts in every nook and cranny of the state. Justices of the peace and sheriffs, together with other minor local officials, came to exert, as Judge Jabez Hammond shrewdly noted, a decisive influence in maintaining state-wide party discipline. For a long time, moreover, the mayors of important cities like New York were designated by the party in power at Albany. Through the instrumentality of all these public officials, the party determining their appointments could effectively exercise control at will in almost all the counties and cities of the Empire State.[2] Indeed, at the Constitutional Convention of 1821, Delegate Rufus King insisted that control over the appointment of some 2,300 justices brought more political power than would all the remaining patronage in New York.[3] A justice of the peace at that time was usually the most influential person in his area and whether he was a farmer or a tender of cattle, he was aware of the political sympathies of every suitor in his court. As a result of the paucity of higher courts, neighbors were forced to go to him, and in adjudicating disputes, it was understood that he would not blindfold himself while holding the scales of justice.

Realizing what an effective means the justices of the peace were for control of local politics, Martin Van Buren opposed the recommendation of the Committee on the Council of Appointment at the Constitutional Convention of 1821 that they be chosen by the people. He argued that if the villagers and townsmen were allowed to choose their own justices of the peace, the latter would lose their independence because of the necessity of currying favor with the leaders of the local political machine. The committee's recommendation, therefore, failed to rectify the evils of the Council. The justices of the peace should operate in an atmosphere free from political pressure and intimidation. To realize this objective the Little Magician suggested that the board of supervisors and the courts of common pleas in every county should each send to the governor a separate list of names equal to the number of justices of the peace allotted to the county. When the two lists agreed the candidates were automatically confirmed; when they disagreed the governor would make the choice from the two lists.[4] Rufus King, a staunch ally of Van Buren by 1821, conceded that behind the noble sentiments of the Little Magician's speeches in behalf of independent justices of the peace lay the goal of bringing "the final appointment . . . to Albany," giving the state headquarters of the party machine the final word in these decisions.[5] If the choice of these key officials were to be placed in the hands of the party hierarchy in Albany, then the dominant political organization in the state could effectively control politics at the "grass roots" level. For similar reasons, the Bucktail chieftains opposed giving to the people of each county the right to elect the sheriffs and county clerks. Van Buren's political opponents exposed his proposal as a ruse to establish the Bucktail party as the dominant political force in the state. Peter A. Jay denounced the Little Magician as desiring the right to make all the important political appointments himself.[6] Others stressed the fact that Van Buren's suggestions would have limited rather than have expanded the rights of the people in running their government.[7]

Van Buren's proposal that the governor should have the final word in selecting the justices of the peace was ultimately incorporated into the seventh section of the fourth article of the Constitution as it passed the Convention of 1821. It won by the vote of 60 to 55 despite the strong opposition of most anti-Bucktails. A few years afterward it was removed from the Constitution, however, so that the right of the people to select their justices of the peace was restored to the respective localities. The Bucktail chief was defeated in his efforts to block the passage of a motion giving to the electors of each county the right to choose their sheriffs and county clerks.

The local political units established a number of techniques to enable them to achieve their objectives. Probably the most popular spot for the dissemination of political propaganda was the tavern or bar. For this was the place where people could and did unbend, enjoy themselves, have a drink, socialize, and engage in free discussion. A skillful proprietor was in an ideal position to guide the conversation along lines that would help to circulate his ideas. If he had any insight into the human psyche, he could exert substantial control over the views of his customers. As the parties became increasingly aware of the bartender's influence, they intensified their efforts to attract him to their group. Thus arose the fame of such establishments as the Tontine Coffee House, Lewis' Tavern, Martling's Tavern, and many others as centers of political activity in the Empire State.[8]

To keep their finger on the pulse of local political happenings in the outlying areas of the state, the parties maintained contacts in the large land companies. For example, Joseph Ellicott, the chief agent of the Holland Land Company on its western lands, virtually assumed the post of leader of the Bucktail party on the Holland Purchase. Although he personally occupied no public positions, he influenced all political appointments throughout that area of the state. On all subjects pertaining to the western sector of New York, political leaders on both the state and national level conferred with him and frequently advocated public policies in accordance with his proposals. Despite the manifold responsibilities resting upon his shoulders, Ellicott found it expedient and necessary to make sure that his voice was heard on such matters as the choice of postmasters, military promotions both in time of war and peace, and the nomination of candidates to public office. Occasionally, his political enterprises menaced his position with the company; thus, in 1813, tenants in the Genesee area levelled accusations against him for attempting to coerce them into supporting the gubernatorial aspirations of Daniel D. Tompkins.[9]

The local and county units of the party gradually developed a repertoire of techniques that would promote electoral victory. For example, Ebenezer Foote, the Federalist political boss of Newburgh, utilized handbills in 1795 to stimulate public enthusiasm, and he also provided transportation to and from the polling booths for his sympathizers who had no other way of getting there.[10] By 1810, similar techniques were being employed by the Republican leaders of Delaware County in order to enlarge their electoral margins. Indeed, the Republican Committee of Correspondence for Delaware County decided on January 10 of that year to divide the county into a minimum of three or a maximum of eight districts for each of which some "young and active person" would be selected whose job was to have a "personal communication with every elector" in order to discover his leanings on public questions. With the information culled from these interviews, the political leaders were able to draw up lists of probable Federalists and Republicans, making possible more accurate evaluation of relative party strength and more intelligent allocation of campaign resources.[11] The records are full of complaints against powerful landlords such as James Duane, William Cooper, and Stephen Van Rensselaer who did not hesitate to exert undue pressures on their tenants at election time.[12] Finally, attempts were made to allow unqualified voters to cast a ballot during elections.[13]

Intimate relations also existed between state leaders and New Yorkers who held jobs in the federal government. For example, after Martin Van Buren had been chosen a United States senator in 1821, a steady correspondence persisted between him and state leaders in an effort to coordinate public policy. De Witt Clinton's famous Green Bag Message of 1821 showed that the Little Magician exerted pressure on the federal government to have certain postmasters in New York removed from office. Shortly after the election of 1820, Clinton publicly accused the Monroe Administration of using the federal patronage in order to influence the outcome of the balloting in the Empire State.[14] In an effort to buttress his charge, Clinton undertook a thorough search for supporting documentation. He wrote to Henry Post: "I want authentic testimony of the interference of the National Gov't in our elections. Our friends must be up and doing on this subject."[15] The papers Clinton collected were so voluminous that he had to place them in a green bag when he submitted them to the legislature together with a message on January 17, 1821. The testimony included a letter from Martin Van Buren to Henry Meigs, a relative of Return J. Meigs, the Postmaster General, in which the New York senator expressed several complaints: "Our sufferings owing to the rascality of deputy Postmasters is intolerable and cries aloud for relief . . . and unless we can alarm them by two or three prompt removals, there is no limiting the injurious consequences that may result from it." Van Buren proceeded to offer several recommendations for the removal of officials allegedly guilty of interfering with the circulation of pro-Tompkins campaign literature, as well as suggestions for their replacement. In less than a month, all of Van Buren's wishes had been complied with down to the minutest details. De Witt Clinton asserted that Van Buren's letter revealed "plainly that the aid of the General Gov't is necessary in the election and this aid was unquestionably afforded."[16] Clinton further accused James Monroe of complicity in fulfilling Van Buren's mandate. William W. Van Ness remarked: "If I am not mistaken, President Monroe will never cease to regret that he has *lent* himself to Martin Van Buren and his coadjustors."[17] Clearly, the maintenance of contact between local and national leaders was a fundamental aspect of political organization in New York at this time.

Martin Van Buren's frequent visits with Thomas Ritchie and William H. Crawford in 1823 and 1824 also indicate the extent to which he strove to make the voice of the Republican party in New York an effective influence in presidential politics. In March, 1823, Van Buren met with William Crawford in Washington where they mapped out the strategy to be used by the Georgian in his bid for the presidency during the coming year.[18] The New York senator subsequently spent much of the following June with Thomas Ritchie of Virginia in order to unite the political organizations of the two states in the vanguard of the Crawford forces. John Calhoun commented: "Between the Regency at Albany and the Junto at Richmond there is a vital connection. They give and received hope from each other, and confidently expected to govern this nation."[19] In the spring of 1827 Van Buren took a trip to the South in order to bolster support for Andrew Jackson's presidential aspirations. He conferred with party leaders in such key states as Virginia, North Carolina, South Carolina, and Georgia. In the course of a most revealing letter about the trip, Van Buren cited his dreams for a closer integration between state and national politics, and his efforts to enlarge the voice of the Empire State in national counsels. He argued that the trip

> will enable me to be much more useful to my Republican friends by extending my acquaintance and the number of my personal friends over the States as far as that can conveniently be done. Personally this was important to me but politically considered I regard it as of greater importance to our cause. It is certainly true that for the past our public men have confined their intercourse and views too exclusively to home concerns. The consequence has been that out of the state they were but little known and when their friends at home stood in want of their influence abroad it could not be given. It appeared to me that there never was a better opportunity for me to correct as far as it lay in my power this error because the circumstances of the moment enabled me to visit other States under the most favorable auspices and because I left behind me in Albany a host of talent and experience it would have been an excess of vanity in me to have suffered stood in need of my personal assistance.[20]

Today one takes for granted the pre-eminent interest of the public in national politics as compared to state or local politics; as a result, it might surprise many that a study of

New York politics during the early nineteenth century would seem to indicate that the opposite situation existed at that time. As seen in newspaper editorials, handbills, and political pamphlets that have been preserved, for example, there was much more attention given to the gubernatorial contests in 1816 and 1820 than to the presidential races of those years. The same truth is even more sharply indicated for the period before 1812. The *New York American,* the *New York Evening Post,* and the *Albany Argus* from January, 1819, to March, 1820, moreover, disclose that slightly over three times as many columns were devoted to the Bucktail-Clintonian political wrangling than to the question of whether Missouri should be admitted as a slave state. The Monroe Doctrine received hardly more than passing notice in the newspapers of New York when James Monroe uttered its principles in 1823.

In trying to estimate the concern of New Yorkers with national as compared to state politics in the early nineteenth century, the election of 1824 provides us with conflicting data that are a challenge to historical interpretation. On the one hand, the virtually exclusive domination of the election campaign by such issues as the congressional caucus and the popular choice of presidential electors would indicate a very great interest among New Yorkers in national affairs. In view of the great domestic questions that could have been raised as subjects of political debate, it is remarkable that two issues that hardly affected New Yorkers as such at all, aroused so much fervor among the people as to exclude almost completely the discussion of other matters more directly relevant to their needs. In addition, the active participation of the Bucktail Party in the campaign in behalf of Crawford's candidacy also suggests great interest in the state regarding national politics.

There are other considerations that tend to cast doubt over the hypothesis that New Yorkers had a greater interest in the national election than the state contest in 1824. For example, with the exception of the Bucktail campaign for Crawford, there was little concerted effort in 1824 among the candidates for public office in the state to foster support for any of the contenders for the presidential prizes. In fact, most of the people who were running for the New York legislature in 1823 did not commit themselves at all on the question of presidential preference, although it was these people who were to choose the presidential electors in the fall of the following year. In addition, while Calhoun stimulated sentiment in New York for electoral reform and the end of the congressional caucus as a method of nominating candidates, most of the people in the state who spoke on these fundamentally national issues in 1824, did not declare themselves publicly in favor of any particular candidates. Some articles in the public press explicitly berate the populace for its indifference to presidential matters. Editorials in the *New York American* in 1823 exhorted the Empire State's citizens to take a more active interest in the national side of the campaign, to demand from all aspirants to public office their views on the presidential question.[21] Itself committed to John Quincy Adams, the paper argued that since unanimity as regards the best candidate of the Republican Party was impossible, the matter ought to be openly discussed. Moreover, since the men chosen for the legislature in 1823 would vote for the presidential electors the following year, it was essential for the people to know which aspirants for the presidency they favored most. Despite the importance of the question the public seemed insufficiently concerned about it to raise the issue. Probably one reason why the presidential question was not more strenuously agitated in the state campaign of 1823 was the hope that the legislators would repeal the law regulating the choice of presidential electors. This hope is well illustrated in the *New York Statesman* of September 11, 1823: "We are compelled to believe that as the people will have an opportunity to express their sentiments on the presidential question by the choice of electors in the autumn of 1824, it would be better to ask no pledges in relation to that subject at present." But, more basically, the apparent silence of New York political leaders on the subject of presidential preferences may reflect relative indifference on the part of the people toward national politics despite the popularity of the issue of electoral reform.

The virtual absence from the People's Party campaign

literature in 1824 of opinions regarding the various presidential candidates suggests a lack of concern on their part with the national election. To be sure, the People's Party attacked the Bucktails' support of William Crawford upon whose brow an antidemocratic stigma could be branded because of his nomination by a congressional caucus, but they voiced no presidential preferences of their own. Apparent indifference to the national election is also reflected in the nomination by the People's Party of De Witt Clinton as governor, a man who disliked John Quincy Adams, although most of the leaders of the People's Men were known to prefer the Massachusetts statesman for president.[22] A slack interest in the national as compared with the state election is also indicated by the fact that on almost all of the posters and advertisements of the People's Party in the various counties of the state, the names of the candidates for state office always occupied a more prominent position and were printed with bolder type than those of federal candidates. Even the names of candidates for state Assembly were more prominently displayed than those who ran for the House of Representatives![23] This observation regarding the placement of the names of various People's candidates on campaign posters, significant in itself, notably strengthens the impression of relative indifference to the national contest on the part of the People's Party.

While state politics at this time may generally have concerned New York's citizenry more than federal elections, there were probably special reasons, in addition, for the almost total neglect of the presidential contest by the People's Party in its state campaign. For one thing, the People's Party came into existence in consequence of a local problem—the revision of the state electoral law. As a result, it exerted most of its efforts to rectify the problem, which was its principal *raison d'être*. Moreover, since the people had no power to select the presidential electors, there was little point in spending one's time discussing a matter about which the populace could do nothing. In addition, the People's Men had no Martin Van Buren directing the campaign, an uncommonly ambitious politician who was working for realignment of national party lines. Finally, having chosen a gubernatorial candidate whose presidential views differed from those of the majority of the party, the leaders of the People's Party tended to be reticent on the matter lest they alienate some votes.

How is one to reconcile such great public interest in questions like the congressional caucus and popular choice of presidential electors, which pertain exclusively to national politics, with seemingly widespread indifference to the matter of which presidential candidate received the support of the state? It is possible that New Yorkers really were much concerned with the national side of the election, and that the ostensible apathy in relation to the question of presidential preference stems from the fact that in 1824 the people could not yet choose their presidential electors directly. But if they were at all interested in the presidential question, it is not unreasonable to assume that they would have at least required their candidates for the state legislature, whose job it would be to choose the electors, to express themselves publicly regarding the merits of a particular candidate for the presidency. It is more probable that the national political contest did not interest the people at this time nearly so much as the state election. The great popularity of such issues as the congressional caucus and the popular selection of presidential electors, therefore, must be laid, not to their being an expression of a concern with the national aspects of the campaign or a desire of the people to participate more actively in presidential politics, but rather to the fact that they were a symbol of the battle for democracy in New York. Since 1820, New Yorkers had been engaged in a struggle for the reform of the state's political institutions. The caucus and the choice of electors by the legislature were the last vestiges of the dying aristocracy. The unreasonably insulting epithets hurled at the enemies of these reforms and the exaggerated importance assigned to these measures in the campaign literature lend further support to the notion that their real significance lies in symbolizing the fight for political reform rather than being a genuine source of discontent.

Like the popularity of the caucus and electoral reform

issues, the active Bucktail campaign in behalf of Crawford is also not a valid indication of predominant state interest in the national contest. The Bucktail support of Crawford was primarily the result of Van Buren's influence in the councils of the organization, and the New York senator was exceptional in this period for his extensive involvement in and preference for national affairs. In 1824, as noted previously, Van Buren travelled extensively all over the country in order to consult with local leaders on Crawford's behalf. His trips, which were so widespread that they necessitated his being absent quite frequently from the sessions of the eighteenth congress, included a conciliatory offer to the Federalist party in Massachusetts.[24] As the Bucktail hopes for electoral victory in the Empire State dwindled in 1824, Van Buren concentrated increasingly on attaining Crawford's triumph on the national level. He hoped that the power and prestige that would accrue from an allotment of the federal patronage would cancel out the humiliation and disgrace of defeat within the state. Moreover, Van Buren indicated to his associates that after Crawford had won the presidency, he would be willing to support whatever adjustments in the electoral system the people desired.[25]

It is rather striking that most political leaders in New York during the early nineteenth century, even those who held office at one time in the national government, frequently expressed a preference for state positions rather than federal ones. When Robert R. Livingston's duties as Secretary of the Department of State and Foreign Affairs interfered with his responsibilities as chancellor of New York in 1782, he gave up the former office. John Jay resigned as chief justice of the United States Supreme Court in order to become governor of New York in 1795. Five years later, Thomas T. Tillotson resigned from the House of Representatives in order to become secretary of state in New York, while De Witt Clinton, elected to the United States Senate in 1802, resigned a year later to accept appointment as mayor of New York City. Daniel D. Tompkins resigned soon after his election to Congress in 1804 to become an associate justice of the New York Supreme

Court, and even more significantly, after being elected vice president of the United States in 1817, he ran for the New York governorship in 1820. In addition, Silas Wright, though re-elected to Congress in 1828, left the job in order to become comptroller of the state of New York, which position he held until 1833; later he quit as senator to be governor. Finally, Azariah C. Flagg, despite frequent opportunity to obtain a high federal post, spent his entire political career performing service on a state level.

A description of the Jacksonian movement in New York points up some extremely revealing facts regarding the inter-relationships of state and national politics. Considerations of state and local affairs between 1825 and 1828 were unquestion-ably treated as matters of much greater importance than na-tional ones. The party of the Regency completely detached it-self from matters of national import in 1825 in an endeavor to restore state-wide political power to itself. Despite disagree-ment with Adams' public and patronage policies, the Buck-tail publication, the *Albany Argus,* limited its attack to an occasional reprinting of unfriendly editorials from other papers.[26] Van Buren was not sure that even this was desirable, but Marcy persuaded him that Croswell was exercising due caution.[27] At the moment, the Bucktails were determined to keep to themselves any unfavorable ideas they might have about the President and his running of the national adminis-tration.

Even during 1826, after the Bucktails had re-established their state-wide basis of power and had become even more discontented with the actions of John Quincy Adams, the Regency politicians remained extremely circumspect in their comments on the Washington administration. In the course of 1827 there was a steady acceleration in the Regency's participa-tion in the national political contest. By March, attacks on the president and his cohorts were featured in almost every issue. But even in the closing days of 1827 when the Bucktail leader, Silas Wright, convinced of the wisdom of an early nomination of Andrew Jackson, urged his colleagues to the same conclu-sion, he also added the significant qualification that nothing "must be allowed to hazard our position at home."[28] The Canton Congressman remarked on another occasion that "even Mr. Van Buren would jeopardize the Presidential election itself rather than risk a breaking up of our ranks at home or of destroying our strength and harmony in the present legislature."[29] The New York politicians were keenly aware that the primary basis of their power lay in the state and that participation in national politics was a luxury to be enjoyed only by those who had first secured the necessary local backing.

In spite of the principal concern of New York political leaders with local matters during this period, the Empire State, which was the largest state in the Union, did exert extremely powerful influence on national affairs. When allied with Virginia, it was hard to beat.[30] The maneuvering of Thurlow Weed in the New York legislature after the election of 1824, moreover, was most important not only in making possible an Adams victory in the state but also in killing Clay's presidential aspirations by preventing his name from being submitted to the House of Representatives as one of three highest contenders for the office.[31] It was New York's Stephen Van Rensselaer who cast the vote in the House that decided that John Quincy Adams was to be the sixth President of the United States.[32] The Antimasonic controversy is an excellent illustration of how an event of local origin strongly affected events not only in New York but throughout the entire nation.[33] Most important, between 1824 and 1828 the groups opposed to Adams remained inchoate and divided until Martin Van Buren, the senator from New York, attempted to revamp the Republican Party on a national level by redefining party principles and distinctions. It was his genius that brought a new form out of the old.[34] Finally, it was New York's switch from Adams to Jackson in 1828 that elected the Tennessean as President.

Not only was interest in national politics subordinate to state and local affairs, but the emergence of a national consciousness was also retarded by sectional rivalry. Thus, antagonism toward the South affected the political behavior of New

Yorkers in the early nineteenth century. The idea was repeatedly expressed during the campaign of 1824 that the South was interfering with the affairs of the people of New York. For example, a handbill published by certain Clintonians in Albany asserted that the "committee of nine" to which the Flagg electoral bill had been referred in the state Senate in order to delay legislative action until after the balloting in the fall, was dominated by a "southern faction" bent on robbing the people "of their dearly bought privilege." Further, the weight of "the Southern Dynasty in our State Legislature is certainly to be deprecated and the state sovereignty is jeopardized when officers of the federal government can meet in a dark corner and prepare the measures of a state legislature."[35] Even a group of Bucktails from Orange County refused to support the Regency's candidate for the presidency, William Crawford, on the grounds of resentment against Southern domination of the federal government. A newspaper entitled the *Independent Whig* declared that it was "attached to that party which is called Bucktail," but that it "still came forward for Mr. Adams alone." The editors affirmed that although they had no personal predilections in Adams' favor, they were "satisfied that under all circumstances the true interests of our country call for his election. AWAKE O NORTH and show yourself in the majesty of strength! Shake off the minions who would barter your birthright for a mess of pottage."[36] These instances of attack against the South both for its interference in New York politics and its monopoly of the offices of the federal government reflect the sectionalist sentiment that was rapidly growing at this time throughout the country.

The popularity of the idea about a Southern conspiracy indicates the overwhelming extent to which New Yorkers were "conscious" of their state or sectional citizenship as distinct from their United States citizenship. One of the most frequent refrains in the campaign pamphlets of the People's Party was the assertion that the Albany Regency was a participant in a conspiracy that enabled the Southern states, especially Virginia, to dominate the federal government, denying New

York the prominence it deserved in national affairs. "Thirty-six out of forty has Virginia supplied us with candidates for the Presidency. Is this equality? Let the yeomanry of the State of New York answer. This state pays more than one-third part of the annual revenue of the United States; and yet she tamely consents to place it at the disposal of her southern friends, who have exercised the right so long that they now claim it by prescription."[37] This is a revealing echo of the sectional hostility expressed in the incidents leading up to the Missouri Compromise, and was a forerunner of the provincial jealousies soon to be aroused in connection with the tariff and slavery.

Martin Van Buren's difficulties in achieving a national union among all the various factions hostile to the chief executive illustrate most clearly some of the problems that arise out of trying to forge a country-wide organization in the face of sectional differences. The tariff question, for example, threatened to arouse antagonism between Jacksonian groups in many parts of the country. In order to secure Southern support the Regency chief had to make it appear as if the Hero and himself were free traders. In New York, however, a high tariff was extremely popular. In an effort to squash rumors that his successful tour of the South in 1827 as well as his absence from Congress when the Woolens Act of 1827 was defeated, indicated an antitariff attitude, Van Buren attended a tariff convention in Albany during the summer of the same year.[38] There he gave a speech that was a masterpiece in evasion. It was so difficult to determine Van Buren's position from his public address that one puzzled listener asked Benjamin Knower which side of the tariff question the New York senator represented.[39] The *Albany Argus* was equally desirous of being as ambiguous and noncommittal on the tariff question as possible. An editorial published in the July 3, 1827, edition of that newspaper made the following assertion: "We confess that we feel an interest in this question, and that we hope to witness the adoption of such salutary and judicious measures as shall lead to a practical advancement of all the interests dependent on such encouragement." In order to forestall a split on the tariff question and to push it into the background, the *Argus* likewise kept to a minimum its comments on the well known Harrisburg Convention of July 30, 1827. Clearly, the articles of the *Argus* during 1827 on the tariff as well as Van Buren's speech at the Albany Convention are prime examples of the attempt to straddle a troublesome issue. The solution of the Bucktails to make vague declarations, characterized by fancy language with little meaning, remains to the present the fundamental device employed to hold together national coalitions in the face of explosive questions.

The ardent efforts of Silas Wright and Martin Van Buren in 1828 to have Congress pass a tariff, however, indicate once again that when the needs of the national organization conflicted with those of the state party, the latter's affairs took precedence. Protariff sentiment in the Empire State was very strong. In the Bucktail party itself were such prominent leaders of the woolens industry as Benjamin Knower whose prosperity depended upon the enactment of protective duties. Consequently, evasion could not constitute a permanent solution of the problem. Silas Wright predicted that since the overwhelming number of New York Bucktails were anxious for tariff legislation, a failure to fulfill their desires would cause a "breaking up" of the party within the state.[40] Moreover, William Marcy warned Van Buren that if he hoped to capture the support of the electorate he must undertake some positive action in behalf of a protective tariff since the people still remembered his "failure to vote on the 1827 measure."[41] The result was Wright and Van Buren's work on what came to be known as the Tariff of Abominations, whose passage, Robert Remini has persuasively shown, was a political necessity for the Bucktails in New York.[42]

The problem of whom to select as Jackson's running mate in 1828 points up the same difficulty of mediating the demands of the state and national branches of the party. For although it was generally acknowledged among Jacksonians throughout the country that Calhoun was to be their choice for vice president, the necessity of keeping De Witt Clinton's friendship compelled the New York Bucktails to refrain from naming anyone other than the governor as the state's selection for the second place on the national ticket. On the one hand, the Bucktails desired De Witt Clinton's support in their efforts to form a coalition in favor of Jackson; on the other, they feared that having realized the impossibility of actualizing his presidential aspirations in 1828, Clinton would attempt to secure for himself the vice-presidency. Silas Wright suggested that the Bucktails could solve the problem best by not naming any particular candidate for vice president in their caucus, thereby discharging themselves "from the responsibility of being the leaders in kicking off Mr. Clinton, or in naming any other man."[43] Opposition to Calhoun by certain prominent Southerners like William Crawford, Sam Houston, and William Lewis plus the fear of provoking De Witt Clinton to nominate Jackson for the presidency before the Bucktails did, persuaded Martin Van Buren, who preferred the South Carolinian for the vice-presidency, to go along with Wright's proposal.[44] Failure of the legislative caucus that named Andrew Jackson for the presidency on January 31, 1828, to support Calhoun for the second place on the ticket strained severely relations between Van Buren and the Vice President. Silas Wright described Calhoun as "a very jealous friend of the Little Magician."[45] Clearly, the policy that most adequately met local needs did not always correspond to the best interest of the national organization. But, in the final analysis, the overriding consideration was that nothing must be done to endanger "our position at home."[46]

V

THE DEMOCRATIC TRANSFORMATION

"In general the politics of that State [New York] are but imperfectly understood out of it."[1] This confession by an observer as astute as James Madison suggests what a bewildering and enigmatic undertaking the study of New York politics during the first half-century of the history of the state constitutes. Numerous personal followings and rapidly shifting factions and regroupings played havoc with the human need to establish order and coherence. The attempt of Dixon Ryan Fox, therefore, to give meaning to party annals during this era is most praiseworthy and deserving of the utmost attention. Fox's thesis, furthermore, has the virtue of being simple and straightforward. He asserts that "whether or not democracy was desirable and practicable was the question uppermost in nearly every party contest. In no long-continued period before or since has there been so definite a philosophical alignment in the politics of the state, the Federalists and later the Clintonians arguing on the one side and the Republicans or Democrats arguing, and successfully, on the other."[2] It is indisputable that the democratization of the state's governmental institutions was the major theme in New York politics at this time. There are many facts, however, that appear to contradict Fox's position on the nature of that process. First of all, an examination of the Federalist party in its later days shows that a substantial segment of Federalists did not join the Clintonian ranks. Moreover, the record of the Clintonian party does not reveal a policy of consistent opposition to the expansion of democracy. Conversely, the anti-Clintonians often posed formidable obstacles in the paths of those who would broaden the base of popular control of the government. Thus, an accurate explanation of New York politics in the early nineteenth century and of the democratic transformation would necessitate some serious modification of Fox's contentions.

There was never any peculiar attraction of the Federalists for the Clintonians. Indeed, a substantial segment of Federalists always opposed the Clintonian wing of the Republican Party. It goes without saying that between 1777 and 1800 the primary enemies of the Federalists were the Republican followers of George Clinton. Even after 1800, however, when the Federalists were compelled to take sides in the feuding within the Republican ranks in order to share some of the fruits of political power, there was never a time when a large percentage of Federalists did not fight against the Clintonians. For example, the Quids or Lewisites, who were the opponents of De Witt Clinton, combined with the Federalists in 1807 to control the legislature and to oust Clinton from his post as mayor of New York.[3] Likewise, although the Federalists did not put up their own candidate for president in 1812, there was sufficient opposition to De Witt Clinton in New York to frustrate attempts to secure an official Federalist endorsement of his candidacy in the state.[4] Moreover, the election of the foremost anti-Clintonian Federalist, Rufus King, as United States senator from New York by the legislature in 1812 suggests that the anti-Clintonian Republicans on occasion voted with the Federalists. For although the Federalist Party had a majority in the lower house that year, it was not large enough to carry a joint session; as a result, King's support must have come from a union of Federalists and anti-Clintonian Republicans.[5] While Fox is unquestionably correct in pointing out that a large number of Federalists supported the Clintonians, it is necessary to stress, in addition, that many Federalists opposed them and joined sides with the other Republican faction in the state.

In 1814, Gulian C. Verplanck, the founder of the Washington Benevolent Society, assumed leadership of a large segment of Federalists opposed to Clinton. Verplanck had served as ringleader of a group that provoked a riot at the Columbia University commencement of 1811 in protest against the action of the provost who denied John B. Stevenson his degree. Stevenson, who was the class valedictorian, was refused his degree because he gave a pro-Republican graduation speech without faculty authorization. When Clinton, in exercise of the judicial powers possessed by the mayor of New York City at that time, heard the case, he severely rebuked the rioters and imposed heavy fines upon them. Verplanck himself was compelled by the mayor to pay a fine of two hundred dollars. Consequently, Clinton unleashed upon himself Verplanck's lasting enmity.[6] Verplanck proceeded to vilify him under the pseudonym of Abimelech Coody in a periodic publication called *The Corrector*. The sheet tried to spoil Clinton's good name by persuading the Federalists that Clinton's conduct merited disgrace and dishonor.[7] Other widely esteemed Federalists such as Judge Jacob Radcliff who had been named by his party in 1810 as mayor of New York City and Hugh Maxwell who had served as the state district attorney were associated with Verplanck's efforts to malign Clinton. Ambrose Spencer, Clinton's brother-in-law, who was hostile toward him at that time, aided the detractors of the New York mayor. All the participants in this undertaking labelled themselves "Washington Federalists," but their opponents referred to them mockingly as Coodies. This group played an important role in bringing about De Witt Clinton's dismissal in 1815 from the office of mayor of New York City.[8]

The literary output of the Coodies included the pamphlet entitled *A Fable* which described Clinton as "a young Irish greyhound of high and exorbitant pretensions."[9] Elsewhere, Clinton was referred to as one who would "sneer at crooked back."[10] Clinton met these attacks by writing an article in which he faintly disguised his identity under the signature of "A Travellor."[11] He acrimoniously condemned all those Federalists who had written against him, but the main object of his attack was the vindictive "rioter" who slandered him so relentlessly. Verplanck was portrayed "as the head of a political sect, called Coodies, of a hybrid nature, composed of the combined spawn of federalism and jacobinism, and generated in the venomous passion of disappointment and revenge; without any definite character neither fish nor flesh, bird nor beast, animal nor plant, but a non-descript made up of all monstrous, all prodigious things, abominable, unutterable and worse than fable."[12] Respite from Verplanck's implacable rancor came only in 1814 when he moved to Europe for two years.

There were numerous grounds for the hostility toward Clinton felt by many Federalists. First of all, from a practical point of view, the Federalists realized that if the entire party attached itself to Clinton, the Republicans would forsake him, and the problem of Federalist isolation would still not be overcome. Moreover, Clinton in an effort to prove that he was an authentic Republican spoke publicly in a degrading and derogatory manner about the Federalists on several occasions. Thus, the *New York American* exclaimed: "In short, Sir, you first insulted the federal party by unfounded vituperations, as you now do by obsequious blandishments."[13] Furthermore, his failure to back Rufus King's bid for re-election to the Senate in 1819 angered many. In announcing his opposition to Clinton's candidacy for the governorship of New York in 1820, King himself explicitly stated to his backers that "Mr. C throws away his claim to my forbearance. I shall not offend in not permitting him to attempt my degradation without suffering in his turn."[14] The noted Federalist leader, William Coleman, announced his intention of trying to unite the anti-Clintonian Federalists and the anti-Clintonian Republicans in support of Smith Thompson for the governorship of New York.[15] Clinton's refusal to reward with political offices many of those Federalists who had supported him for electoral office also augmented the ranks of his opponents in the party of Alexander Hamilton. Among those alienated in this fashion was Josiah Ogden Hoffman who had worked ardently in behalf of Clinton almost a decade. When Clinton declined to give him the recordership of New York City, a post Hoffman had held prior to 1810, he joined the enemy.[16]

Not only were many Federalists opposed to Clinton but they were actively courted by and received the ardent support of the anti-Clintonian Republicans under the leadership of Martin Van Buren. It will be remembered that Van Buren was the most influential person in securing the re-election of Rufus King in 1819 as United States senator. King reacted to the Little Magician's backing in the following way: "The Part taken by Mr. Van Buren has indeed been most liberal, and as I conceive at the risk of impairing his high standing, and influence among his political friends."[17] Moreover, King was prepared to admit that Van Buren's "views and principles deserve my hearty approbation."[18] As a result of these considerations, when Van Buren asked King to give "a public expression" in behalf of the Bucktail candidate for the governorship in 1820, King proved quite willing to reciprocate the "personal Respect and Esteem with which he has inspired me."[19]

Another incident that indicates the close cooperation between the Bucktails and the Federalists at this time involved the resignation of Joseph Ellicott in 1819 as a canal commissioner. It was Governor Clinton's intention to appoint Ephraim Hart as Ellicott's replacement. The Federalists, however, were adamantly opposed to Hart. Consequently, a Federalist representative approached Martin Van Buren and asked him to suggest a different candidate for the Federalist Party to back. The name of Henry Seymour was agreed upon. A short period of quiet but efficient electioneering among the Bucktails and Federalists followed which succeeded in securing a Senate nomination for Seymour, although Hart was chosen by the Assembly. When the two houses met for a joint ballot, Henry Seymour was selected as the new canal commissioner. Thus, a coalition of Bucktails and Federalists managed to thwart Clinton's political will.[20]

The eagerness with which the Bucktails tried to induce outstanding Federalists to join their ranks was evident in 1821 when the Regency-dominated Council of Appointment fired Thomas J. Oakley as attorney general along with thousands of others. An ardent Federalist named Samuel Talcott was the Bucktail choice to replace Oakley.[21] Van Buren had been interested in Talcott since 1819 when the Bucktail leader happened to read some newspaper articles critical of him and his leadership but written clearly and forcefully. When he inquired about the author of the articles, Van Buren discovered that it was a young Federalist attorney with a reputation as an outstanding orator, Samuel Talcott. Van Buren felt that the Bucktail Party would derive immense benefits from the services of a man like Talcott provided he could be persuaded to switch political loyalties. A chance meeting between the two men on a steamboat gave Van Buren the opportunity to initiate a series of discussions that succeeded in transforming Talcott into a stalwart Bucktail by the middle of 1820. Indeed, during the election of that year, Talcott worked energetically in behalf of Tompkins' bid for the governorship. The subsequent choice of Talcott as attorney general exemplifies Van Buren's policy of granting "some distinguished mark of attention" to outstanding and talented Federalists who would ally themselves with the Bucktail Party.[22]

That a substantial number of Federalists had joined the Bucktail ranks became quite obvious by the middle of 1819.[23] To denounce the motives of these apostate Federalists, Pierre C. Van Wyck, a leading Clintonian lieutenant, wrote a witty and sardonic pamphlet entitled *A Martling Man, or Says I to Myself—How is this* that made the opposition appear ludicrous.[24] Personal pique arising from Clinton's refusal to appoint him as recorder of New York City had led Josiah Ogdens Hoffman to switch loyalties. Barent Gardenier and Philip Brasher had abandoned the Clintonians for similar reasons.[25] Empty pledges and insincere obsequiousness were used by the Bucktails to obtain the support of Richard Hatfield and the sons of Alexander Hamilton, people whose names possessed magical, vote-getting appeal. The work of the Coodies under the leadership of Hugh Maxwell and Gulian Verplanck had been triggered by the riots at the Columbia commencement of 1811 and nurtured by the loving care of the Regency. It appears that the Bucktails were as eager as the Clintonians to absorb refugees from the Federalist party.

The last Federalist caucus at which both pro-Clintonian and anti-Clintonian delegates were present was held in January

1820. Elisha Williams split the gathering wide open by his boldly dictatorial assertion that all the delegates must support De Witt Clinton's choice for the post of Assembly speaker. John A. King immediately objected that he would not support the Clintonian candidate, and he further urged that all true Federalists should henceforth refrain from meeting again with party members subservient to De Witt Clinton.[26] A few days later fifty leading Federalists signed a document announcing the termination of the Federalist Party. The signers declared that "after deliberate reflection," they had "resolved to unite . . . unequivocally and without reserve" with the Bucktail Party. This revolutionary decision sprang from "a deep-rooted distrust of the views and character of Mr. Clinton as a politician" as well as from his endeavors "to create a personal faction, and to surround himself with a band of low minded sycophants, and venal dependents." It was clearly more desirable to dissolve the party than to use it basely as an instrument of personal aggrandizement.[27] In addition to most of the anti-Clintonian Federalists mentioned before, the signers included such eminent Federalists as Judge Morris S. Miller; Zebulon R. Shepherd, a former congressman; George Tibbits, an aspirant in 1816 for the post of lieutenant governor; and other prominent contemporary politicians. The ranks of Bucktail-oriented Federalists also embraced Peter Porter, Henry Storrs, and Walter Bowne. Hammond declared that the substantial array of able, wealthy, socially respectable, and dignified Federalists who sided with the Bucktails was unparalleled in extent in the political history of the state.[28]

These Federalist opponents of Clinton wasted no time in their efforts to promote the political goals of the Bucktail Party. Through the *New York American,* their unofficial organ of communication, they proclaimed that the "high minded descendants of the great men" of the state must withdraw all support from the cause of De Witt Clinton's efforts for reelection as governor in 1820. The Clintonians, in retaliation, referred to them sarcastically as "High-Minded Federalists" and discharged them from all obligations to their former political associates.[29] In the battle for a seat to the United States

Senate in 1821 for which Martin Van Buren and Nathan Sanford were competing, the high-minded Federalists lent their
active support to the Regency leader. Dismayed by the behavior of the Federalists, Judge William W. Van Ness reflected
sadly that "most of our Federalist friends have not even voted
for" Sanford, and "probably have thrown their votes away on"
Van Buren, "a man . . . with a decided political character."[30]

A study of Table 1 shows that of the twenty most prominent

TABLE 1
PRIOR POLITICAL AFFILIATION OF LEADING
POLITICAL FIGURES IN NEW YORK DURING THE 1820's

BUCKTAILS		ANTI-BUCKTAILS	
Name	Previous Political Affiliation	Name	Previous Political Affiliation
Martin Van Buren	Jeffersonian	Jacob Barker	Jeffersonian
Benjamin F. Butler	Jeffersonian	De Witt Clinton	Jeffersonian
Edwin Croswell	Jeffersonian	C. D. Colden	Federalist
Charles E. Dudley	Jeffersonian	John Crary	Jeffersonian
Azariah C. Flagg	Jeffersonian	T. A. Emmet	Jeffersonian
J. A. Hamilton	Federalist	Oliver Forward	Jeffersonian
Michael Hoffman	Jeffersonian	Obadiah German	Jeffersonian
Rufus King	Federalist	Charles Haines	Jeffersonian
Benjamin Knower	Jeffersonian	Henry Huntington	Jeffersonian
Morgan Lewis	Federalist	Peter A. Jay	Federalist
P. R. Livingston	Jeffersonian	W. J. Mac Neven	Jeffersonian
William L. Marcy	Jeffersonian	Thomas J. Oakley	Federalist
Erastus Root	Jeffersonian	Henry Post	Jeffersonian
Roger Skinner	Jeffersonian	Ambrose Spencer	Federalist
Samuel Talcott	Federalist	James Tallmadge	Jeffersonian
Smith Thompson	Jeffersonian	John Taylor	Federalist
Daniel Tompkins	Jeffersonian	William Tracy	Jeffersonian
Silas Wright	Jeffersonian	Pierre C. Van Wyck	Jeffersonian
Gulian Verplanck	Federalist	Thurlow Weed	Jeffersonian
Samuel Young	Jeffersonian	Henry Wheaton	Jeffersonian

personalities in New York's Bucktail and anti-Bucktail parties
respectively during the 1820's, 25 per cent of the leadership in
both groups was originally Federalist in orientation. The other
75 per cent had spent their entire political careers within the
fold of the Jeffersonian organization. Thus, both parties con-

tained approximately the same number of former Federalists as ranking members in their party hierarchy.

Some Federalists continued to maintain their independence, opposing both the Bucktails and Clintonians in 1820. A member of this group was William Coleman. He told John King: "After much thought, therefore, I have determined while things remain as they are to keep myself equally aloof from both. 'The plague take both your Houses.' "[31]

Even more important than the issue of whether the Clintonian party absorbed the leadership and membership of the old Federalist organization is the question of whether its policies, like those of the Federalists, consistently represented an aristocratic or conservative point of view opposed to the expansion of democracy. To be sure, one might also ask whether the assumption of Fox and most other historians of our early period that the Federalists were unalterably opposed to the expansion of democracy is completely accurate. While there are probably stronger grounds for holding this view in connection with the Federalists than with the Clintonians, it is revealing to note that there were occasions when the Federalists in New York favored democratic reforms against the opposition of the Republicans. The Federalists whose ranks comprised the largest number of landowners, for example, were the most active in putting through measures to help the negro. In 1799, Governor Jay backed legislation providing for the gradual abolition of slavery in New York.[32] A law of 1817 that designated July 4, 1827, as the date of emancipation of all slaves in the state received the firm support of Federalists in the two houses.[33] Moreover, in an effort to prevent the state's electoral vote from going to Thomas Jefferson in 1800, Alexander Hamilton became the first figure of public importance in New York to urge that a measure be passed through the legislature to divide the state into districts for the choice of presidential electors by the people.[34] Thus, even in regard to the Federalists, our stereotyped ideas do not tell the whole story.

The Clintonians are certainly undeserving of the badge of

aristocracy and conservatism that has been fastened to their lapels. Like the Federalists, they have a progressive record on the negro question. In his opening speech to the legislature of New York in 1820, Governor De Witt Clinton, for example, called attention to the Missouri controversy which had been plaguing the country for over a year. In contrast to the straddling position of the Bucktails, he called for a forthright stand by the state in support of James Tallmadge's bill which, while permitting Missouri to enter the Union as a slaveowning state,[35] would have prohibited the further introduction of slaves into the state and required all children born therein of slave parents to be freed upon reaching the age of twenty-five.

The Clintonians also favored significant political reforms. In an effort to promote De Witt Clinton's aspirations for the presidency in 1812, they provoked the first great revolt against the congressional caucus. His followers issued a remarkable address in which they not only protested against caucus nominations as opposed to the sovereignty of the states and the rights of the people, which were thereby appropriated by a small clique, but condemned them with comparable fervor as destructive of "the freedom of election." The address declared that "acquiescing in the regular nomination at Washington is by many considered as the touchstone of republicanism. The individuals or the states that dare to exercise the right of independent choice are denounced as schismatics, and factionalists; and if already an innovation so recent and so flagrant be called the regular nomination, what will be its influence should time and repetition give it additional sanction? . . . Should the practice become inveterate we do not hesitate to say that to promulgate a nomination will be to decree an election."[36]

It was primarily through the efforts of the Clintonians that the state convention in 1817, with its more representative elements, supplanted the legislative caucus as a method of nominating gubernatorial candidates. In an endeavor to secure for Clinton the nomination of the party as governor, in that year, Ambrose Spencer engineered a plan that would cancel out the small majority of the legislative caucus that he forecast would be opposed to Clinton. Immediately after the caucus had met, Spencer argued that it was unfair that Republicans, who came from counties represented in the legislature exclusively by Federalists, should have no voice in choosing the gubernatorial candidate of the party; consequently, delegates from these Federalist strongholds should be permitted to participate in the proceedings. Clearly, the procedure advocated by Spencer was much more democratic than the practice of limiting the right of nomination exclusively to members of the legislature; indeed, it called into being a state nominating convention, the first in the history of New York. At the same time the proposal was highly expedient for the Clintonians who had already undergone "indefatigable pains to have their extra members on the spot, so that had the motion for an immediate choice, succeeded, the cunning friends of Clinton would have carried him."[37] Van Buren, cognizant both of the political implications of Spencer's motion and of the warm, responsive chord evoked by the democratic suggestion, decided that the best he could do was to postpone action. Hence, he proposed that formal elections be held in the unrepresented counties which would choose a number of delegates from each one equal to the number of its seats in the legislature, and following which the caucus would again meet together as a state convention. The Clintonians, confident of their ability to return an overwhelming majority of delegates who would support their candidate, unhesitatingly backed Van Buren's motion. Their confidence was vindicated when the convention, which had reconvened on March 25, named Clinton as its candidate for governor by the impressive margin of 85 to 41. Despite his strong dislike of Clinton, Van Buren acquiesced in the decision of the convention so that in the subsequent election Clinton polled 97 per cent, or all but 1,479 of the 44,789 votes cast.[38]

The manner in which the state nominating convention was introduced provides the pattern for most of the other democratic innovations that followed in subsequent years: opportunistic politicians, without any permanent or recognizably consistent commitments, pushed certain democratic causes that they felt would promote their ambitions. The "democratic banner" moved back and forth among the different factions depending on the particular circumstances. Dixon Ryan Fox argues that the anti-Clintonian wing of the Republican party in New York was the more democratic contingent, while the Clintonians who allegedly absorbed most of the conservative elements of the Federalist party were aristocratic in orientation and policy.[39] While there are some instances of the anti-Clintonians promoting the cause of democracy, here we have one of the several instances of precisely the opposite situation: the supposedly conservative Clintonians pushed for the more democratic nominating device of a state convention against the opposition and delaying tactics of their presumably more liberal adversaries. This suggests that the traditional categories of interpretation in American politics—liberal-democratic vs. conservative-aristocratic—do not fit the facts. If this is so, we have to find some new explanation of what was at stake in the battle for political power.

The role of expediency in determining one's position on the subject of democratic reform is also evident in Clinton's attitude toward the calling of a constitutional convention in 1821. Clinton opposed the bill introduced by Ogden Edwards in February, 1818, to call a convention to devise a new method of appointment. But, by 1820, his views had undergone a sharp change. The change was probably motivated by the fact that in 1818 his party controlled the legislature and consequently the Council of Appointment, while in 1820 these were in the hands of the enemy who was ready to "turn out the *whole* of the Clintonians from office."[40] But pragmatic reasoning like this, rather than abstract philosophic commitments, governed the decisions of all parties on all matters at this time.

The record of the Clintonians and other alleged conservatives at the Constitutional Convention of 1821 ought to establish irrefutably their right to share the credit for many of the most important governmental innovations in the history of the state. The Clintonian delegates, first of all, voted for the abolition of both the Council of Revision and the Council of Appointment.[41] Indeed, one Clintonian subsequently complained that the method of appointment adopted by the convention was still too undemocratic; he felt that the appointing power under the new constitution would bestow upon the future governors "princely prerogatives," which would be limited only by an "aristocratic Senate" without the more democratic Assembly having any voice at all in the procedure.[42] The Clintonians also supported the measure vesting the veto power in the governor with a two-thirds vote of the legislature necessary to overcome it. They likewise backed a proposal to grant to the electors of each county the power to choose their justices of the peace, sheriffs, and county clerks. Among the anti-Bucktails who spoke up on behalf of giving the populace the right to select these local officials were Ambrose Spencer, William W. Van Ness, Peter A. Jay, and J. R. Van Rensselaer.[43] The cause of negro suffrage similarly found ardent friends among the foes of the Albany Regency at the convention. Peter A. Jay sought vigorously to have the word "white" stricken from the proposal of the committee to which the subject of the suffrage had been referred that every male white person, twenty-one or older, who had within one year paid taxes, or been assessed and actually worked on the highways, or been enrolled and served in the militia should be entitled to vote for all officers of the government elected by the people. He declared: "They were born as free as ourselves, natives of the same country, deriving from nature and our political institutions the same rights and privileges which we have."[44] The entire delegation of Federalists and Clintonians supported Jay's amendment when it was voted upon. According to Hammond, the negro voters generally cast their ballots against Bucktail candidates, and this accounts for the Regency's attempt to deprive negroes of the franchise as well as the Clintonian desire to insure the colored man the right to vote.[45] Thus, once again we see how party interest determined the position of the politicians on public questions. Politicians supported measures to expand political rights when it profited them and opposed the expansion when it injured them. The amendment reducing the term of the governor from three to two years also won the unanimous support of the Clintonians, although they split on the issue of revising the judicial system.[46] While the Clintonian delegation opposed some of the convention's proposals, this is hardly the record of a group philosophically committed to the cause of limiting the voice of the people in affairs of government.

That the Clintonians stood for the cause of political democracy during the election of 1824 is almost a self-evident proposition. Indeed, it is perhaps the most striking illustration of the Clintonians enthusiastically waving the banner of reform against the dogged opposition of the Bucktail Republicans. It was the Clintonians, not the Republicans, who strove to enable the people to choose their presidential electors directly and to replace the caucus with the convention as the accepted method of nominating candidates for public office.

A final indicator of Clinton's democratic sympathies is his reputation as the protector of the Irish immigrants of New York against both the Federalists and nativistic oppressors of Tammany Hall.[47] The Irish revered him because during his term as United States senator he successfully spearheaded a move to reduce the period of naturalization from fourteen to five years; moreover, he improved their political and financial condition by advocating the repeal of the Alien and Sedition laws. One grateful son of Erin praised him for standing "foremost in preparing and carrying into law the existing mode of naturalization." In addition, Clinton "rebuked with effect that churlish and savage jealousy" that sprang up among some of New York's citizenry who were hostile to foreigners. Perhaps, most importantly, Clinton was loved for his efforts to enable Catholics to become members of the legislature without having to take the qualification oath customarily required of all representatives in the Assembly and Senate.[48] His sympathy for the church was also reflected in his position that a priest on the witness stand could not be compelled to reveal testimony disclosed to him through confession.[49] His public addresses on St. Patrick's Day reverberated with calls for the emancipation of Ireland from political and religious persecution.[50] The profound affection and reverence the Irish felt for him is manifest in a tribute given to him by Thomas Addis Emmet and William James MacNeven after he had lost his position as mayor of New York City in 1815. "We prefer the moment of your retreat from office, for the expression of our deep sense of your manifold and important services to the public."[51]

The converse of the argument that the Clintonians were not consistent opponents of the growth of democracy is the contention that the anti-Clintonian wing of the Republican party cannot be considered as the undeviatingly faithful upholder of the cause of the people. Like their opponents, they waved the banner of democracy only at moments when it was advantageous for them to do so. When they believed that their interest would best be served by opposing a certain democratic reform, they did not hesitate to do so and to defend their move by the appropriate rhetoric.

Numerous instances during the early nineteenth century indicate that the anti-Clintonian wing of the Republican party often sought to thwart the will of the people rather than to give it effect. In 1807, for example, Morgan Lewis, the Republican nominee for governor, was criticized not only for his membership in a "numerous and pride-bloated" family but for the questionable methods employed to secure his nomination at a legislative caucus. His opponents complained: "Our representatives were sent not to make our governors, but to make our laws; and with blushes have many of them confessed, that they were drilled like soldiers, and compelled to sign the nomination, under pain of being denounced and calumniated in the newspapers."[52] Martin Van Buren, who became the chief of the Bucktails, moreover, did not complain in 1810 that the Federalists were using the undemocratic device of "fagot holding"[53] to increase their following in the state, but rather he was annoyed that they were more adept at using it than he. He asserted that of the six hundred fagot votes cast in Columbia County, the Republicans secured approximately one-third. The number could have been larger but for the fact that "in Chatham our friend Dorr after he had made about a Dozzen got one of the *Judas Breed* into his Camp who gave up his Deed to the Federalists—this broke us up there—in Claverack our friends made more than they did—in this city they made more than us—and in the lower town where we had no body to make or to be made they played the very devil with us." Van Buren's ultimate conclusion is that the Republicans have been too honest: "If some friends had laid off their scruples earlier we would have reduced their majority to about 250 which is all they are honestly entitled to."[54] The anti-Clintonians, finally, resorted to outright theft in 1815 when their candidate for speaker of the Assembly won by a fraudulently secured majority of one since the deciding vote should have been thrown out. The clerk of Ontario County had "most corruptly and flagitiously" certified Peter Allen rather than his Federalist opponent, Henry Allen, because on some of the latter's ballots, which were more numerous, his first name appeared in an abbreviated form rather than being written out in full.[55]

One of the foremost students of the Tammany Society, which was always the central hub of the opposition to De Witt Clinton, claims that after the War of 1812 the society hindered rather than helped the movement toward a wider suffrage in New York.[56] To be sure, at the outset the primary *raison d'être* of the group had been to achieve universal manhood suffrage and to abolish laws for the imprisonment of debtors. However, most of the leaders in the group had used the organization to obtain public office, so that by 1817 most of them owned substantial parcels of property. Indeed, at that time, a third of the membership consisted of bankers, a third of merchants, and a third of politicians. As a result, they were no longer especially concerned about securing for the poor man the right to vote, particularly since most of the lower classes were predominantly Clintonian in sympathy.[57]

The record of the anti-Clintonians on the slavery issue also tends to detract from their reputation as authentic democrats. It was widely known that the Bucktails were "in general lukewarm on this subject, and many of them opposed to the [Tallmadge] restriction."[58] Moreover, in order to avoid making his feelings on the subject a matter of public record, Daniel D. Tompkins "fled the field . . . of battle" on the day that the

Congress voted on the Missouri Compromise.[59] The common gossip about the state capital was that Tompkins discountenanced any limitation on slavery in the territories, and the Clintonians did their best to give the rumor even wider circulation. Further, in contrast to Clinton's forthright stand on the Tallmadge amendment, Van Buren also sought to avoid a public commitment on the matter. He refused to participate in a public meeting sponsored by Henry P. Jones, one of his Bucktail colleagues, to arouse widespread support in behalf of the Tallmadge amendment; but he did agree to permit the use of his name in connection with the meeting. Nevertheless, when he was subsequently asked to sign resolutions passed at the gathering in behalf of the Tallmadge amendment he declined on the grounds that the resolutions reflected obviously political and partisan designs.[60]

The behavior of the Bucktails at the Constitutional Convention of 1821 ought to demonstrate indisputably how inaccurate it is to credit the anti-Clintonians with establishing a genuine equal-rights democracy in New York. To be sure, it was the Bucktails who took advantage of public resentment against some constitutional abuses to lead a movement for reform in 1821 in an effort to acquire the reins of political power from their opponents. If it could dislodge Clinton from office, the Bucktails were willing to "revolutionize everything. . . . They talked of dividing counties—calling a State Convention—extending the right of Suffrage—abolishing the Council of Appointment—districting the State for Senators anew—and many other schemes."[61] But even at the convention called at their behest they opposed certain democratic measures that they felt would hinder them politically, such as the popular election of justices of the peace, county clerks, sheriffs, and negro suffrage. Van Buren believed that by bringing "the final appointment . . . to Albany" of the justices of the peace who exercise so much power in the local constituencies, he could tremendously strengthen his control over the state.[62] The prominent Bucktail delegate, Samuel Young, argued that the negro was incapable of exercising the right of suffrage responsibly and sensibly.[63] Moreover, on most topics of executive and legislative reform, the vast majority of Bucktails adopted a moderate position virtually identical with that held by the majority of Federalist and Clintonian delegates at the convention. The vote on Carpenter's plan for judicial change is further indicative of a frequent occurrence at the convention —the crossing of party lines in regard to questions before the gathering. The facts clearly do not support an interpretation of the growth of democracy in New York that ascribes all the important advances to the Bucktails who had to fight the conservative and aristocratic Clintonians every inch of the way.

The election of 1824, which is really the acme in the battle for democracy in New York, is perhaps the most striking instance of the Clintonians upholding the standards of democratic reform against the dogged opposition of the Bucktail Republicans. The Clintonians fought for the direct selection of presidential electors by the people and for the elimination of the congressional caucus as a method of nominating presidential candidates. The Bucktails, in contrast, wanted to prevent the enactment of these democratic measures.

The fact that the Bucktails were the group that supported Andrew Jackson's aspiration for the presidency in 1828 explains, in part, the connection in the popular mind between the Bucktails and democratic reform. There are, however, no objective grounds for establishing this relationship. First of all, the radical transformation of the political institutions of New York that changed the democratic theory of the early Republic into democratic practice occurred before and wholly apart from Andrew Jackson's rise to a position of political prominence in the state. The basic alterations took place at the Constitutional Convention of 1821, which sharply broadened the suffrage, corrected the worst abuses of the appointive system, and made the executive, legislative, and judicial departments of the government more responsive to the will of the people. The election of 1824, as the climax of this democratic upheaval, realized the final establishment of the nominating convention and the origin of the movement that secured for the people the privilege of choosing their presidential electors. By the autumn of 1825, an electoral law based on the districting system was passed. Moreover, whatever restrictions remained on the suffrage after the reforms of the Convention of 1821 were also wiped away in 1825.[64] In short, the basic issues of political democracy were resolved without the consistent aid of the Bucktails and before the Jacksonians took command.

While political democracy had been largely achieved in New York by 1825, Andrew Jackson did not play an important role in the politics of the state until the end of 1827 when the Regency finally committed itself to membership in the Jacksonian camp.[65] Moreover, the Tennessean was not supported by the politicians in New York because of his reputation as a reformer. Indeed, his position on the burning issues of the day was virtually unknown. The only thing that was sure was that his popularity as a military hero would bring him many votes. Silas Wright declared that he had no qualms regarding the "desirability of Jackson as a soldier"; he was, however, "not so sure about his politics."[66] When Van Buren decided to back Jackson's bid for the presidency, he had no knowledge or commitment from Jackson regarding fundamental public questions or the latter's position on the revival of "old party feelings"; but he was content to have the party press hail the Tennessean as the "Soldier Boy of the First War of Independence, the Hero of the Second. He saved the Country, Let the cry be Jackson, Van Buren, and Liberty."[67] Although the Bucktail leaders who formed the core of Jackson's support in New York may have envisioned Old Hickory as the leader of a new national party devoted to the principles of Thomas Jefferson, they formulated no specific program of democratic reform. Nor did Jackson's tenure as President of the United States result in one iota of change in the political structure of New York. Thus, notwithstanding the popular myth that Andrew Jackson was the great leader in the battle for the equal-rights democracy that we enjoy today, there appears to be little connection between the two in New York.

The lack of association between Jackson and democracy has been likewise stressed by Richard McCormick, though from a

somewhat different angle.[68] He has demonstrated that none
of the electoral contests in which Jackson was involved constituted "a mighty democratic uprising" in the sense that
people voted in unprecedentedly large numbers. When one
compares the participation of the electorate in the presidential
contests during the Jacksonian era to the highest voter turnout
in the states prior to 1824, to the results of gubernatorial contests during the Jacksonian era, and to the tremendous out-
pouring of the voters in the election of 1840, the former seems
singularly unimposing.

VI
ECONOMICS AND POLITICS

The support the New York Bucktails gave to the effort to charter the Chautuqua County Bank in 1831 was offered "with a view to advance the interests of the party in the county."[1] This frank evaluation of Bucktail motives by Oben Edson, the county's historian, emphasizes the important role expediency played in the making of political decisions on economic problems. Economics is obviously an inescapable part of life. Yet its relation to politics and public policy is not always simple. Party divisions do not, as some would have us believe, necessarily reflect economic conflicts. New York politics in the early nineteenth century clearly shows the very limited expression that interparty battles afforded varying economic aspirations. There was little difference between the social and economic background of the membership in the numerous party organizations. Moreover, important public measures in such key economic areas as banking, the tariff, internal improvements, and land policy had factions for and against in each of the major political groupings. Sectional differences often played a much more significant role than party affiliation in determining one's position on the fundamental economic issues of the time.

Throughout this study we have argued that there were no uniformly consistent party divisions over the major issues of the struggle for political reform. Instead, at different times all parties both supported and opposed various reforms, each particular decision contingent on what was politically expedient at the moment. This absence of an ideological gulf between the contending factions suggests that the political parties of New York did not represent distinct classes but rather consisted of groups whose interests and outlooks did not diverge sharply from one another. This, in fact, turns out to be the situation. At the Constitutional Convention of 1788, for example, small, independent farmers were the dominant group in both the Federalist and Antifederalist camps. Moreover, wealthy landlords were distributed in approximately equal proportions among the two parties.[2] Richard McCormick's research confirms the same point. Thus, he has shown that both the upper electoral class and the lower electoral class were to be found in numbers of similar magnitude in all of New York's major parties.[3] First of all, he uses the election of 1816 in which the Federalists mobilized their forces in full battle array for the last time in a gubernatorial, congressional, and state election in order to discover the factional loyalties of the various social classes that could vote.[4] Table 2 shows that the nonfreehold voters favored the Republican Party in only a barely higher proportion than the wealthier citizenry.

TABLE 25
DISTRIBUTION OF PARTY AFFILIATION
BY ELECTORAL CLASSES IN NEW YORK, 1816

Party	Vote for Governor	% by Party	Vote for Congress	% by Party	Non-freehold Voter Congress	% by Party
Republican	45,412	54.0	67,757	54.9	22,345	57.0
Federalist	38,647	46.0	55,514	45.1	16,867	43.0

Moreover, the expansion of the suffrage that followed the Constitutional Convention of 1821 did not materially alter the balance of power since the newly enfranchised voters did not have any special party preference. Consequently, although the enfranchisement of the common man raised the proportion of voters to adult white males from 33 per cent to 84 per cent, there was virtually no difference in the distribution of the votes between the Bucktails and Clintonians, New York's major parties at this time. In 1820, prior to the liberalization of the suffrage, Clinton polled 50.9 per cent of the 93,437 ballots cast in the gubernatorial contest. In 1824, when the size of the electorate had jumped to 190,545, Clinton secured 54.3 per cent of the vote. Two years later, Clinton obtained the backing of 50.4 per cent of the 195,920 citizens who went to the polls. In all likelihood, the increase in the number of votes cast came from groups that had previously been ineligible to vote or had been denied the right to participate in the balloting for governor. Certainly, the New York experience would corroborate the point of view that social and economic class, as defined in terms of suffrage restriction, was an insignificant factor in determining political preferences. For the new voters, who came from economic groups that had previously possessed no voice in public affairs, joined the Bucktails and Clintonians in fairly even numbers.

The fact that economic status did not influence party affiliation is also reflected in the lack of clear-cut party differences on the important economic questions of the time. As far as the chartering of banks is concerned, for example, the legislative debates were not between some groups that felt that banks were a good thing and others that regarded them as evil ventures, but rather differences centered around the question of whether one ought to enrich oneself by acquiring stock in newly chartered institutions, or whether one's stockholdings in already existing companies would be jeopardized in value by the creation of rival banking operations.[6] The absence of party uniformity on the subject of banking is evident from the large number of both Federalists and Republicans who were involved in the incorporation of the Manhattan Company in 1799. Although Aaron Burr was responsible for steering the bill of incorporation through the legislature, it elicited strong bipartisan support. The company's first Board of Directors included both Federalists and Republicans. When the proposal for the incorporation of the bank was reviewed by the Council of Revision, it required the cooperation of a Federalist like Judge Benson and a Republican like Chancellor Robert R. Livingston to transform the bill into a law.[7] The role of opportunism rather than ideology in determining the party's position on the banking question is likewise reflected in the opposition of the Republican Party to the rechartering of the First National Bank in 1811 although they proposed the chartering of the Second National Bank in 1814 and 1815. They fought the First National Bank because of Federalist domination, while they supported the Second because they hoped to monopolize the economic power that would flow from it.[8]

The focus of corruption in the New York legislature from 1791 to 1838, when the granting of a bank charter required a special act of the legislature, was to be found in the maneuvers for the incorporation of these financial institutions. The leadership of the party in power used the distribution of bank stock as a reward for service to the organization. In order to insure the benefit of this power, the state legislature passed measures between 1804 and 1818 that forbade private banks to issue notes, thereby limiting all banking activity to chartered corporations. These laws were passed by overwhelming majorities embracing all parties and factions of the state; thus, all groups in the legislature were equally anxious to reap the harvest of these provisions.[9] Moreover, although Fox claims that the Federalists and Clintonians were more favorable to businessmen who advocated liberal incorporation of banks, the fact is that between 1791 and 1820, the Republican-controlled legislatures incorporated more than twice as many banks as the Federalist-dominated bodies, and that between 1815 and 1825 the legislature, irrespective of whether it contained a majority of Bucktails or Clintonians, incorporated approximately three banks a year.[10] That the differences in policy between the Clintonians and Bucktails during the early 1820's toward the Holland Land Company were centered around a struggle for control of the Niagara Bank at Buffalo indicates still further how opportunism, the desire for profit, rather than class ideology, determined party attitudes on the state banking system.[11]

Quite often, a political party backed the incorporation of a bank in a credit-short community in an effort to strengthen its position among the voters. Thus, the Chautuqua County Bank was chartered in 1831 through the strong backing of the Bucktails to meet the demands for better credit facilities necessitated by an expanding commerce, a growing lumber industry, and the manufacture of potash and pearlash. The close connection between banking and politics is even more vividly reflected in the efforts of the National Bank of New York in 1830 to secure an open commitment of patronage from the state Democratic Party to insure that the public's subscription to its stock should be completely filled. William James, Jr., one of the bank's directors, urged upon Azariah C. Flagg, the state comptroller, the propriety of helping out one's friends. He declared that since the government could "do their business with any institution they please, then we would naturally expect *that patronage* and could it be known that such a result would follow, we could fill the bank in two hours."[12] Thus, the political parties used banks as a method of strengthening their position, and the banks used the parties to achieve their ends. Sometimes, the effort to use banks as a political instrument led both parties to adopt an identical position. Hence, Jabez D. Hammond remarked that anti-Jacksonians owned a majority of the bank stock in New York so that they heartily supported the Tennessean in his efforts to prevent the rechartering of the Second Bank of the United States.[13]

Since the political parties in New York did not represent distinct classes, and members from each of the major social groupings in society were to be found in all the parties, it is only natural that there should be differences of opinion within the parties on important economic questions that benefited some constituent elements while they injured others. The protective tariff that aroused a great deal of concern in the Empire State during the 1820's typifies intraparty ambivalence and conflict. The Bucktails embraced both protariff and antitariff wings. Although Martin Van Buren avoided references to the tariff when he could, he was known to be against protecting manufacturers.[14] To the extent that Silas Wright, Azariah Flagg, William Marcy, and Michael Hoffman could be said to favor tariffs at all, they desired duties that would benefit the farmer alone.[15] A group of Bucktail manufacturers, however, such as Knower, Dudley, and Olcott, indignantly protested against a negative attitude on the tariff and staunchly fought for an increase in tariff rates.[16] Peter R. Livingston was so insistent on this point that he threatened to abandon the party unless it followed a more ardent protariff position.[17] In order to maintain party unity the Bucktails tried to straddle the fence on the protective tariff. Their enemies accused them of "noncommittalism" as a result of these numerous efforts to sidestep the question. The Bucktails defended themselves by saying that the protective tariff was not a party issue, and their newspapers described the many tariff gatherings without comment.[18]

The Clintonians exhibited the same kind of intraparty split on the tariff as the Bucktails did. By 1828, the *Albany Argus* was protesting that the Albany central committee, made up of tariff sympathizers, was but a "Clintonian-Federal caucus" since only three of its twenty-five members were genuine Bucktails.[19] The Clintonian-supported New York Society for the Promotion of the Arts and Manufactures, which was made up of farmers and city merchants, proclaimed as its purpose the provision of "relief to the agricultural interests of the state, by encouraging the growth, introduction, and stationary residence within it, of a manufacturing population adequate to the consumption of its agricultural produce and to the fabrication of its raw materials."[20] Other anti-Bucktail groups such as the editors of the *New York American* vociferously opposed the tariff. They claimed that a rise in duties would compel farmers to pay higher prices for what they needed, so that an elevated standard of living could be enjoyed by manufacturers "whose evident prosperity increasing with each year required no sacrifice from trade or agriculture."[21] Moreover, the enactment of a protective tariff would endanger the future of the Union since the anger of those parts of the country which derived no profit from the raised duties would be aroused against the section which was its beneficiary. Even within the section that secured economic benefit from the protective tariff, there would be agitation from those citizens who were not directly involved in the protected industry. Finally, the growth of industry that would result from increased protection threatened to put the handicraftsmen out of business since they would be unable to compete against the low wages paid to the laboring force drawn "from the foreign rabble, cheap men devoid of skill, now flocking to our ports."[22] Clearly, neither of the great political parties in New York was united in its position on the protective tariff.

Another widely discussed economic subject during this era, governmental support for internal improvements, illustrates a similar lack of distinct differences in the attitudes of the parties in New York. To be sure, De Witt Clinton was the great hero of internal improvements in the Empire State. In 1811, he had accompanied Gouverneur Morris to Washington in order to seek federal help for the New York canal. During the following year the legislature, in response to his beseechments, persuaded the Ohio congressional delegation to solicit aid from the national government to construct a canal in New York state.[23] Three years before the completion of the Erie Canal, Clinton expressed his opinion in a speech before the state Senate and Assembly that the western states which had initiated preparations to construct inland waterways should be subsidized by the general government in order to facilitate the actualization of the "magnificent plans they had projected."[24] There was an effort in 1824 to nominate De Witt Clinton as vice president in order to enhance the possibility that his policies for national development would be carried into effect.[25] Other prominent anti-Bucktails expressed sentiment favoring federal aid for internal improvements. Charles G. Haines published a volume in 1818 entitled *Considerations on the Western Canal from the Hudson to Lake Erie,* a summary of his views advocating the use of

federal monies for canal construction in the Empire State. The astounding statistic that the expense of shipping a cannon from Washington to Lake Erie was four or five times the cost of its manufacture was used by James Tallmadge to buttress his arguments in behalf of governmental assistance to projects for internal improvements.[26] The prominent Clintonian newspaper, the *Albany Daily Advertiser,* cited the messages of Thomas Jefferson to justify its contention that national help for roads and canals had long been envisioned by the greatest leaders of our country.[27]

The Bucktails, especially after they realized the great political advantages to be gained, often espoused the cause of internal improvements with enthusiasm equal to that of the Clintonians. To be sure, in 1816 Martin Van Buren expressed public opposition to De Witt Clinton's proposals for the immediate construction of a canal connecting Lake Erie and the Hudson River. The New York senator argued that additional estimates and surveys ought to be undertaken before beginning a project of this magnitude.[28] According to Nathan Miller, the Little Magician recognized the popularity of the canal idea, and he wanted to get on the bandwagon, but only after insuring himself against the imputation of servilely imitating and copying his opponent. By advocating further study of the subject, he could maintain that the Bucktails were as "canal-minded" as the Clintonians but "far more cautious, more scrupulous, and operating on a higher standard of responsibility than their political rivals."[29] Further Regency support for internal improvements is reflected in an assertion found in the January 14, 1822, edition of the *Albany Argus:* "We rejoice to find that a bill making an appropriation for repairing this [Cumberland] road has passed the Senate of the United States by a vote of 26 to 9." On April 10 of the same year the Bucktail-dominated Assembly put forth a resolution requesting governmental assistance to improve navigation on the Hudson River. In 1826, William B. Rochester, known to favor Henry Clay's American System,[30] was nominated by the Bucktails for governor, while Nathaniel Pitcher, who resided in the area traversed by the Erie Canal, but who also had a following in the southern counties because of his proposals as a state road commissioner, was given second place on the ticket. Other prominent Bucktail spokesmen for internal improvements were Chancellor Robert R. Livingston, Joseph Ellicott, and Samuel Young.[31] Young's interest in the subject extended to the writing of a treatise staunchly urging generous federal help for internal improvements. Perhaps the most fervent Bucktail advocate of national development was Peter B. Porter of Buffalo. Porter was a wealthy merchant who also invested in turnpikes and monopolized the carrying trade across the Niagara River. He declared that the government of New York had long seen the value of constructing a canal, and they only waited "in the expectation that the General Government will aid them in this work." In response to those who argued that the Constitution did not give Congress the right to subsidize the building of roads and canals, he contended that the chartering of the national bank for which the Constitution also offered no specific authorization, was a precedent sufficiently broad to encompass federal aid for internal improvements. He declared with vehemence on the floor of Congress: "If you can constitutionally create banks for the accommodation of the merchant but cannot construct canals for the benefit of the farmer—if this be the crooked, partial sideway policy which is to be pursued, there is a great reason to fear that our western brethren may soon accost us in a tone higher than the Constitution."[32]

Side by side with these warm expressions of support for governmental aid to internal improvements by both parties are other assertions by responsible party spokesmen condemning such activity. Even De Witt Clinton often contradicted himself on this subject. In a speech before the state legislature in 1825 he declared that the rights of the states would be jeopardized by the involvement of the federal government in projects for internal improvement; indeed, he denounced the interference of Congress in interstate commerce. In his message of 1827 he reiterated his hostility to the "possession or exercise by or . . . investment in the national authorities" of the right to build waterways or turnpikes.[33]

Senator Jordan of the People's Party sponsored a resolution on the floor of the New York Senate in 1826 that would have sharply restricted the power of Congress to aid the states in the development of their resources.[34] There were also prominent Bucktails who voiced dismay at the prospect of federal involvement in internal improvements. Michael Hoffman asserted that the very claim by the federal government of the right to construct canals is a dangerous violation of "our Democratic principles."[35] Silas Wright gave public expression to these same sentiments in a resolution before the state Senate in 1826.[36] Martin Van Buren, the most distinguished leader of the Bucktails, declared before the United States Senate in December, 1825, that the Constitution gave no authorization to the federal government that could justify its participation in the building of state roadways or canals. Indeed, he maintained on another occasion that even if Congress' role were restricted to financial assistance so that the construction and control of the project remained in the hands of the state, this would still constitute a violation of the compact between the states. Further, only the state could negotiate contracts with private companies to take on the job of construction.[37] Once again, it is evident that a number of conflicting views were held by leaders within both parties, and occasionally even the same man might reverse himself at different times. Unquestionably, just as in the case of the incorporation of banks and the protective tariff, so also in regard to the subject of internal improvements, the political parties of New York did not provide clearly defined alternative approaches. Instead, the party positions were vague, confused, and unstable.

Ambivalence and ambiguity also characterized party attitudes on the development of manufacturing in New York. On the one hand, prominent Bucktail manufacturers such as Benjamin Knower, Peter Sharpe, and Clarkson Crolius who made hats, whips, and pottery respectively fervently supported the enactment of legislation favorable to the growth of industry.[38] The *Albany Argus* published several articles encouraging the instruction of the populace in the operation of machinery.[39] On the other hand, however, there was a division of opinion in Bucktail circles as to whether textile manufacturing should be encouraged by releasing all factories engaged in this enterprise from the payment of any taxes as well as by freeing their employees from service on juries or in the militia. The opposition to favored treatment grew steadily until by 1824 the Bucktail senators successfully passed a bill through the state legislature that outlawed the granting of any assistance to manufacturers in the state.[40] The eloquent Bucktail spokesman, Gulian C. Verplanck, in addition, strove in the state Assembly to have laws passed to make the incorporation of new manufacturing concerns more difficult.[41]

The same kind of intraparty split emerged in anti-Bucktail circles. A textile firm located in Whitestown, New York, the Oneida Manufacturing Company, included among its stockholders De Witt Clinton, John Taylor, and Stephen Van Rensselaer.[42] Other well-known spokesmen for the stimulation of domestic industry were Ambrose Spencer and Philip Hone.[43] Nevertheless, the ranks of the anti-Bucktails had such prominent opponents of industry as J. R. Van Rensselaer and William W. Van Ness who voiced their contention at the Constitutional Convention of 1821 that manufacturing endangered the stability of society, and the mill owners and workers were not as politically trustworthy or reliable as the merchants and landlords.[44] This overlapping of attitudes on industrialization hardly supports an interpretation of New York politics that would assign the roles of protagonist and antagonist respectively to the Clintonians and Bucktails.

The improvement of agriculture also failed to produce division along partisan lines. Jesse Buel, who owned the *Albany Argus,* was among the foremost proponents of the organization of an agricultural society to improve the farming methods practiced in Albany County.[45] De Witt Clinton, however, fired popular interest to an even greater extent by supporting the establishment of a state board of agriculture which would provide supervision and money for the local and county groups.[46] The concern of an overwhelming number of New Yorkers in measures to improve agriculture is also evident in the tremendous nonpartisan majority in the state legislature that voted $30,000 to aid the county societies in their endeavors to promote more efficient farming.[47] Finally, the founders and leaders of New York's Society for the Promotion of Useful Arts, which at that time included agriculture, represented all of the political factions and groups within the state.[48] It is unequivocally true that no significant economic issue in the Empire State during the decade preceding Jackson's election to the presidency generated partisan alignments. In all parties there were always opposing groups on these questions. Fox is certainly wrong in arguing that the Bucktails uniformly stood for the needs of the small farmer and town laborer while the Clintonians consistently upheld the demands of the great landlords, merchants, and manufacturers.[49]

Not only is it false to label the Clintonians aristocrats and the Bucktails democrats since party positions frequently shifted and there were substantial numbers of party members on all sides of the various economic issues, but as far as at least one question is concerned—land policy—one can make a good case for proving that the Clintonians backed the common man while the Bucktails supported the wealthy landowners. Ever since George Clinton had successfully challenged the political domination of the landlord gentry under the leadership of Alexander Hamilton, the Clintonians had been hailed as the "champions of the debtor farmers." Attorney-General Thomas A. Emmet, one of De Witt Clinton's most faithful lieutenants, investigated the legitimacy of the land titles of the Van Rensselaer estate on behalf of the state in 1812 with such care and diligence that political pressure led to his rapid replacement in office by Abraham Van Vechten who had the reputation of being the "landlord's lawyer."[50] De Witt Clinton's brother-in-law, Ambrose Spencer, in the same year, made several proposals to lighten the financial burden of debt-ridden tenants in his capacity as chairman of a commission appointed by the legislature to study possible changes in the laws regarding land tenure. He felt that the state had the obligation of rescuing the tenants from the difficult straits they got themselves into as a result of their rashly entering into imprudent contracts. Consequently, he recommended that landlords should be prohibited from forfeiting leases, although they could maintain the legal remedy of suing for damages in a court of equity. Moreover, such punitive measures as "fines" and "quarter-sales against alienation" should be done away with since they constitute "exceedingly objectionable . . . and rigid and unreasonable burdens."[51] But the most persuasive proof of the overwhelming concern of the Clintonians for the poor farmer and insolvent tenant is found in their valiant encounter during the 1820's with Joseph Ellicott, the chief agent of the Holland Land Company in western New York, and his Bucktail supporters.

Beginning in 1819, the Clintonians were involved in a perennial conflict with the administration of the Holland Land Company. The first incident began as a result of a series of articles in the *Niagara Journal* of Buffalo, attacking the company in strong and uncompromising terms.[52] The articles were signed by "Agricola," who was known to be Albert H. Tracy, a popular lawyer, a member of the House of Representatives at that time, and an ardent supporter of De Witt Clinton. The author condemned the company for charging exorbitant sums for their land, for refusing to sell huge tracts no matter how much was offered for them, and for pitilessly disregarding the public and private needs of the people who settled upon their property. In addition, the company was reproached for extorting outrageous increases in payments when tenants renewed their contracts; moreover, its earnings were sent abroad, reducing the circulating capital within the state. Tracy also urged changes in the law that would compel the Holland Company to expend larger sums for the construction and maintenance of highways and schools. Under the prevailing ordinance the burden of taxation fell exclusively on landowners who had actually settled in the area, thereby freeing absentee landlords from any obligation. Finally, the youthful attorney advocated legislation that

would compel the company to restore to the settlers the difference between the price of their renewed contract and the
original principle plus simple interest. Although Tracy was
not the first to voice these criticisms of company policy, his
felicitous style together with the wide circulation of the
organ in which he published his articles helped to popularize
his views.

The publication of Tracy's position engendered a protracted
public controversy with the Bucktails ranged on the side of the
company and the Clintonians upholding the interests of the
tenantry. Two Bucktail newspapers, the Niagara *Patriot* and
the Batavia *Spirit of the Times,* spearheaded the attack on
Tracy's writings in the Clintonian Niagara *Journal.* The
leading members of a public meeting, held at Cook's Inn in
Niagara County on October 28, 1819, to translate Tracy's
complaints into concrete legislative proposals were Clintonian
in political orientation. Oliver Forward, who was chairman of
the gathering, was a Clintonian assemblyman, while Tracy
himself was an active member of the committee that formulated
the group's resolutions. The meeting petitioned the legislature
to enact legislation to compel nonresident landowners to share
the burden of building and maintaining such public facilities
as roads, bridges, and schools. The Clintonians, moreover,
were not at all bashful in trying to convince the debt-ridden
tenants that the only way of ameliorating their condition lay
in the electoral victory of a Clintonian ticket.[53]

In order to reduce opposition to the Clintonian program
of land reform, flowing from the strong political influence of
Joseph Ellicott in his capacity as agent for the company,
De Witt Clinton urged the legislature to approve the purchase
by the state of the Holland Company's real estate holdings.[54]
The Clintonian-dominated Assembly responded favorably to
the governor's proposition, while the Magnus Apollo's supporters in the Senate, under the leadership of Gideon Granger,
also fought for its passage. The overwhelming number of
Bucktails, however, voiced opposition to the proposed purchase. Martin Van Buren favored the maintenance of the
status quo so that in order to "preserve the public interest"

it was necessary to take whatever measure "defeats Mr. Clinton's and Mr. Granger's political plans."[55] However, David E. Evans, a Bucktail senator who had sixteen years of experience working in the land office at Batavia, tried to awaken the Regency to the perilous political consequences that would flow from outright opposition to Clinton's proposals, which were extremely popular among the rank and file. Most of the settlers felt that the sale of the company's holdings to the state would be followed by a more favorable adjustment of their financial liabilities; consequently, the party that could claim credit for having the measure passed could expect the preponderant percentage of western voters to register their gratitude at the polls.[56] When the Bucktails realized the political implications of their opposition to the purchase, their attitude softened considerably, and the Bucktail-dominated Senate easily passed a resolution appointing a committee, at least to examine the question. The Assembly accepted the resolution except that they changed the members of the committee. Instead of the three Bucktails named in the Senate resolution, the lower body substituted the commissioners of the Land Office who were politically loyal to De Witt Clinton.[57] The Senate did not have the opportunity to review the amendments of the Assembly because the time of adjournment was so close at hand. As a result, no further action was taken. In view of acrid partisan sentiment on the subject, it is unlikely that a compromise slate of committeemen could have been chosen, even if the Senate had taken up the issue. No one ever raised the proposal again.

After the Clintonians had failed to effect their aims through a purchase of the Holland Company's holdings in western New York, they tried to achieve their goals by applying pressure on the company to remove Ellicott from his office as agent. The political grapevine quickly disclosed to the Bucktails that the Clintonians were trying to have Samuel Hopkins appointed in place of Ellicott. Hopkins was a wealthy and reputable landlord from Connecticut, who had invested substantial sums in the development of land holdings along the Genesee River, east of the property owned by the

Holland Company. In order to prevent the carrying out of this plan, Van Buren exerted pressure on the company administration at the highest level to insure Ellicott's retention. The Regency chief revealed to Busti, the general agent of the Holland Company in America, that he was distraught by the Clintonian attempt to arouse the ire of the populace against company policy; moreover, Clinton's attempt to make the company subserve his political ambitions was destructive of the public good, and deserving of the severest condemnation. In contrast to the selfish and vicious Clinton, Van Buren declared his readiness to protect the rights of the company in the face of the strongest pressures, as long as the company remained steadfast in its alliance with the Bucktail party.[58] Although the Bucktails did not succeed in preventing Ellicott's removal, they did force the choice of a compromise candidate. For Jacob S. Otto, a close business associate of Busti in Philadelphia, was selected instead of Hopkins as the company agent at Batavia. Thus, once again, differences over the policies of the Holland Land Company produced clear partisan alignments.

The struggle of the Clintonians in behalf of the tenants and resident landowners against the Bucktail-supported administration of the Holland Land Company continued for nearly a decade. In 1827, the Bucktails in the state legislature successfully prevented the passage of a bill that would have equalized the burden of taxation by compelling absentee landlords to pay the same rates as resident landowners.[59] As late as 1829, the Bucktail-dominated Senate managed to block passage of a bill approved by the Assembly, which was Clintonian in sympathy, that would have distributed more equitably the yoke of taxation for road building. The chairman of the committee of the Assembly that originally formulated the bill was Oliver Forward, the dedicated Clintonian lieutenant. The opposition of the Bucktails in the Senate on this measure was so adamant that they would not even debate the question; as a result, the bill failed for want of consideration.[60] Similar bills came up nearly year after year but the opposition of the landowners was sufficiently powerful to block them until 1839. During the 30's the Jacksonians, who were composed primarily of former Bucktails, lined up with the company, while the Antimasons, who comprised many former Clintonians, opposed it.[61] By showing that most of the basic economic issues in New York produced no clear partisan alignments, our earlier discussion proved the falsity of Fox's contention that the Bucktail Party was the main support of the poor farmer and laborer while the Clintonian organization backed the rich landowners, merchants, and manufacturers. But the story of the tenant-landlord controversies during this era provides an even stronger refutation of Fox's position, for not only were the Clintonians not the spokesmen of the rich and influential landowners of the state, but they were even the precise opposite—the heroes of the small landowners and tenants of New York against the tyrannical policies of the Bucktail-supported land companies. Thus, the Clintonians contributed significantly not only to the development of political democracy in New York but also to the evolution of economic democracy in the Empire State.

If the state did not divide on the most important economic issues along partisan lines, on what basis did the state divide in these matters? By and large, sectionalism rather than partisanship was the primary consideration. This is seen most conspicuously in the area of internal improvements. In 1809, for example, De Witt Clinton was informed that his efforts to construct a state canal were under attack by a group in Kingston that wanted to build a turnpike instead. The opposition was motivated by the "contemptible locality of calculation" that thwarts the long-range goals of able statesmen.[62] When the canal proposal was debated in the legislature, opposition was centered in the middle and lower counties of the state.[63] Everyone knew, moreover, that sectional interests were such that any plans for a northern canal would have to be coupled with plans for a western one as well. Thus, a single law incorporated the Northern and Western Inland Lock Navigation companies. De Witt Clinton's trips around the state in behalf of the Erie Canal project during 1816 quickly taught him that the counties of the Champlain Valley considered a canal in their area of the state a prerequisite of their supporting the Erie proposal. Clinton wrote to Joseph Ellicott that the plans for the two canals would have to "proceed pari passu."[64] Most of the hostility toward the projected Erie Canal arose in New York City, whose populace felt that it would have to shoulder the expense of the undertaking although it received no direct benefits. To allay this antagonism, the legislature passed a law stating that only lands bordering the canal would be taxed to pay for the canal. Sectional considerations are manifest in other methods used to obtain revenue for the purpose of covering canal costs such as the imposition of a sales tax on salt manufactured in the western counties of New York as well as the payment of a duty by all steamboat passengers.

Governor Clinton's recommendation in 1825 that a highway be constructed to link Lake Erie with the lower Hudson elicited the strong disapproval of the inhabitants of the area served by the Erie and Champlain canals. The residents of northern New York were content with the existing facilities, and were recalcitrant to the assumption of an additional financial burden so that the southern counties of the state could enjoy better roads.[65] Party affiliation had very little to do with a politician's opinion on this question. While Gamaliel Barstow, a staunch Clintonian from Tioga County, and Erastus Root, the prominent Bucktail leader who lived in the area that would be served by the new road, were foremost advocates, Francis Granger, a Clintonian lieutenant from Ontario County, and Samuel Young, the well-known Bucktail spokesman, expressed sharp disapproval of the measure.[66] The bill for the proposed state road was ultimately defeated in the legislature during April, 1827. Judge Hammond asserts that fifty-five of the sixty-four votes cast against the bill in the state Assembly came from areas adjacent to the Erie and Champlain Canals.[67]

Sectionalism as an important factor governing policy decision is manifest during this era on numerous occasions. The vote in the state legislature on an act of 1831 to allocate funds for canal building shows how distinct patterns were emerging in New York—the north and east became progressively "creditor-conscious" while the south and west grew "debtor-oriented." The sixteen counties of the northern and western part of the state that would benefit from the stimulus to the economy provided by the new construction favored it by a vote of 24–4, while the Hudson River counties, most of the assemblymen from New York City, and the counties from Richmond in the south to Washington in the north overwhelmingly opposed the bill.[68] In addition, after New York City had been afflicted by a serious fire in 1835, a measure to provide relief through the monies of the Canal Fund elicited disapproval from areas of the state such as Chenango Valley which wanted all the resources of the fund to be used for internal improvement projects more directly beneficial to them.[69] Nathan Miller asserts that there were three basic sectional alignments within the state—the Hudson River counties, the Erie Canal counties, and the Champlain Canal counties. The first comprised Richmond, Kings, New York, Rockland, Westchester, Putnam, Orange, Ulster, Dutchess, Greene, Columbia, Albany, and Rensselaer; the second, Oneida, Madison, Oswego, Onondaga, Cayuga, Seneca, Wayne, Ontario, Monroe, Orleans, Livingston, Genesee, Niagara, Erie, Tompkins, and Yates; the last consisted of Saratoga, Washington, Warren, Essex, and Clinton.[70] Clearly, sectional interest rather than partisan affiliation was the fundamental determinant of one's position on these burning economic problems. People from all political parties were to be found on all sides of the most significant public issues facing New Yorkers during the momentous first part of the nineteenth century.

VII

THE ROLE OF IDEOLOGY IN POLITICS

"The New York Republicans were divided into three factions, represented by Clinton, Livingston, and Burr interests; and among them was so little difference in principles or morals that a politician as honest and an observer as keen as Albert Gallatin inclined to Burr as the least selfish of the three."[1] This is Henry Adams' description of the political complexion of the Empire State at the opening of the nineteenth century. On the other hand, Dixon Ryan Fox has asserted that the principle of "democratic reform" was the decisive determinant of political conflict and the meaning behind the endless partisan maneuvers.[2] Moreover, Robert V. Remini has argued that Martin Van Buren, often considered to be the most ruthless and opportunistic politician of that generation, was primarily motivated by the desire to establish a national party dedicated to the basic Jeffersonian principles from which the Republicans had deviated during the administrations of Madison, Monroe, and Adams.[3] Who is right? To what extent did principles or expediency influence the course of New York politics during the pre-Jacksonian era?

The absence of sharp ideological conflict in New York during the early nineteenth century is suggested by the fact that all political groupings called themselves "Republican." Although the Regency liked to think of itself as the last authentic heir of the original Republican Party, all factions used the "Republican" caption. Thus, for example, the anti-Bucktail Utica Convention, which was held in September

1824, entitled its proceedings "State Convention, Republican Nomination,"[4] thereby indicating that the members of the People's Party considered themselves the spokesmen of true Republicanism rather than the founders of a new organization. The scramble for electoral victory in New York was not a battle between Republicans and anti-Republicans but a quarrel of groups, both of whom looked to the same parent party. The one-party system that prevailed throughout the Era of Good Feelings was not yet formally breached in 1824. The People's Men contended that the Republican Party and the state had been "degraded and disgraced by a cabal of aspiring and desperate politicians in their own bosom," and they were out to correct the situation, not to establish a new party. Thus, Fox is wrong in restricting his use of the term "republican" to the Bucktails. There simply is no truth to his assertion that "Clintonian and Federalist were often interchangeable terms, and the word Republican was reserved for followers of Van Buren and his coadjutors of the Tammany Society."[5]

All of the major political organizations also tried to legitimize their existence by associating themselves in some way with Thomas Jefferson. Van Buren's opposition to James Monroe resulted from a belief that the latter had "weakened the traditionally cohesive qualities which had originally united the Jeffersonians."[6] The Little Magician's primary ambition during the 1820's, according to Robert V. Remini, was to forge a national coalition of faithful "keepers of the Jeffersonian conscience."[7] But the followers of De Witt Clinton were just as emphatic about their connection with the Jeffersonian heritage. The central committee of the People's Party published a circular dated October 30, 1824, whose express purpose was to disprove an apparent rumor that Thomas Jefferson "never spoke favorably of De Witt Clinton." The phamphlet declared that "Mr. Jefferson made no hesitation in saying that De Witt Clinton was one of the greatest men in the western world." According to the publication, there were five basic reasons for Jefferson's alleged affinity with Clinton. The former governor had "a happy manner in com-

POLITICS IN NEW YORK STATE

municating his liberal views for the benefit of mankind"; he
had done "more than any other person to cement and brighten
the chain of the union of the states in his persevering course
to unite the great western waters with the Atlantic"; he adhered
steadily to the "great cause of States' rights following the example of his venerable uncle George Clinton"; he always
pursued that course which he conceived would best promote
the interest of his country, disregarding the effect it might
have on his popularity; and the father of the Erie Canal was
a man of artistic and scholarly propensities. Apart from the
question of the validity of the assertions in this handbill, the
document is illuminating in that it reveals the universal
veneration that was accorded Thomas Jefferson at this time.
Each of the contending political parties claimed Jefferson as
its patron saint and accused the other of heresy.[8] It was thus
a matter of the utmost importance to all aspirants for public
office to prove that they were true Republicans, respected by
the sage of Monticello himself, and not opportunistic Federalist renegades in disguise.

As late as 1840, the leaders of the Whig Party felt that their
chances for political success would be enhanced by making
explicit their Jeffersonian pedigree. Erastus Root, who became
one of the foremost Whig spokesmen, asserted that of the three
Jeffersonian electors who were still living at the time of the
Harrison-Van Buren battle for the presidency, and of the nine
surviving legislators who cast ballots for the Jeffersonian
electors, all but one were members of the Whig party. Root
advocated the naming of these men on the Harrison ticket in
the belief that such a slate would be "unequivocally of the
Jefferson school," and would consequently "repel effectively
the charge of federalism too successfully made against us."[9]

Although both of the principal contenders in the Empire
State during the pre-Jacksonian era were factions of the
Republican Party, and both claimed to be authentic standard-
bearers of Jeffersonianism, the Bucktails were more effective
in selling their self-image and also more aggressive in trying to
pin the tag of Federalism on their Clintonian opponents. To
be regarded as a Federalist was tantamount to political death.

As De Witt Clinton put it: "The odium attached to the name of Federalist has been a mill-stone round the neck of true policy."[10] The Regency proclaimed in 1824: "De Witt Clinton is again presented by the federal party for your suffrages." His principles were compared to a "box of glass, labelled, 'keep this side up'—contents Hartford Convention, Peacepartyism, Toryism, British Influence, Essence of Aristocracy, and Federalism." It was claimed, moreover, that those who were most boisterous in their support of the new electoral law proposed in 1824 were "federalists, who, with Clinton, rejoiced at the disasters of our army."[11] There were no objective grounds for these charges since, as we have shown in Chapter V, the Federalists were attracted with approximate equality of numerical strength to both the Bucktail and Clintonian parties.[12] It is revealing that the *Albany Argus,* which attacked the Clintonians more vehemently than any other publication for their Federalist sympathies, was itself led by editors who were former Federalists.[13] The number of Bucktail leaders who, like John Armstrong, Chancellor Robert R. Livingston, Peter Porter, and many others, were converted to Republicanism from Federalism was legion. In addition, many Federalists detested Clinton. Indeed, the entire group of founders of the *New York American* in 1819 consisted of well-known Federalists such as Josiah Ogden Hoffman, Johnston Verplanck, Hugh Maxwell, two sons of Alexander Hamilton, and one son of Rufus King, who sought to provide an organ of expression for anti-Clintonian Federalists. The *American* lambasted the Magnus Apollo for oscillating between "unfounded vituperations" and "obsequious blandishments" in his attitude toward the Federalist Party. The newspaper maintained that all Federalists who adhered to the Clintonian cause lacked "the spirit to feel resentment for your injuries" as well as "the honesty to resist your temptations."[14]

There were obvious objective grounds militating against an alliance of the Clintonian and Federalist forces. First of all, if the bulk of the Federalist Party openly adopted a pro-Clintonian posture, the Republicans would have deserted Clinton en masse, and the Federalists would not have solved the problem of political isolation which led to their sorry plight in the first place. Moreover, Clinton, in an effort to purge himself of the sin of Federalism and to prove his genuine Republicanism, was often compelled to make derisive public statements about the Federalists; thus, he once asserted that they would rather rule in Hell than serve in Heaven.[15] His failure to appoint loyal Federalist followers to public office and his refusal to support Rufus King's bid for re-election to the United States Senate in 1819 were also instrumental in creating a strained relationship between the Clintonians and a substantial portion of the Federalist party.

The virtually nonexistent part played by ideology in New York politics during the early nineteenth century is vividly evident in the political behavior of the Federalists and in the attitude of the various Republican factions toward them. As far as the Federalists were concerned, the primary determinant of their predilection toward one candidate or another was the question of proscription. The desire for public office led to the apostatization of many Federalists to the Republican side. A group of Federalist leaders in New York who had gathered together in 1816 to discuss the problem of defection comforted themselves with the thought that the desertions of the unfaithful "increase our purity more than they diminish our strength." They withdrew the clasp of friendship from former colleagues who were willing to sacrifice "integrity" for the "power, the pleasure or the emolument of office."[16] In reality, however, after 1816 there were no major questions of principle that divided the parties. The importance of sea power disappeared as a public question as a result of Madison's successful effort to strengthen our naval forces. Moreover, the financial problems encountered in trying to pay for the Second War of Independence as well as the glaring weaknesses of the state banking systems made the existence of a national bank more palatable to the Republicans. Finally, the subjects of the tariff and internal improvements which had divided the parties internally before the war continued to produce intraparty splits after the conflict. Rufus King attributed an increasing number of public scandals involving Federalists in the government to the declining lack of concern with matters of principle and doctrine. He asserted that the "degradation" and "depreciation" of the Federalist organization sprang from the presence within its membership of "too many who in nothing of worth differ from our opponents."[17]

The fact that there were no substantial ideological conflicts between the Federalists and Republicans enabled the Federalists to move more easily in and out of the different Republican groupings. It also intensified the efforts of the competing Republican factions to increase their numerical strength by the addition of former Federalists to membership rolls. When one considers that in 1816 the Federalists cast 40 to 50 per cent of the total vote in a number of eastern states including New York, it is clear that the ability to draw substantial Federalist backing could shift the balance of power markedly in one's favor.[18] By 1824, the Federalists were so widely dispersed among the numerous splinter organizations within the Republican Party that Robert Walsh was led to make the following statement: "Federalists and Democrats are so intermingled as the advocates of each of the candidates, that neither of them can deem himself especially obliged to one denomination more than another."[19]

The Republicans who avidly sought Federalist votes were confronted by a dilemma. On the one hand, the active recruitment of Federalist members would swell their margins at the polls; on the other hand, too complete an alignment with former Federalists would evoke cries of betrayal of the principles of Jefferson and result in a loss of support. The attempt to grapple with this problem is reflected in the Bucktail approach to the Federalists. In an endeavor to secure Federalist backing, Van Buren bestowed political favors on certain highly esteemed Federalists like John Duer. However, to prove his authentic republicanism he was led to oppose the political aspirations of other Federalists such as David B. Ogden, whose bid for the post of United States attorney in New York City was blocked by Van Buren.[20] Whenever Van Buren was on the verge of bestowing too much influence on new converts he was warned to retard their elevation out of fear that "jealousies will be excited."[21] To prove its authentic republicanism the Bucktail-oriented *New York Enquirer,* which supported Andrew Jackson for the presidency in 1828, insinuated that the Federalists were guilty of anti-Americanism when the editors wrote that "all who opposed the late war, . . . who got up the Hartford Convention, . . . and who, of course, are opposed to Gen. Andrew Jackson" be invited to join the Adams forces.[22] The prominent Bucktail editor of the *National Advocate,* Mordecai Noah, deprecated the Federalists as "cunning fellows" who detest Republicans, who would never "give us a crumb," and who desire to be friends only when hopelessly and "egregiously beat."[23] Nevertheless, Noah was willing to swallow the implications of his own rhetoric when the Bucktails could derive some political benefit by cooperating with the Federalists. Hence, he wrote Van Buren that the Federalists in New York City "would go Heart and hand with us" in the balloting of 1820 provided that "their Mayor, Recorder, and a few others . . . be preserved."[24] Clearly, the Bucktails were ambiguous and ambivalent in their treatment of the Federalists. The result was a strange scene of sly angling for Federalist support that constantly alternated with bitter accusations about the Federalist character of the rival party.

The extent to which the Federalists were simultaneously wooed and condemned is manifest in the efforts of all the presidential candidates to capture Federalist backing in 1824 and at the same time to remain untainted by such support. After he became president John Quincy Adams expressed his gratitude for Federalist help by choosing six prominent members of that party to fill important public posts.[25] On the other hand, many Federalists opposed Adams' bid for the presidency primarily out of resentment for his "apostasy" from the Federalist Party and his hatred of Alexander Hamilton. Daniel Webster discovered that most Federalists in New York City disliked Adams although he had considerable backing from Federalists in other parts of the Empire State.[26] John Calhoun's endeavor to attract Federalists to his banner included overtures to James A. Hamilton whose father the South Carolinian praised as creating "the only true policy for the country."[27] Nonetheless, in order to avoid any impugnation of his Republican purity he advised his followers in New York that the bulk of his organization must consist "as far as practicable" of "supporters of the late war."[28] Even William Crawford who more than any of the other candidates tried to campaign on a platform of "pure Republicanism" attempted to draw Federalist votes.[29] Indeed, the Federalist-oriented *New York Post* was persuaded in August, 1824, to support openly Crawford's presidential aspirations. Andrew Jackson was the most open in his recruitment of Federalist backing since his popularity as a military hero in the Second War of Independence immunized him from the charge of being a Federalist in disguise. The general's followers in New York did not hesitate to publicize a letter written by Jackson to James Monroe in 1816 urging the appointment of a South Carolina Federalist to public office. Old Hickory expressed the opinion that since points of differences between the Federalist and Republican parties had ceased to exist, the national government ought to make appointments to public office on the basis of merit rather than prior party affiliation.[30] However, Jackson's managers also had the problem of explaining away the Tennessean's boast that he would have hanged all the participants in the Hartford Convention. William Coleman declared that Jackson's statement sprang from misinformation and did not truly represent his feeling.[31] Clearly, the attempt by all the major Republican factions to lure Federalist votes and the easy passage of Federalists into the various groupings of the Republican party provide emphatic testimony to the lack of marked ideological difference between the political parties.

The inconsequential part played by doctrine, ideology, and principle in New York politics is also manifest in the inconsistency of the party leaders on public issues and their frequent reversal of previously held views in the face of public pressure. Thus, for example, the Bucktails, who had waged the election campaign of 1824 on the basis of opposition to any proposed change in the method of selecting presidential electors, abandoned this position a couple of months before the autumn balloting. The Regency, concerned by its inability to sell its case to the people and worried about the outcome of the election, decided to alter its strategy. In September Samuel Young, the Bucktail candidate for governor, published a formal statement declaring himself in favor of repeal of the existing electoral law. Since Young had uttered sentiments favorable to a reform of the procedure for choosing presidential electors before his nomination for the governorship by the Bucktails, this formal declaration produced no public shock. However, when Erastus Root, the Bucktail candidate for lieutenant governor who, as presiding officer of the state Senate, had refused even to permit discussion of the electoral question, also made public his predilection for the popular choice of presidential electors, the reaction of the populace was electrifying. The ludicrous turn of events represented the desperate attempt of doomed politicians to win salvation.

The very fact that the Bucktails chose Samuel Young as their candidate for the governorship in 1824 shows how little doctrinal position played a role in state politics. For Young was nominated even though the Republicans knew well that he ardently supported an improved electoral law and preferred Henry Clay to William Crawford as President.[32] Thus, the fact that Young was a prominent and widely respected attorney from Saratoga County, had compiled an outstanding record as Speaker of the Assembly, enthusiastically promoted the Erie Canal project, and was one of the very few men who could successfully match wits with Clinton were apparently sufficient to overcome the "minor" difficulty that he disagreed with most of the major objectives of the party that nominated him. The nomination of Young is an expression of the politics of expediency in action, that brand of politics that would rather be wrong than not be president.

The primacy of opportunistic considerations also helps to explain the treatment accorded Albert Gallatin during the presidential campaign of 1824. In an effort to draw Pennsylvania into the Crawford camp, the Republican followers of the Georgian had nominated the famous secretary of the treasury for the post of vice president. However, Gallatin proved anathema to the South, and the emergence of Andrew Jackson, who was tremendously popular in Pennsylvania as a candidate, annulled Gallatin's usefulness to the party. Consequently, Republican leaders through the urging of Martin Van Buren sought to improve Crawford's chances of victory by securing "the voluntary withdrawal in a manner proper" of the Pennsylvanian's candidacy.[33] When Gallatin was told of the organization's wishes, he graciously resigned his position on the ticket. Indeed, he even penned a congenial note to Martin Van Buren, who had masterminded the whole procedure, informing him of his decision to withdraw as a result of the feeling among some party leaders that "the continuation of my name was injurious to the Republican electoral ticket," and in order to "facilitate a plan you had in view of substituting another candidate."[34] Thus, no question of principle or ideology entered into the initial choice or subsequent retirement of Gallatin as a candidate for the vice-presidency. Utility as a vote getter was the sole factor of importance governing the selection of a nominee.

Since popular appeal was the only important qualification of a candidate, the Regency, under Van Buren's guidance, had no qualms about replacing Gallatin with Henry Clay. It was hoped that Clay's addition to the Crawford ticket in New York would compensate for the anticipated losses in support that flowed from the Bucktail stand on the congressional caucus and the popular choice of presidential electors. Clay's large following in the West would also offset a Jacksonian triumph in Pennsylvania. Neither Van Buren nor any of his cohorts were apparently concerned that Clay's "American System" clashed with the allegedly significant dedication of William Crawford to Thomas Jefferson's belief in limited government.[35] Only Clay's refusal to abandon the presidential race for a second slot on the Crawford ticket prevented the union of the two forces.[36]

Perhaps the most vivid illustration of the primacy of expediency over matters of ideology was the projected union in late 1825 and 1826 of the two arch political foes in the Empire

State during the pre-Jacksonian era, Martin Van Buren and
De Witt Clinton. The strong showing of the Bucktails in the
state election of 1825 led Clinton to seek an alliance with Martin Van Buren as a prerequisite to furthering his ambitions
for the presidency. In December, 1825, Edward Livingston
disclosed to Van Buren the governor's intention to make overtures of peace to the Regency leader. Clinton paid the Little
Magician "sundry compliments," and in return for Bucktail
support of the governor's presidential aspirations, Clinton
"wished you to succeed him in the government of New York,
or if Mr. C. was President you might have under the General
Government what you wished."[37] Van Buren refrained from
making any rash or impulsive commitments, but he was sufficiently enamored of the idea to keep it alive during 1826 by
supporting Clinton's nomination of Samuel Jones for the
post of chancellor.[38] Clinton reciprocated this conciliatory gesture by offering a circuit judgeship to a Bucktail. If the Bucktails were considering Jackson as their candidate at all, and
the New York senator probably already had it in the back of
his mind in 1826, the alliance would seem to make some sense,
especially if Clinton could be persuaded to abandon his own
presidential ambitions and back his old friend, Andrew Jackson. One of the main factors that prevented Van Buren from
consummating the coalition was his awareness of the bitter
anti-Clintonian sentiment that animated a large segment of
his party. The deep-seated personal antagonism that so many
Bucktails felt toward Clinton halted Van Buren's inclination
toward joining forces. As a result, he was unable to persuade
the Bucktails to forego a contest against Clinton in 1826 for
the governorship.[39] Nevertheless, an uneasy truce persisted
between the two men until Clinton's sudden death in 1828
ended all hopes of amalgamation. Hence, no problems of
ideology or principles influenced the discussions regarding an
alliance, or proved an insurmountable obstacle to such a
union.

The absence of an ideological gulf separating New York's
parties can also be ascertained from the widespread support

the Jacksonian cause elicited from all political groupings in the state. First and foremost, of course, were the Bucktail Republicans under the leadership of the Albany Regency. Although they did not recognize that Jackson would make a strong candidate until a few years had elapsed after Adams' election in 1824, it was the Bucktails who provided the leadership, the organization, and the strategy that resulted ultimately in the Hero's victory in the state. The personal popularity of the military chieftain was undoubtedly an extremely important factor in attracting the backing of these astute politicians. Although Jackson had not personally associated himself with any movement for democratic change, his supporters linked his name with the rhetoric of reform. Van Buren was convinced that "a temperate but firm and unreserved expression of the Democratic sentiment through the medium of the press" was "all that is necessary" to unify all the disparate groups in the Jacksonian camp.[40] The power of democratic slogans is also reflected in an excerpt from a resolution published by the Republican Young Men of Saratoga County: "Resolved that the cause of Jackson is emphatically the cause of the people—that the contest in which we are engaged is between the democracy of the country on the one hand, and a lordly purse proud aristocracy, on the other; between an honest patriotism and a devoted attachment to the spirit of our republican institutions, on the one hand, and an unholy and selfish ambition, and a contempt for the principles of our republic, on the other."[41] Besides appealing to mechanics, artisans, and farmers with the "common man" oratory, the Bucktails also sought for Jackson the Irish vote and that of other immigrant groups who were at the same time being repelled by the nativist propaganda of such Adams newspapers as the *New York American* and the *New York Advocate*.[42]

The Clintonians also possessed their ardent supporters of Andrew Jackson. Indeed, Jackson's earliest supporter in New York was probably De Witt Clinton. In fact, the famous governor had been the sole politician of prominence in the Empire State who had backed the General in 1824. An amiable relationship between Clinton and Jackson can be traced back to 1818. In that year, at a banquet in Nashville, Tennessee, Old Hickory toasted the New York governor, declaring him "the promoter of his country's best interest." During the following year, Jackson aroused the ire of the Regency at a dinner given in his honor in New York City by praising Clinton before an audience full of Bucktails as the "enlightened statesman and governor of the great and patriotic state of New York."[43] The bond between the two men becomes even more apparent from Clinton's assertion that only in Jackson could he find "a sincere and honest friend." Expressions of friendship from others were "dictated by policy and public sentiment."[44] Clinton's backing of Jackson was also motivated by a dislike and jealousy of John Quincy Adams. The two came from the same part of the country, stemmed from similar backgrounds, and held kindred points of view. As a result, the envious governor regarded the chief executive as his arch political rival. The Jacksonian cause in New York actually did not gain very much through Clinton's support since most of his party brethren favored Adams for the presidency. It was only a few die-hard Clintonians like Messrs. Colden, Bogardus, Viele, Birdsall, and Bryant in the state legislature who shared the governor's views in regard to the General.

Another source of Jacksonian support in 1828 were a substantial number of Federalists who were either former followers of President Adams, offended by his patronage policies, or frustrated independents, convinced that a successful political future necessitated their joining the general's ranks. The Federalists were especially anxious to join the Jacksonian forces since Old Hickory's public image was so popular and his publicity men so effective that he could bestow "the appellation and favor of 'a Republican' to" anyone who backed him as well as remove "the stigma and woes of 'federalism'" from such an individual.[45] It was James A. Hamilton, the son of Alexander Hamilton, who had the big job of trying to enlist old Federalists of substance in the Hero's cause. Federalists who backed Jackson quickly learned to parrot the democratic rhetoric. Thus, Ebenezer Baldwin, a leading Federalist from

Albany, proposed that voting be made compulsory for all citizens.[46] It is similarly noteworthy that Jackson appointed numerous Federalists to public office after he was elected.[47]

It should be observed that Jackson won New York City by 8,000 votes where there was a relatively large number of working-class people and 28,000 of the 160,000 Irish who resided in the state. He likewise carried the counties of Sullivan and Delaware, which were Irish centers.[48] The ability of Jackson to draw support from such disparate groups, many of which were diametrically opposed, provides ample evidence for the thesis that no deep-seated problems of principle or ideology were at stake in the election.

It would not be entirely accurate to say that there was a total absence of genuine issues dividing the political organizations of the Empire State during the pre-Jacksonian era. For in 1826 an important matter intruded itself upon the politics of New York, threatening to transform completely the alignment of parties within the state—Antimasonry. The unsolved abduction in the autumn of 1826 of William Morgan of Batavia, New York, a Mason who threatened to disclose the secrets of the order, quickly aroused a public furor.[49] Meetings held all over the state condemned the Masons as an undemocratic and subversive organization destructive of the public order. Since the greatest antagonism toward the Masons existed in the western counties, in 1827 the Bucktails nominated for the state legislature candidates from this area who were known to have no affiliation with the Masonic order.[50]

By the beginning of 1828, the opponents of Freemasonry started to develop a political consciousness. They held a convention at Le Roy in Genesee County on March 6 that advocated laws to make the Masonic order illegal. The delegates, a large percentage of whom supported Adams for the presidency, decided to hold another convention during the coming summer at Utica to nominate candidates for public office in New York friendly to the aims of the movement. In order to remove this intrusion from the political scene, the Bucktails made an effort to calm the emotionally charged public atmosphere by sponsoring the appointment of a committee by the state legislature to investigate the Morgan incident. In April a committee under the chairmanship of Daniel Mosely of Onondaga was chosen, but its efforts were of little value.[51]

The discovery during the spring of 1828 that Andrew Jackson was an active Mason while Adams had been unaffiliated with this group drew the lines of party battle more sharply than ever within the state. Van Buren became extremely concerned about the seriousness of the Antimasonic question the excitement over which was "far greater than I supposed," making it a matter "that required looking into."[52] Had the supporters of John Quincy Adams in New York been more successful than they were in uniting the Antimasons under their banner, the controversy would have proved more injurious to the Bucktails than was actually the case. Thurlow Weed of Rochester, the editor of the *Anti-Masonic Enquirer,* was the foremost proponent of a union between the Antimasons and Adams men in the state. His efforts in this direction failed, however, since many friends of the administration in Washington were practicing Masons.[53]

The failure of the administration and Antimasonic parties to amalgamate gave the Regency much cause for satisfaction. Benjamin Butler was prompted to remark that the "oracle of antimasonry has blown the administration sky high into Adams' lighthouse."[54] Nevertheless, the Antimasonic furor in the state succeeded in scaring the Regency to the extent that they felt that victory in the gubernatorial contest of 1828 could be had only if they nominated their strongest personality for the chief executive's post—Martin Van Buren.[55] The Little Magician, who wanted to be secretary of state in the event of a Jackson victory, accepted the nomination only because the welfare of the party required him to do so. It was understood, however, that he would be free to resign the governorship if Jackson won the presidential contest.

Antimasonry clearly turned out to be a major issue influencing the decisions of New York's political parties in the late 1820's. Its significance is most fully disclosed in its having driven the Jacksonians to nominate Martin Van Buren for the governorship, their strongest, most reliable, and last resource. The Antimasonic uproar continued during the period of Jackson's ascendancy and played an even greater role in the politics of the 30's than it did in the 20's.

Was Martin Van Buren, undoubtedly the most influential New York politician during the 1820's, an idealist or an opportunist? Was he striving to achieve the realization of a definite set of principles, or was he moved only by considerations of self-interest? The problem of motivation is tricky and puzzling, indeed. One is often inclined to abandon the search, and follow the counsel of the biblical sage who declared that "man looketh on the outward appearance, but the Lord looketh on the heart."[56] Human beings are denied entrance into others' minds. Nevertheless, a man's words and deeds do provide testimony, however imperfect, that enables us to make judgments regarding his motivation. Martin Van Buren has been the object of conflicting judgments. Some have labelled him "an American Talleyrand," while others have characterized him as a farsighted statesman who laid the foundations of a national party dedicated to the ideals of Thomas Jefferson.[57] If we can understand the role ideology played in this major personality of the times, perhaps we will have come closer to comprehending the role of ideology in the political life of the state as a whole.

One of the paradoxes in Van Buren's political behavior was his sharp condemnation of federalism but his warm attitude toward Federalists. He tried to associate all of his enemies with the discredited Federalist Party. Thus, he endorsed the view that De Witt Clinton, together with the Federalists, "rejoiced at the disasters of our army" during the War of 1812.[58] Despite this kind of assertion, the Little Magician actively courted the backing of the Federalists. He was the most influential person in securing the re-election as United States senator in 1819 of the dean of New York's Federalist party, Rufus King.[59] By 1819, the number of Federalists who had joined the Bucktail ranks was quite substantial, and included such notables as James A. Hamilton, Josiah Ogdens Hoffman, Barent Gardenier, Philip Brasher. It would appear that Van Buren's conduct was dictated by purely expedient considerations. Because of the opprobrium attached to the word "Federalist," he tried to fasten it on all his opponents. On the other hand, the desire to secure additional votes led him to seek out the help of individual Federalists. If it be argued that Van Buren accepted help only from Federalists who had repudiated the principles of their party in favor of the ideals of the Bucktail Party, there is no evidence that such repudiation was a prerequisite to entrance into the Bucktail ranks. Indeed, the New York senator tried to attract the backing of Samuel Talcott while the latter was still an avid Federalist and a caustic critic of the Republicans.[60] Nevertheless, Van Buren probably had in mind to convert him ultimately, and even if initially he was moved by expediency to win the support of a man like Talcott, there may have been other considerations involved as well.

The difficulty of disentangling Van Buren's motives is particularly evident in his opposition to the appointment of Solomon Van Rensselaer to the office of postmaster. On the one hand, Van Buren's decision seemed to be determined by deepseated principles. He was anxious to effect "a radical reform in the political feelings" of the nation in addition to a "general resuscitation of the old democratic party." Under these circumstances, if the appointment to high public office of a known Federalist such as Solomon Van Rensselaer were acquiesced in, the selection of a Republican over a Federalist in the future could be achieved only by "soft, soothing milk and water petitions . . . instead of that manly simplicity and characteristic boldness which distinguished the conduct of our public men in the early years of Mr. Jefferson's administration."[61] Nevertheless, an examination of other factors in the situation would suggest that politics, not principle, was primarily responsible for Van Buren's position. There was concern, for example, that a Van Buren failure to prevent the appointment of Van Rensselaer would show that the Little Magician couldn't influence the distribution of patronage in Washington as effectively as he had done at Albany. Moreover, the fact that Rufus King supported Van Buren's stand would indicate that the Little Magician's position was based primarily on expediency since King would never have acquiesced in the proscription of a Federalist on principle.[62]

It is difficult to justify on any grounds other than expediency Van Buren's projected alliance with De Witt Clinton in 1826. Actually, the New York senator's relationship with De Witt Clinton varied over the years in accordance with the personal benefits to be derived from such a connection. His career began as a vigorous leader of the Clintonian contingent of Columbia County. His efforts in 1812 not only persuaded several Federalist electors to support De Witt Clinton's bid for the presidency but also prevailed on Madisonians not to vote at all lest they disclose their subservience to the Virginia dynasty by opposing a favorite son of New York. After the Clintonian branch of the Republican Party was defeated in 1815, Van Buren joined the Tompkins segment of the organization convinced his own ambitions would be best promoted by such affiliation. His status in the party rose steadily during the next decade as a result of his skillful leadership against the Clintonians. His desire to augment the Jacksonian forces in New York during 1826, however, led him to consider seriously the desirability of re-establishing an alliance with the Magnus Apollo. Charles King described Van Buren's efforts at union as "coquettish" and possessing the "appearance of open prostitution."[63] Thus, interest rather than ideology dictated the Regency leader's association with De Witt Clinton.

Van Buren's reversal of position on the question of building the Erie Canal also appears to be rooted in "realistic" rather than "theoretical" considerations. In 1816, the Bucktail helmsman voiced opposition to the proposed construction project, and managed to table action on the matter through a series of parliamentary maneuvers. During the following year, however, the Little Magician did a complete "about-face" on the issue. Van Buren claims that his prior opposition was based, not on the propriety of the canal construction itself, but rather on the necessity of gathering further data before undertaking such a gigantic enterprise.[64] It is undeniable, nevertheless, that the New York senator had changed his mind after the canal proposal had succeeded in restoring De Witt Clinton to political life, following the latter's "demise" in 1815.[65] When the widespread public popularity of a procanal policy was established, Van Buren jumped onto the canal bandwagon in order to improve his own vote-getting ability. It would be unfair to discount completely the sincerity of the reasons Van Buren proffered for his initial antagonism toward the canal. On the other hand, it would also be the height of naivete to disregard the circumstances surrounding his change of mind.

Those who assert that Van Buren had political objectives that transcended personal ambition usually ascribe to him the aspiration of creating a new national party that would champion limited government, the "old party feelings" that were the authentic embodiment of Jeffersonian democracy. The Little Magician's acrid opposition to the appointment of Solomon Van Rensselaer as postmaster at Albany was rooted in fear that James Monroe was destroying the purity of the Jeffersonian party by attempting an "amalgamation" of the Federalists and Republicans.[66] A "general resuscitation" of the "old democratic party" was required to halt these dangerous tendencies toward "fusion."[67] Moreover, the New York senator's hostility toward John Quincy Adams stemmed from the federalism that permeated all of the latter's announced policies. Adams was also guilty of pursuing Monroe's policy "to obliterate . . . party distinctions of the past and to bury the recollections of their causes and effects in a sepulchre."[68] When Van Buren tried to persuade William Coleman to join the Jacksonian Bucktails in 1828, he gave a complete exposition of his theory on "states rights," and offered numerous examples of Adams' interference in matters that legitimately belonged within the purview of the state.[69] It seems, however, that one must take with a grain of salt Van Buren's constant harping on the theme of purifying the Republican party in accordance with the principles of Thomas Jefferson. The numerous Federalists who joined his forces and whom he appointed to high positions regardless of their philosophic commitment indicate that he was not concerned with keeping federalism per se out of the government but rather anti-Bucktail Federalists.

Van Buren's efforts in behalf of Andrew Jackson in the campaign of 1828 have also been explained as part of an attempt to preserve the fundamentals of Jeffersonian democracy via a new national coalition. In 1826, Van Buren said he would support the Tennessean provided the latter put his election "on old systems," and added "his personal popularity to the yet remaining force of old party feeling."[70] To produce a "better state of things" it was indispensable to nourish and defend the "old party feeling yet remaining" from the unbridled hostility of President John Quincy Adams and his Secretary of State, Henry Clay.[71] Adams' great sin was an excessively broad conception of the proper sphere of government activity which exceeded the limits prescribed in the Constitution. The "old party principles" that were of such great importance to the Little Magician were primarily states rights and limited government. When Van Buren finally decided to support Jackson in January, 1827, however, he had not received any assurances regarding Old Hickory's adherence to the "old party feelings." Silas Wright was rather wary about going along with Van Buren's choice of Jackson since the party was "not so sure about his politics."[72] Clearly, the New York senator's selection of Jackson revealed that he had decided to subordinate all other concerns to what appeared to be political necessity. Van Buren's declaration in behalf of the general, despite the latter's silence on matters the Regency leader had earlier declared to be prerequisites for such support, shows only that considerations of expediency prevailed in determining Van Buren's decision, not the total absence of ideological concerns. Despite the absence of assurances from Jackson, Van Buren may have felt that the important role he was playing in the creation of a new party structure would enable him to control the views of the Hero.

Van Buren also justified his attempt late in 1824 to persuade Henry Clay to become the Bucktail vice-presidential candidate as a move toward the creation of a national party founded on "old Jeffersonian principles." He declared that a coalition composed of Clay's western following and Crawford's eastern supporters "would make a great and powerful party capable of sustaining the interests of the country." Even more significantly, Van Buren felt that such a political organization would be quite similar to "the old Republican Party of the Union and one I would be willing to stand or fall with."[73] But Clay's policies diverged rather sharply from the limited sphere of government activity envisioned by Jeffersonian philosophy. A strong federal government, spending large sums on roads and canals, a protective tariff, and the United States Bank loomed large in the Kentuckian's program, although such matters would elicit the scorn of faithful "keepers of the Jeffersonian conscience."[74] If the New York senator was sincere about wanting to create a national party dedicated to Jeffersonianism, how could he choose as his candidate for vice president a man who stood for policies which, in the Regency leader's eyes, were a perversion of Jefferson's principles? Did he think that Clay would be helpless to put his policies into effect as vice president? Did he feel that Clay could be persuaded to abandon his views on government? Or was Van Buren interested only in a strong candidate who would bring a substantial following of voters with him, and was all the talk about "old party feelings" simply empty political rhetoric? All one can be sure of about Van Buren is that he passionately wanted to win, and he would do almost anything to secure victory. Whatever ideological concern he may have possessed was always subordinate to the attainment of electoral triumph. Ideology always played second fiddle to expediency and opportunism in Van Buren's career, as it did in New York politics generally during the 1820's.

VIII
POLITICS IN THE LIFE
OF THE COMMUNITY

Richard T. Ely once quipped: "Every political question is becoming a social question, and every social question is becoming a religious question." This incisive observation points up the interrelatedness of all areas of life. Politics particularly cannot be isolated from the other major concerns of mankind without disturbing the organic unity binding together all human endeavor. If politics impinges on all aspects of our behavior today, it pervaded the lives of Americans in the early nineteenth century even more so.

When election time rolled around in the Empire State during the pre-Jacksonian era, it was far more than just a time when people decided whom they would like to represent them in public office. The elections were colorful and noisy occasions when all sorts of wiles were employed to stimulate the mind and excite the emotions of the populace. Campaigns were the principal American sport, but a sport played with the utmost earnestness. The contests gave the public a chance to have a good fight. The voters chose sides and fought by means of both word and deed in behalf of their respective candidates. Many a hoarse throat testified to the cheers and yells shouted by the multitudes. Increased liquor consumption resulted from the numerous victory toasts that were drunk at picnics, poleraisings, and banquets. Broken limbs, bruises, and scratches also bear witness to the zeal with which enthusiastic partisans threw themselves into the fray. The most popular subject for parlor talk was the election. Both friends and strangers could find common ground for conversation in the approaching electoral campaign. The energy of the multitudes expended today in such diversions as the movies, the theater, and highly professionalized sports activity, found its release a century and a half ago in politics. Those who participated in the contest developed a team spirit and acquired a sense of belonging that helped to dispel loneliness and isolation. Political leaders raised the level of public excitement to feverish proportions, ignited the passions, and halted the mind's effort to think objectively and rationally. The rival campaign committees competed with each other to put on a better show. After the balloting was over, the multitudes returned to their abodes and found pleasure in recalling the experiences of the campaign. These reminiscences satisfied them until the time came to get ready for the next election.

The pre-eminent role played by politics in the life of the Empire State is revealed also in the extremely violent rhetoric that was used in the course of the electoral campaigns. Since the whole future was believed to turn on the outcome of the balloting, the struggle for votes was waged relentlessly and without restraint. The contest in 1820 between Daniel D. Tompkins and De Witt Clinton is an example of the "bitterness and desperation" that marked most electoral battles at this time.[1] The personal character of each man was unjustifiably defamed by overzealous partisans of the other. Although no substantial issues were involved, the campaign was fought like a crusade. Martin Van Buren accused Clinton of collecting "around him a set of desperadoes, who instigated by the hope of official plunder, will never be content to limit their depredations to the boundaries of the State but would, if successful here, without doubt extend their incursion abroad."[2] The Bucktails labored "with holy zeal and almost more than human industry" to attain victory for Tompkins. They regarded Clinton as a "serpent" who had to be politically exterminated.[3] When the Regency failed to oust Clinton from the governor's chair, the dismay that follows naturally from defeat was magnified into an all-pervading gloom that penetrated "the pit of their bones and the core of their hearts."[4]

The same extremity of language and gesture is evident in the campaign of 1824. The removal of De Witt Clinton from his office as canal commissioner, despite his outstanding achievements in this area and his refusal to accept remuneration for his efforts, is an instance of what the *New York Evening Post* aptly termed "envenomed malignity."[5] The Regency ridiculed Clinton as a "traducer" and "persecutor" of the masses. He was also accused of arrogance, ill temper, want of integrity, hypocrisy, and cynicism.[6] The rhetoric of the Clintonians toward their opponents was equally excessive in its violence and extravagance. The Regency was condemned for trying to impose a "slavish bondage" upon the people of New York.[7] The Bucktails were led by a "cabal of aspiring and desperate politicians" who had "disgraced, degraded, and betrayed" the best interests of the state.[8] The motives and goals of the enemy were as "ugly as Cain."[9] The language employed by the Chinese Communists about Chiang Kai-shek is hardly more vehement or malevolent than the verbal jousts exchanged by New York's political parties.

The deadly seriousness with which politics was conducted in the early nineteenth century can be ascertained likewise from the frequent duels over public controversies. John Swartwout, one of Aaron Burr's most ardent lieutenants, challenged De Witt Clinton to a duel because of the latter's allegedly underhanded and despicable disregard of legitimate Burrite interests in the Republican Party. In the resulting battle, Swartwout caught two shots in the leg while Clinton's injury was limited to a ball in the coat.[10] In 1807, Philip Hamilton lost his life in an appeal to arms resulting from a political question. Similarly, William Coleman, the editor of the *New York Evening Post,* killed Captain Thompson, the harbor master, in a combat fought in 1803. Of course, the most dramatic incident of this kind was the duel held in Weehawken, New Jersey, during the following year in which Aaron Burr with the same shot ended both the life of Alexander Hamilton and his own political career.

Opposition in political affairs often led to personal animosities that would endure for years. The conflict between the Livingstons and Clintons that erupted within the Republican Party during 1805 lasted a lifetime. In reaction to the Clintonians who forged a union with the Burrites at Dyde's Hotel on February 20, 1806, the Livingstons met on the twenty-fourth in the Long Room of Abraham Martling's tavern where they denounced their political foes. The Martling Men, as those who participated in this convocation were called, proved a troublesome thorn in De Witt Clinton's side until his death in 1828.[11] The deep-seated nature of partisan opposition was so intense that it provoked Martin Van Buren to muster his followers for an unrelenting effort to prevent a fellow New Yorker, John Taylor, from being appointed to the post of Speaker in the House of Representatives. Although Taylor was also the choice of the President, Van Buren claimed that he bore the stigma of Federalism and Clintonianism. The Regency leader's declaration in November 1821 that Taylor "could not be Speaker" was dutifully obeyed by the Bucktail congressmen from the Empire state; and despite an earnest effort by the administration, Taylor's opponent, Philip B. Barbour, squeaked through to victory by a narrow margin of two votes.[12] The Monroe administration allegedly represented all political parties—Federalists, Clintonians, and Bucktails, no substantial issues of public policy were at stake, and the prestige of the Empire state would be enhanced if a native were to hold the office of Speaker. Nevertheless, the New York Bucktails, to a man, conspired to defeat Taylor's aspirations. Personal antipathy thereby prevailed against all the other rational considerations that would have dictated a different course for the Bucktails. These events led Gales of the *Intelligencer* to remark, "there must be something peculiar in the political distinctions in New York."[13]

The proliferation of political attitudes and animosities into nonpolitical areas of life gives rise similarly to the assumption that politics played a major part in most New Yorkers' lives. In Utica, where political feeling ran particularly high, each political party had its own social club with a well-trained instrumental band that played drinking ballads that savagely attacked the opposition. A number of banks in New York City and Albany denied service to anyone who was not a Federalist.[14] A woolens mill that was established in Trenton Falls, New York in 1812 refused to sell stock to Republicans.[15] Father Romeyn, a Catholic priest from Rhinebeck, whose political sympathies were Federalist in nature, refused to christen a newly born child with the name of Thomas Jefferson as the mother and father had desired. Instead, the young boy was given the name of John Adams much to the astonished dismay of his parents.[16]

Although extreme emotionalism, misrepresentation, and rancorous quarrels were long acknowledged to be standard elements of political life in New York, there were some people who were disturbed by it. A New Yorker named Henry Storrs wrote in 1824 that "there is nothing relating to our own State which can honor our political character abroad. The profligacy of the time, the thirst for public office and emolument, and the unwearied and artfull [sic] efforts to corrupt and purchase others have truly sunk our state in public estimation. If there is any virtue or honor or pride of character of firmness left in the State which can operate on our legislature, I do not by any means despair of an honorable result at their meeting in November."[17] Many New Yorkers probably had similar thoughts and kindred hopes as they marched to the polls on November 3, 1824.

In view of the heatedness and extensive emotional involvement of so many New Yorkers in their state's politics, it is surprising that during the election of 1824, which stimulated greater interest than any previous electoral contest, nearly a third of the voters remained apathetic. In the balloting of that year, Clinton received 55 per cent of the vote, 104,782 going to him and 85,912 to his opponent. The voter turnout in New York for this election was 56.1 per cent of the adult white males, a notably higher proportion than had ever before voted in the state. Nevertheless, it represents only about two-thirds of the adult white males who were eligible to vote.[18] If $33\frac{1}{3}$ per cent of the voters chose not to exercise their right of suffrage, one might legitimately ask how anxious the disenfranchised group was to acquire the vote at this time. I think the sources show indisputably that questions of democratic reform aroused more interest than any other issue in the decade from 1815 to 1824. Nonetheless, it was apparently true then, as it is now, that a large portion of the population is unmoved by virtually any matter of public concern. We never cease to be amazed by public polls showing that a substantial number of Americans do not even know the name of the president of the United States. Similarly, in 1824, there was an ample percentage of New Yorkers upon whose consciousness the election of 1824, for all its importance and significance, impinged but little.

The eagerness with which men sought public office provides another indication of the pre-eminent place of politics in the lives of New Yorkers in the era between Jefferson and Jackson. In the absence of other avenues to status and fame, politics afforded the most likely way to success. In a very revealing document, Edward Everett, the well-known Massachusetts Federalist, explains why the pursuit of public office was so intense in the United States:

> In England where families are hereditary, the hereditary family politics are of vast consideration. . . . Besides this, mere Rank is of vast consequence there, and fills the utmost ambitions of many persons in a large class of Society. Here it is unknown. Prodigious accumulations of fortune exist there, conferring of themselves very extensive influence and power, and making mere office a small thing with its possessors. The outgrown naval and military establishments open a career, in which the ambitions find scope for their talents. In place of all these, we have nothing, to which the ambitions can aspire, but office. I say nothing, because all the private walks of life are as Wide open in England as here, and afford in that country, as well as in this, occupation for much of the Active talent of the Community. But office here is family, rank, hereditary fortune, in Short, Everything, out of the range of private life. This links its

possession with innate principles of our Nature; and truly incredible are the efforts Men are Willing to Make, the humiliations they will endure, to get it.[19]

It was undoubtedly the desire for public office that motivated the maneuvers after the election of 1824 that led ultimately to the choice of John Quincy Adams as president by the House of Representatives. A pledge or, at the very least, an informal understanding that Adams would choose Henry Clay as Secretary of State induced the Kentuckian's followers to switch support to the candidate from Massachusetts. Moreover, a meeting with Daniel Webster, held shortly before the balloting in the House, produced an arrangement whereby Adams promised to appoint certain Federalists to high public office. This arrangement enabled Webster to secure the backing of New York and Maryland for Adams, the margin that gave him the presidency.[20]

Everett's observation that family background did not of itself secure one firm status within the community is reinforced by the fact that the political views of even old and established families did not diverge sharply from those of the general community; moreover, there was not necessarily unity of viewpoint within a particular family. Henry Adams was quite right in characterizing New York as "a society, in spite of its aristocratic mixture, democratic by instinct."[21] George Dangerfield described Robert R. Livingston, one of the most famous representatives of one of New York's most venerable families, as "a man looking in two directions—forward as a scientific farmer, backward as an aristocrat."[22] The aristocratic bent of the Livingstons was expressed by their possession of slaves and the administration of their properties as quasi-feudal estates. Their democratic sympathies are evident in their support of the American Revolution and the ideals of Thomas Jefferson. Indeed, the chancellor made an effort to persuade the legislature of New York to adopt the Virginia Resolutions.[23] There were, in addition, sharp differences of opinion within the Livingston clan. The Livingstons were far from united in their switch from the Federalist to the Antifederalist Party of New York in 1790. The family was also capable of producing staunch conservatives like Peter R. Livingston and fanatical radicals like John Morin Scott.[24]

Similar moderation and variety characterized the political outlook of other famous families of the Empire state. There was a sharp split among New York's well-established families at the Poughkeepsie convention of 1787 over whether or not to ratify the new federal constitution.[25] Although most of the aristocratic families in the state opposed the results of the Constitutional Convention of 1821, there were some like the Kings and the Jays who supported them.[26] It was difficult to ascertain a unified stand on the part of any group in 1824 regarding questions like the tariff and internal improvements.[27] Finally, the Van Rensselaers were scattered about the camps of all the presidential candidates during the election of 1824.[28]

Despite the similarities in philosophical outlook between the established families and the bulk of the populace, there was a deep-seated resentment of the "aristocracy" by a large portion of the people. This probably resulted more from the social snobbishness of the former than from any profound class conflict. The patronizing and condescending attitude of the aristocrats is exemplified by a comment of Philip Schuyler to John Jay. After the election of George Clinton as governor in 1777, Schuyler, who was a member of one of New York's oldest and wealthiest families, declared: "Clinton's family and connections do not entitle him to so distinguished a preeminence." This assertion, however, represented a purely subjective emotion, and was in no way an aspersion against Clinton's capacity or intentions. That the remark was an expression of inner feeling rather than opposition to a program of action can be determined from the remainder of Schuyler's comments. Schuyler continued: "He is virtuous and loves his country, he has ability and is brave, and I hope he will experience from every patriot support, countenance, and comfort."[29] The steadily growing democratic sentiment within the Empire state from the very beginning generated a political consciousness among the people that challenged the "superiority" of the old families. This opposition to the family aristocracies is described in a very revealing letter by Walter Livingston:

I plainly see the leveling principle of which our Constitution savors too much has already taken root. You say the cry is the Livingstons intend making their peace. The truth is that they are envied and jealousy is endeavoring to divide them from the country. They would be happy if we did attempt to make our peace, they don't want to see a gentleman have influence in the Country. In forming the Constitution, they deprived us [the Livingstons] of sending a Representative to the house of Assembly which right is an unalienable right we held by law, usage, and Pattent [sic]. The antient [sic] and inestimable Priviledges [sic] to be plucked from a family without more ceremony than a Carob from a Tree? While I was serving them faithfully [as a deputy commissary], I was placed in such a predicament as would have reflected disgrace had I continued to serve. As soon as I quitted the service I was ordered to return. I retir'd to my farm, as I was laid aside by the Public. The country took me up [and] elected me one of their Representatives. I am now waiting to attend on that duty and am censured for my conduct. An Angel cannot please the populace long. . . . I fear the little aristocracy which we formerly enjoyed in this State is torn up by the root.[30]

With each successful assault on the family aristocracies, another external indication of status disappeared with the result that politics and the pursuit of public office became more important than ever as avenues of social ascension.

Two other considerations of major significance help to explain why politics affected all aspects of one's life during the pre-Jacksonian era with an intensity rare today. First, life in the rural areas of New York, with its seclusion, bordered on the primitive. Sparse were the pastimes that relieved the doldrums of one's daily toils. It was easy to confound pent-up pep looking for an outlet with dedication to an ideal. The result was the creation of enduring and acrimonious controversies. Clearly, without alternative diversions for one's energies, many found in politics a release from the strains and stresses of their regular routine as well as a satisfying hobby during leisure hours. Secondly, at this early period in American history, the legitimacy of an opposition party in a democracy had not yet fully taken root. The inability to recognize political competitors as a constructive and necessary element in a working party system generated rancorous animosity toward all those who challenged your position. This was almost the inevitable outcome in an age whose view of the world was still characterized by religious dogmatism and sharply drawn categories of right and wrong. In the 1850's, Judge John Woodworth recalled the turbulence and ferociousness of political conflict that existed in the Empire State during the opening years of the nineteenth century, and wrote gratefully about the improved conditions. When anyone complained about the problems of political life in the middle of the nineteenth century, the revered judge would repeat the sage counsel of King Solomon: "Say not then, what is the cause that former Days were better than these. For thou dost not inquire wisely concerning this."[31]

IX

NEW YORK AND THE REST OF THE UNION

The events in New York during the first quarter of the nineteenth century both influenced and were influenced by events in the rest of the country. Moreover, although each state is a unique entity in certain respects, there are striking parallels between the developments in the Empire State and elsewhere. A comparison in such areas as the evolution of democratic reform, the relation between economic issues and politics, the nature of the political system, and the growth of sentiment for Andrew Jackson is especially illuminating.

Just as the Federalist party of New York often led the battle for democratic reform, the Federalist organizations in other states were frequently in the vanguard of democratic innovations. They played a particularly important role in the movement for the revision of state constitutions. In New Jersey, for example, dissatisfaction with the original state constitution grew to substantial proportions because of the overlapping jurisdictions of the executive, legislative, and judicial branches of the government, and because of the extremely high requirements for exercising the right of suffrage and holding public office. Although from time to time the legislature had raised the issue of governmental reform, nothing concrete was achieved until the Federalist-controlled Assembly of 1799 resolved to hold a constitutional convention if the majority of the electorate should indicate approval of such a move in the balloting of 1800.[1] The revision movement was generated almost exclusively by the Federalists who had to combat the opposition of the Republicans, an opposition founded "not on the basis of need, but of expediency."[2] Similarly, the Federalists had been the foremost proponents of the bill that passed the Pennsylvania legislature on March 28, 1825, permitting the people to decide by a public referendum whether or not they wished constitutional reform.[3] Finally, the support of the Federalists proved essential for the passing of Connecticut's democratic state constitution of 1821.[4]

Many other instances prove beyond a doubt that the Federalist party was not the arch foe of reform that Republican propaganda and American historiography have made it out to be. It was the Federalist-dominated legislature of Massachusetts that in 1804 democratized that state's system of choosing presidential electors. Previously, the legislature had named the electors, two from the state at large and the rest from lists submitted by the congressional districts. Under the new procedure, however, the people chose the electors from a general ticket.[5] Moreover, religious traditionalism and democratic ideology were close allies in Massachusetts politics.[6] Further, some of the richest and most powerful Federalists of Maryland led the movement for increased suffrage. Prominent Federalist leaders in North Carolina, such as John Stanly of New Bern and John Iredell of Edenton fought on the side of political reform. Clearly, the prominent Federalist in New Jersey, William Griffith, was not alone in his contention that property was not a justifiable criterion for granting the right to vote. He asserted: "Every citizen has (besides property), his liberty, his life, and his just rights in society to be protected; and these are equally important and common to all members of the community."[7]

The lot of the New York Federalists after 1800 also befell their brethren in other states. After the turn of the nineteenth century, there was no real chance for a Federalist to be elected governor of Pennsylvania although the party continued to go through the form of naming candidates for that position. The Federalist Party of Pennsylvania nominated its last gubernatorial candidate in 1814. Two years later, it chose its last presidential nominee. The Federalists were finished as far as national politics was concerned. The only path of political progress for the Federalists within the state was to ally themselves with various factions of the Republican Party. There were individual counties within the state, however, where the Federalists continued to obtain substantial majorities well into the nineteenth century. Adams, Lancaster, Delaware, Philadelphia, and Bucks counties were regarded as Federalist strongholds until the middle of the 1820's. Other areas that voted for Federalist candidates at least part of the time were Allegheny and Erie counties in the western part of the state.[8] The story of Federalism in New Jersey or Connecticut is not much different.

Just as the Federalist party did not always strive to limit the rights of the common man, so the Republican party cannot be credited with consistently trying to broaden his privileges. In New Jersey, for instance, although the Republican Party dominated the legislature by large majorities from 1802 to 1812, no democratic changes occurred. The ownership of property was maintained as a prerequisite for exercise of the suffrage. There was no lessening of the financial means that holders of public office were required to possess. There was no amelioration in the lot of debtors. There was negligible improvement in the facilities for public education. Moreover, the Republicans admitted that many members of their own party as a result of background, upbringing, and social status were more aristocratic than democratic in orientation.[9]

Actually, in regard to most of the issues connected with the expansion of democracy there were no clear-cut party divisions. In 1807, for example, New Jersey's voting requirements were substantially modified with very little argument and the support of both parties. Although the Republican Party controlled the Assembly 27–13 and the Council 8–5, the suffrage bill won 31–5 and 11–1 in the two houses respectively. Clearly, this legislation cannot be regarded as a party question. Similarly, in New Jersey, both the Republicans and the Federalists had procaucus and anticaucus factions.[10] There was likewise no party division on the suffrage question in Rhode Island, while Federalists and Republicans from Massachusetts also agreed "on all fundamentals."[11] Even in the South this was the case. Few issues of a constitutional or political nature arose in Tennessee that divided the factional squads in the state; in Maryland, both Federalists and Republicans used the expansion of the suffrage as a way to get votes; the contest over extending the vote in South Carolina was also not a party fight.[12]

To the extent that one can determine definite divisions over political questions in the states, the differences were often based on sectional rather than party considerations. During the 1820's, western Pennsylvania promoted alterations in the governmental structure in contrast to the eastern part of the state where there were strong adherents of the status quo. In North Carolina also, questions of political change, which involved mostly reforms of the county system of government, caused an east-west split. It is likewise true that in New Jersey local and sectional interests were often more important than party considerations in determining decisions. Northern Jersey ordinarily opposed southern Jersey in its efforts to use population as a basis for determining the number of representatives a county ought to have in the state legislature. Similarly, the northern and southern parts of the state divided on the question of whether congressional candidates should be chosen by districts or by a state-wide general ticket.[13]

Not only in New York did parties consist of constantly shifting factions with no uniform adherence to certain principles, but the same was true almost everywhere in America during the first quarter of the nineteenth century. Perhaps Pennsylvania and New Jersey provide the most striking parallels to the situation in the Empire State. When differences of opinion arose on the solution of problems by New Jersey's legislature, these resulted from discrete, concrete questions, and not from an abstract set of philosophic doctrines. In other words, practical and pragmatic considerations were the primary determinants of one's point of view;

consequently, coalitions and alliances were in a constant state of formation and re-formation with each new public issue.[14] The absence of clear-cut party distinctions enabled the prominent Pennsylvania Republican, James Buchanan, to declare he was "fond of being considered a democrat in the liberality of his principles, whilst he desired the support of the Federalists as their Magnus Apollo."[15] Michael Leib, one of the most virulent and vituperative of the Keystone State's Republican leaders, declared: "There is not an Honest man in the Federal party"; yet he ran and was elected to the state Assembly as a Federalist. Party differentiations were so vague that one Pennsylvania newspaper in its election reports forgot "to state that there were upon the Democratic Ticket the names of several Federalists . . . and upon the Federal Republican ticket the names of several Democrats."[16] The leadership of the Keystone State's Democratic Party was itself confused as to who made up the organization, and what its objectives were. There was neither stable platform nor enduring principles to give the organization definite shape. Personalities rather than policies were the focus of political conflict. For example, Simon Snyder, who served as governor of Pennsylvania from 1808 to 1817, was the most significant centripetal force within the Democratic-Republican party. His role was so predominant that the term "Snyder party" in Pennsylvania, like the term "Clintonian party" in New York, became synonymous with the organization it represented. Finally, the same lack of firmness in party differences that made possible the startling rapprochement between Martin Van Buren and De Witt Clinton had its counterpart in Pennsylvania when John Binns forged an alliance with William Duane in 1819. This union of forces resolved an antagonism that for fifteen years provided one of the few recognizably consistent elements in the political forays of the state. William Rawle must have expressed the amused perplexity of many when he commented on the Binns-Duane coalition in his journal: "Such are the strange involutions of parties."[17]

When parties did take a stand on issues connected with

democratic reform, the fundamental consideration was expediency, that is, party victory. In New Jersey, for example,
despite the universally recognized need for constitutional
reform in 1800, the Republicans opposed calling a convention
because they felt that they could not control the course of
events in their favor.[18] Similarly, opportunism determined the
vote of New Jersey's legislators on the question of whether to
elect representatives to Congress according to districts rather
than on a general ticket. Despite differences within the
parties based on sectional considerations, the Federalist party,
which stood to gain more from the district system, pushed
the measure through the legislature in 1799. In the following
year, when the Republicans obtained a majority in the legislature, they restored the general election system, saving for
themselves in the next congressional election all five seats
available. When New Jersey Federalists regained a majority in
the state legislature in 1812, they repealed the law calling for
election of congressmen from the state at large and replaced
it with a provision dividing the state into three congressional
districts, each of which would select two representatives. The
law, enacted to increase the influence of the Federalists,
achieved its goal when in the first election held under the new
system, the Federalists won four out of six congressional
seats.[19] Opposition to the caucus provided both Federalists
and Republicans who were hostile to Pennsylvania's incumbent chief executive in 1816 with an issue well suited to unseat
him from his throne of power. Likewise, the call for reform
during 1820 in Pennsylvania was combined with a demand
for wider distribution of the patronage. The opponents of
Governor Findley, called the Hiesterites, who exclaimed "any
honest man against Findley" were just as vociferous in
declaring "Give us a fair share of our country's political
honors, offices, and emoluments."[20] In 1825, when action in
behalf of constitutional reform in Pennsylvania was initiated
by a disgruntled faction of Republicans, the Old School men,
and Federalists who aspired to strengthen their influence in
the government, hostility to a revised constitution came from
the incumbent politicians who succeeded in obstructing the

reform movement.[21] The decision of Massachusetts' Federalist-controlled legislature in 1804 to provide for the selection of presidential electors by the people from a state-wide ticket was determined by "fear that some Republicans might slip in" under the old method according to which the legislature appointed the electors on the basis of lists received from the congressional districts.[22] In North Carolina, the People's Ticket, which led the anti-Crawford forces and vociferously attacked the caucus, was itself guilty of "raising little caucuses all over the state." Politicians were not averse to using the very institutions they condemned when it was to their benefit.[23]

In view of the great emphasis in previous chapters on the point that the Clintonian branch of the Republican party in New York often led the struggle for political reform, it is illuminating to note that De Witt Clinton was frequently regarded as a hero by reform parties in other states. For example, the anticaucus Republicans of Pennsylvania in 1817, the Hiesterites, were ardent supporters of De Witt Clinton for the presidency. One political leader wrote: "It is an important election. Should Mr. Hiester succeed, I presume the plan would be a coalition with Governor Clinton to secure all the Eastern and middle states to Maryland . . . for his presidency in 1821. That would yield 18 votes."[24] William H. Crawford predicted that if Hiester were elected "De Witt Clinton would receive the suffrage of that state."[25] Clinton's popularity was rooted in his attack on the caucus in New York and his initiation of the Erie Canal project. In Ohio also, the anticaucus Democrats strongly backed Clinton for President in 1824. During the two years prior to the election, the party sponsored many public gatherings that approved resolutions condemning the legislative caucus as a method of nomination and activating committees of correspondence to strengthen Clinton's chances for victory. Clinton was regarded by many notables in Ohio politics as the only candidate who could attract many erstwhile Clay supporters in the West as well as draw the backing of a substantial number of voters in the Northeast who might otherwise cast their ballots for John

Quincy Adams. A union of these two sections behind Clinton might well have proved a winning combination. The "grass roots" support for Clinton was very strong in Ohio, and had New York reacted more hospitably to the presidential aspirations of her native son, Clinton would have made a powerful candidate in the Northwest.[26]

The same absence of party differences on issues related to the growth of democracy existed in regard to the foremost economic questions during the first quarter of the nineteenth century. In New Jersey, for example, through the leadership of able men in both parties, fourteen new banks between 1812 and 1820 received charters from the state government. There was absolutely no partisan division evident in the movement to incorporate these new financial institutions; rather, the primary factors, which the legislators examined, concerned "value, feasibility, profit, and location within the state."[27] Moreover, the top-ranking personnel of these banks was drawn equally from members of both parties.[28] Internal improvements were likewise not a party issue in New Jersey. During the first decade of the 1800's, dozens of turnpike proposals, most of which were backed by the Republicans, passed the legislature; but the Federalists cooperated, seeing the chance for profits. Prominent Federalists like John Rutherfurd, John Neilson, William Paterson, John Bayard, and James Parker invested substantial sums in the turnpike companies. There were numerous Republicans who were also vitally interested in the turnpike business. Indeed, opponents of the toll roads complained that the "discordant names of Democrat and Federalist hath become harmoniously attuned to the persuasive [sic] and dulcet sounds of interest; in short, the most cordial cooperation hath taken place between the peculators of both parties and their coalition hath been complete."[29] Bipartisan support also accompanied plans for the construction of bridges and canals.[30] Further, bills to reduce the legal rate of interest from seven to six per cent for the welfare of the debtor, and to abolish imprisonment for debt, which were passed by the New Jersey legislature in 1819 and 1823 respectively, did not arouse conflict based on parties. Finally, the wide gamut of problems in the Garden State about which no partisan differences arose included attitudes toward the War of 1812, recovery measures from the Panic of 1819, public education, and the extension of slavery.[31]

Massachusetts reflected the same lack of correlation between economic status and party affiliation that was true of New York and New Jersey. The fishermen, farmers, freeholders, bankers, and merchants of Massachusetts were scattered widely throughout both the Federalist and the Republican parties. Thus, for example, although the Federalist party was controlled by prominent and wealthy merchants, there was a substantial percentage of people in the state who declined to support the Federalist organization in spite of their economic interests. These included the fishermen of Cape Cod, Martha's Vineyard, and Nantucket whose affiliation with the Republican party flew in the face of the material well-being to be derived from joining the Federalists.[32] In addition, powerful merchants like David Henshaw and J. K. Simpson were Antifederalists. During the 1820's and 1830's, moreover, the rural inhabitants of the state found their way in large numbers into both the Jacksonian and Whig parties. Both parties, finally, had their own banks.[33]

Professor Richard McCormick has shown in his study of North Carolina that differences in economic status did not determine in any appreciable way party alignments within the state. North Carolina, like New York, had a dual suffrage system: citizens who met a taxpaying qualification could vote for governor and members of the lower house of the state legislature, while fifty-acre holders could vote for state senators as well. In three noteworthy electoral contests, those of 1840, 1844, and 1856, the fifty-acre freeholders distributed their votes between the Whigs and Democrats in approximately the same proportion as the taxpaying voters. Thus, in 1840, while 53.7 per cent of the freeholders voted for Whig candidates, 52.7 per cent of the taxpaying electors made that decision. None of the electoral contests yielded between the two classes of voters a differential of more than 2 per cent, an almost negligible quantity. Hence, a man's possession of fifty or more acres of real estate did not materially alter his political sympathies.[34] Differences in North Carolina were based on sectional rather than party considerations. The more backward regions of the west and south were lined up against the affluent middle east on such questions as federal construction of internal improvements and bank reform. The bankers and creditors who were concentrated in the middle east had to combat the antibank sentiment expressed by the numerous debtors who dwelt in the western and southern sections of the state. The inhabitants of the west, on the other hand, advocated an elaborate program for internal improvements in order to enlarge their profits from an expanded trade made possible by better roads and increased canal construction. The more prosperous inhabitants of the middle east, who would have to pay the lion's share for these internal improvements and whose own section was in less need of such projects for development, provided the bulk of the opposition.[35] Quite clearly, in economic matters as well as on political questions, there were no clear-cut differences between the parties in numerous American states during the first quarter of the nineteenth century.

The paucity of clear-cut and consistent party differences on major issues in New York seemed to reflect the absence of a well-defined political system in that state, and the situation in most other parts of the country was similar. In Massachusetts, for example, although the Federalists had an uninterrupted chain of electoral victories until 1823, they were inclined to view the period of James Monroe's presidency as an "era of good feelings" during which partisan differentiation was nonexistent. Further, while the Federalist party had succeeded in dominating political affairs within the state for many years, the organization had to concede that it was gradually losing its grip. The climax occurred in 1824 when Federalism waged its last political battle as a distinct party, going down to an ignominious defeat in the contest for the governorship in that year. What followed was a period of "confusion" and "flux" that lasted for the rest of the decade.

Without national leadership to provide guidance and with the local organizations quickly breaking up, Massachusetts Federalists split in 1824 over the problem of whether or not to support the presidential aspirations of their state's favorite son, John Quincy Adams. Members of the party who were concerned about the development of manufacturing within the state pardoned Adams' personal affronts and supported his bid for the presidency. Others, however, such as Theodore Lyman, Jr., whose father had been a leader of the Essex Junto, and Congressman Francis Baylies, who had participated in the Hartford Convention, could not bring themselves to make peace with Adams. The swiftly dissolving old party organizations in Massachusetts were not soon followed by clearly discernible new ones. Even the attempt to identify variations in point of view at this time is fraught with the temptation to draw lines of separation more sharply than is justified by the realities of the situation. It was anybody's guess as to how, when, and if stable parties would emerge from the turmoil and imbroglio of Massachusetts' political life.[36]

The blurring of party lines in Massachusetts increased during the next four years. The complicated factionalism of Massachusetts is suggested by the numerous nominating conclaves held prior to the election of 1828. Suffolk County alone was the scene of four separate conventions. Two groups, the "Federal Republicans" and "Democratic Republicans," favored Adams, while two other factions, with names identical to those above, named Andrew Jackson as their choice. Adams' Massachusetts supporters included old Federalists like Daniel Webster and venerable Republicans like Levi Lincoln.[37] Political commitments, nevertheless, were not very firm. David Henshaw, for example, joined the Adams forces in 1825 and was elected to the state Senate the following year as a candidate on the Adams ticket. The coalition was scarcely more than a year old when it was destroyed as a result of differences over the Charles River Bridge Case. Andrew Jackson also had a motley group of backers. Besides leading Republican leaders such as David Henshaw (after his rupture with Adams) and John K. Simpson, there were many noteworthy Federalists such as Theodore Lyman, Jr., Lemuel Williams, a well-known New Bedford attorney, and Moses Stuart, a prominent professor at the Andover Theological Seminary. Adams censured these Federalist supporters of Jackson. Indeed, he reiterated his former accusation that in 1807 the Federalists had committed treason against the country.[38] It was not until the 1840's that stable and meaningful party divisions emerged in Massachusetts.

In New Jersey, also, party alignments were ephemeral and transient during the first three decades of the nineteenth century. In 1797 Jonas Wade and Recompense Stanbury were hailed as Republican leaders; twelve months afterward, they ran for public office on a Federalist slate.[39] Although the Federalist party officially terminated its activities as a state organization soon after the conclusion of the Second War of Independence, it endured as a vital institution for a number of years in several New Jersey localities as it did in New York; indeed, it was alleged that Federalists continued to comprise at least forty per cent of the state legislature for as long as twenty years after the party had been placed in opposition status. In fact, Isaac H. Williamson, who served as governor of the Garden State for twelve years beginning in 1817, was accused by some of his political enemies of having Federalist sympathies. Nonetheless, this prominent attorney and scion of a well-known Elizabeth Town family, was named to his post for three successive years by a unanimous vote in a Republican-dominated legislature. Partisan calculation was similarly lacking in the appointments made by a joint meeting of the legislature in 1817 for Chief Justice of the state, Attorney General, and Clerk of the Supreme Court. The Republican legislature chose two Federalists, Theodore Frelinghuysen of Essex and Garret D. Wall of Trenton, as Attorney General and Clerk of the Supreme Court respectively.[40]

Party lines in New Jersey virtually vanished after 1824. Nine of the state's thirteen counties gave Jackson a majority of their ballots in 1824. The other four, who went for Adams, were Essex, Middlesex, Salem, and Cape May. However, at the same time that Essex County, the foremost center of Republican sentiment in the Garden State went for Adams, the other strongly Republican counties of Hunterdon, Sussex, Morris, and Monmouth went for Jackson. On the other hand, Middlesex and Cape May, two Federalist fortresses, went to Adams, although Somerset and Burlington, two other bastions, belonged to Jackson. Obviously, the old party lines were not holding very firmly. To complicate the situation further, there was practically a complete reversal of circumstances four years later. Whereas in 1824 nine counties voted for Jackson, in 1828 nine counties voted against him. Similarly, whereas Jackson won the Garden State's electoral vote in 1824 but lost the election, in 1828 Jackson failed to carry New Jersey but won the presidency. These oscillations and transformations produced a fusion of Federalists and Republicans that made former distinctions unrecognizable.[41]

The same lack of clarity in regard to political differentiations occurred elsewhere, too. Tennessee politics, for example, manifested a pattern of numerous transient groupings based on personal attachments. The climax of this confusion in Tennessee took place in 1819 after which two major parties, differing over the principal question of government attitude toward banks, began to emerge instead of the traditional factions that had been grouped around attractive personalities.[42] In North Carolina, during the election of 1824, competing for votes were four factions that differed slightly on the major questions of the day; and the number of their followers changed radically from day to day.[43] Ohio, the most important of the western states during the 1820's, was also characterized by numerous unstable factions that played havoc with old party distinctions. Thus, the Federalists in Ohio found their way in substantial numbers into all the major groupings for the election of 1824 including the Adams, Clay, Crawford, and Jackson camps.[44] Quite clearly, the pattern of transient factionalism which was drawn in New York state during the early nineteenth century reflected a design found in many places throughout the country. The American political system in 1828 was still at a very primitive stage of development.

When did the United States become an equal-rights democracy? The popular legend is that Andrew Jackson's years in the White House were the crucial turning point in the democratization of American political institutions. Yet not only in New York, but throughout the country, the most important reforms occurred before and totally apart from Old Hickory's tenure as president of the United States.

As far as suffrage is concerned, voting requirements were liberalized in the vast majority of places well before the end of the first quarter of the nineteenth century. The widening of the franchise was particularly early in Pennsylvania. The Constitution of 1790 declared that every freeman, who had reached twenty-one years of age, "having resided in the state two years next before the elections, and within that time paid a state or county tax, which shall have been assessed at least six months before the election, shall enjoy the rights of an elector." In the absence of a general state tax at this time, most of the populace qualified for the voting franchise by payment of a highway or property levy that the counties imposed. Thus, the Keystone State had achieved quite early for almost every male, at least, the right to vote. Indeed, she was way ahead of New York as well as other states in this respect.[45] The democratization of Maryland's political institutions also occurred very swiftly. To be sure, the state constitution of 1776 was the handiwork of wealthy aristocrats, and was designed to protect the interests of the landed gentry. Nevertheless, within twenty-five years every free white male could vote providing only that he had resided within the state twelve months and in the county six months. By the end of the first decade of the nineteenth century, all property requirements for the holding of office had similarly been removed.[46] Hence, a state constitution, which had been regarded as a paragon of conservatism at the time of the American Revolution, had been altered so drastically that it was esteemed as a thoroughly democratic document even before the War of 1812. After 1807 the suffrage in New Jersey included almost all free white males, or about twenty-one per cent of the population.[47] Among the other Northern states, Connecticut abolished property qualifications for voting in 1818, Massachusetts in 1822, and, of course, New York in 1821. Further, among the new states entering the Union by 1820, the right of every man to vote had either been enacted into law or acquired through practice in Ohio, Indiana, Illinois, Mississippi, Alabama, Maine, and Missouri.[48]

The early date marking extension of suffrage in most of the states is accentuated still more by the fact that an unauthorized enlargement of the electorate generally preceded changes in the law. As far back as 1790 in Maryland, for example, almost 100 per cent of the adult white males voted in the town of Baltimore, while seven counties boasted participation in elections exceeding fifty per cent. By the beginning of the nineteenth century, over sixty per cent of Maryland's adult males cast ballots in six counties, while the electoral statistics of 1808 record a turnout unequalled by most other states even toward the end of the Jacksonian era.[49] By 1800, moreover, from eighty to one hundred per cent of New Jersey's adult males were regularly voting although no amendments had been made to the conservative state constitution of 1776. The handling of election controversies reveals unequivocally that the ownership of property as a prerequisite to voting had been discarded by the people long before the constitution officially rescinded such requirements.[50] Studies of Massachusetts, in addition, have tended to minimize the importance of property requirements as a factor limiting the size of the electorate there.[51] The unanimous agreement of North Carolina's principal state historians that before 1848 there was no widespread movement for the removal of the freehold qualification to vote, suggests that more people succeeded in exercising the right of suffrage in the state than were, in fact, permitted by law.[52]

The other great subject of political reform in the early 1800's concerned the voice of the people in nominating candidates for public office. As the congressional caucus was used to nominate presidential candidates, on the state level the legislative caucuses determined who would run for local offices. The earliest case on record of a state legislative caucus is the meeting in Rhode Island during 1790 that named candidates for the offices of governor and lieutenant governor.

Shortly thereafter, Pennsylvania followed the example of Rhode Island in using the caucus to choose its nominees for the governorship. The nomination of John Jay as governor in 1795 by a joint meeting of the Federalists from both houses of New York's legislature marked the adoption by the Empire State of this method of electing candidates.[53] There were a number of objections that one could raise against the caucus method of nomination. It blurred the distinctions between the executive and legislative departments, increasing their interdependence. Since the meetings usually took place in the state capitol, the party in control of the government also managed to dominate the caucus proceedings, while groups with no representatives in the legislature were denied any voice in the selection of candidates. Members of the legislature had no authorization from the people to choose nominees for public office, and the members of the caucus almost always selected a man from their own ranks to be the candidate. Public hostility against these abuses led to their gradual elimination.

Just as agitation against the state legislative caucus reached a climax in New York in 1817 with the holding of the first nominating convention in the Empire State so in Pennsylvania a group of Independent Republicans who gathered at Carlyle in that year were hailed as "the entering wedge in the destruction of caucuses, corruption, and intolerable hypocrisy."[54] The convention delegates publicized the absence in their ranks of public officials, the selection of a site other than the state capitol for the meeting, and the choice of each of them by their respective constituencies for the specific purpose of naming a candidate for the governorship. This democratic innovation by the "Independents" led the party in power to democratize its own nominating procedure to the extent of inviting delegates from districts unrepresented in the legislature to participate in the caucus at Harrisburg. The sole issue of substance in the Pennsylvania campaign of 1817 was the proper method of nominating candidates for public office. According to the Independent Republicans, the balloting represented a "contest between those in power, who wish to continue there by means of a corrupt system of caucusing and official influence, contrary to the spirit of our institutions; and the great body of the people of all parties who wish to preserve uncontaminated those institutions."[55] Interestingly enough in Connecticut, also, important changes were made in the method of nomination in 1817.[56]

The caucus, both state and congressional, was attacked and modified in many states during the opening decades of the nineteenth century. As early as 1807, a "mixed caucus," comprising legislators and especially elected delegates from districts without representatives in the legislature, was established in Rhode Island. In 1823, the legislative caucus in Massachusetts widened its membership to include outside delegates. During the same year, the legislatures of Tennessee, Maryland, and some other new states in the West passed resolutions condemning the practice of the congressional caucus.[57]

The battle against the caucus dominated the election of 1824 not only in New York but also in most of the other states. Herman Hailperin concluded from his study of Pennsylvania politics in the 1820's: "The real issue in the campaign of 1824 was the manner of selecting the President."[58] The groups opposed to the candidacy of William Crawford in the Keystone State responded with enthusiastic approval to John Calhoun's contention that the essence of the difference between Crawford and himself was "not a question of man, but of principle, between those who are willing to trust the election to the people at large, and those who wish to govern the people through the agency of a few intriguing politicians in the several states."[59] For the anti-Crawfordites realized that the best chance for the defeat of the Georgian and the victory of their own candidate lay in a vociferous denunciation of the caucus. The decisive vanquishment of Pennsylvania's legislative caucus occurred on March 4, 1824, at the Harrisburg Convention that met to choose a slate of presidential electors. The gathering had all the elements that constitute political conventions. The assembly was convoked by the Jacksonian party in Pennsylvania, and received delegates, elected by local party organizations from each county in the state, proportional to the size of its population. Hence, the task of nominating candidates for public office was no longer within the exclusive province of the state legislature, but fell rather upon the especially selected delegates of the people.

In the West also, the caucus was the most frequent object of attack in the election campaign of 1824. The democratic innovators from that section of the country condemned the caucus as a source of collusion, wrongdoing, and fraud. Its defenders were allegedly apostate Federalists who desired to duplicate the despicable treacheries of the Hartford Convention. The enemies of the caucus in Ohio derived satisfaction from the fact that only one member of that state's delegation to Congress (Benjamin Ruggles) had "been seduced from the path of duty, to the imminent hazard of his popularity and usefulness" by participating in the congressional caucus of February, 1824.[60] Ruggles' behavior, which differed from that of his fellow Ohioans in the Congress, was also condemned as a defiance of the sentiments held by "the great body of people of this state." In the anti-Crawford centers of the South such as North Carolina, the primary source of unhappiness with the existent political institutions in 1824 also centered around the choice of candidates for public office by means of the caucus together with the selection of presidential electors by the legislature.[61]

The number and prominence of the rival candidates, the bitterness of the contest, and the existence of only one national party have established the traditional view that the election of 1824 was primarily a contest between rival personal leaders. To be sure, personalities were influential in determining the size and distribution of the vote. However, a survey of the campaign shows that the strongest and most frequent appeals to the voters were based on public issues with which the candidates were identified rather than on their personalities. The foregoing paragraphs have stressed the central importance of the caucus together with the method of choosing presidential electors as political issues. In addition, there were important economic questions. In Pennsylvania, the protective tariff and internal improvements were frequently debated in 1824.[62] The same problems dominated public attention in Ohio. Indeed, the *Stuebenville Gazette* wrote that "the question is not now whether this candidate or that candidate is a democrat or a federalist, but whether he is a friend or an opponent to domestic industry and internal improvements."[63] North Carolina, besides being concerned with the tariff and internal improvements, was worried about policy toward banks and the extension of slavery.[64] Public education, the legal rate of interest, the treatment of debtors, banking policy, the protective tariff, and internal improvements troubled the populace of New Jersey most in 1824.[65] Clearly, public issues were of great, if not determining, influence all over America in the election of 1824.

The fact that the election of 1824 marked the climax in the process of democratizing the fundamental political institutions of New York state led us to the conclusion that 1824 was the most crucial year in the evolution of an equal-rights democracy in that state. There are indications that 1824 was also a critical year for political reform elsewhere in the country. Herman Hailperin asserts that "the popular triumph of . . . 1824 was the beginning of a democracy" in Pennsylvania.[66] The greatest political reforms of Massachusetts, according to Arthur B. Darling, resulted "from the demise of the old Federalist party in 1824."[67] Moreover, Albert Ray Newsome declares that the election of 1824 in North Carolina marked the triumph of a "political revolution" in that state: "The memorable election of 1824 in North Carolina was a democratic upsurge which repudiated political methods and leadership well-entrenched by a generation of dominance."[68] In addition, the degree of voter participation in North Carolina up to 1824 reached heights unsurpassed in any electoral contest of the Jackson period.[69] Indeed, Richard McCormick has shown that in the overwhelming majority of states there was greater public participation in the elections prior to Andrew Jackson's victory as president of the United States than took place during the years when Old Hickory occupied the highest office in the land.[70] Undoubtedly, an equal-rights democracy was not achieved everywhere in America at the same time; but it was achieved in most states before Andrew Jackson became president. Further, in many states the final obstacles to democracy were removed in 1824, the year of the last presidential contest prior to Jackson's election. Consequently, if it is at all possible to determine exactly when the United States of America became an equal-rights democracy, it appears that 1824 is the most crucial and climactic year of a process that stretched over many decades.

One of the most striking aspects of government in New York during the first three decades of the nineteenth century was the primacy of state over national politics, a situation reversed today. Here again one finds numerous parallels throughout the country. In North Carolina, for example, the citizenry was customarily indifferent toward presidential elections. Although the congressional representatives chosen in August, 1823, would designate in caucus the party candidate for the presidency, the vast majority of voters in North Carolina did not take this into consideration when they cast their ballots. In the Fayetteville district, when "A Citizen" asked the congressional nominees, John Culpepper and Archibald McNeill, to make public their choice for president, they refused to issue a forthright statement. Indeed, the districts of Morganton and Charlotte were the only places where a semblance of dialogue on the presidential question took place, but even there the discussion was "reluctant, cautious, and restrained."[71] Moreover, in spite of the vitality that characterized the battle for the presidency in 1824, the number of ballots cast in the national contest was only 36,036, or just about 66⅔ per cent of the vote tallied for the state election of the same year.[72] Further the relative indifference of North Carolina regarding who should be elected President, compared to their overwhelming concern with the issues of democracy posed by the election of 1824, was eloquently expressed by the *Catawba Journal*. This local periodical declared that since the fundamental purpose of the election, which was the defeat of the caucus method of nominating candidates, had been achieved, "let who will then be president; our main object is accomplished—the charm of caucus nomination is dissolved, the sovereignty of the people has been maintained, and North Carolina assumes that rank among her sister states, which the character of her citizens, her resources, her steadfast adherence to republican principles, so justly entitles her to."[73]

In other states also there are many indications that local questions were of much greater importance to the voter than national ones. In Ohio, throughout the early nineteenth century, presidential campaigns evoked but little concern, the tally consistently lagging far behind the turnout in state contests.[74] Even in 1824, in spite of the intense campaigning and the acerbity of its closing episodes, the total balloting in the presidential election was only 50,024 while 76,634 votes, or over one-third more, were cast in the gubernatorial race.[75] New Jersey legislators spent much more energy on internal problems such as the proper approach of the government toward insolvent debtors, public education, economic difficulties, the creation of new banks, and the building of roads than they gave to issues of national importance like the protective tariff, the extension of slavery, the Panama Congress, or the Monroe Doctrine.[76] Similarly, in Massachusetts, the subjects of "free bridges, lotteries, and the sale of liquor" were much more likely to excite the populace at this time than the broader questions linked with national destiny and purpose.[77]

It is extremely significant that in nineteen of the twenty-three states that were members of the Union by 1824, the highest known percentage of adult white males voting in them up to that critical year occurred in state rather than national political contests.[78] The gubernatorial contests in most of the states consistently drew close to seventy per cent of the electorate to the voting booths. Some of the states recorded astronomically high percentages: Delaware in 1804 when 81.9 per cent of the adult whites voted, Vermont in 1812 with 79.9, New Hampshire in 1814 with 80.8, Tennessee in 1817 with 80.0, Alabama in 1819 with an unbelievable

96.7 per cent, and Mississippi in 1823 with 79.8. The evidence also shows that for at least some states, the election figures are higher in contests involving the choice of state legislators than in balloting for a governor. These percentages for participation in state elections acquire even more striking proportions when it is noted that only 26.5 per cent of the eligible voters in the United States exercised their right of suffrage in the presidential election of 1824. To be sure, this percentage expanded to almost twice its original size during the next twelve years, but, even so, there is not one instance prior to 1840 where the national average in a presidential contest exceeded or came close to the national average obtained in state elections. Thus, even while a personality as colorful and attractive as Andrew Jackson occupied the White House, the people remained much more concerned with local than national affairs. During the period of Old Hickory's incumbency, the voter turnout in thirty-four of the fifty gubernatorial contests, which were held in states where presidential electors were also chosen by the people, was larger than in the parallel balloting for the chief executive's post in Washington. Without exception, the states of Rhode Island, Delaware, Tennessee, Kentucky, Illinois, Mississippi, Missouri, and Georgia cast a larger number of votes in the gubernatorial than the presidential elections.[79] Unquestionably, there were few Americans in the early nineteenth century for whom national questions were of greater import than state matters.

In addition to a primary interest in the state, there was also a developing sectional consciousness during the 1820's. Just as New Yorkers complained about southern domination of federal offices, similar complaints of exploitation by different sections of the country issued forth throughout the land. In Ohio, where feelings ran particularly high against the southern part of the country, numerous speakers and writers proceeded to harangue the "southrons."[80] Congressman T. H. Hall of Edgecombe, North Carolina, also viewed political conflict from a totally sectionalist perspective. Indeed, he reduced the issues in the election of 1824 to a question of whether North Carolina should "take the man who is bound to us by birth, habits, identity of interest and political sentiment" or choose a man who was ignorant of and uninterested in the South.[81] The *Raleigh Register* declared that "if the *southern people* wish *restrictions* upon state sovereignty, and other measures, whose end shall be *abolition of slavery,* by *emancipation among us,* then of course, Mr. Adams should be preferred."[82] In a similar vein, *The Star* argued that "a President from a non-slave holding state can never be the man whom the policy of North Carolina should support. . . . Plain and simply . . . the sentiments of the north are too widely different from those of the south."[83]

Intersectional rivalry was sometimes softened by intra-sectional jealousy as in the case of North Carolina, which resented its reputation of being led by Virginia. Many North Carolinians who desired to assert the independence of their state and to throw off the lamented political subordination to Virginia refused to support William Crawford for the presidency in 1824 because of his Virginia nativity and his great popularity in that state.[84] On the other hand, some citizens favored Adams primarily on the ground that he opposed Virginia's control of the national government.[85] John Calhoun, in an effort to promote his chances for the presidency, also stressed the importance of North Carolina's combatting the widespread impression that she was "the mere appendage" of the colossus to the north.[86] Beyond a doubt, the America of the early nineteenth century was parochial in its outlook, and lacked the cohesion that is provided by an overriding loyalty and dedication to the needs of the nation as a whole.

"The Election of 1828 will be regarded by posterity as we regard the events of 1776 and 1798 as worthy of lasting commemoration." This prophecy by the Jacksonian committees of correspondence regarding the future's judgment of Old Hickory's triumph has been fulfilled in the interpretation of this era by most of the nation's great historians. The Jacksonian movement is popularly regarded as initiating numerous political reforms throughout the country, providing the poor man opportunity to participate in the control of the government, marking the political maturity of the common people, stimulating the formation of new state constitutions, and popularizing the idea that the president should come from humble origins. From what we have shown earlier in this chapter, however, it should be quite clear that the Jacksonians' connection with the development of political democracy has been vastly exaggerated not only in New York but in the entire country. For the basic issues of political democracy were substantially resolved before the Jacksonians took command, completely independently of their aspirations to power.

Richard McCormick has revealed, moreover, that the period of Jackson's occupancy of the White House did not constitute a "mighty democratic uprising" in the sense that more Americans cast ballots in the elections of that time than had ever done so before. The fact is that voter turnout during the Jacksonian era seems relatively meager when compared to the swarms of people who exercised the suffrage in 1840, to the ballots cast in the gubernatorial contests of the 30's, or to the maximum votes tabulated in state elections prior to 1824. Although 56.3 per cent of the nation's electorate voted in 1828, voter participation exceeded all past records in only six of the twenty-two states in the Union at that time. Further, while six states reported that over 70 per cent of their adult white males had cast ballots in 1828, as many as ten states had reached these high proportions in earlier electoral contests. In addition, despite Old Hickory's great popularity in 1832 and the serious questions that were debated in the campaign of that year, the number of ballots cast was smaller by two per cent than the voter participation in the previous presidential election.[87] Such statistics hardly justify the conclusion that the Jacksonian movement was a "roaring flood of the new democracy . . . foaming perilously, near the crest." Finally, the foregoing evidence would tend to disprove the contention that prior to the Jacksonian era the average person was either indifferent to or prevented from exercising his right of suffrage by insurmountable restrictions.

Not only is there no objective correlation between the career of Andrew Jackson and the evolution of democracy in the United States, but it can even be shown that people did not vote for "Old Hickory" because they *thought* he was a political reformer. In Pennsylvania, for example, it was Jackson's "military character and reputation for integrity in all matters that gave him such a large and devoted following."[88] Moreover, although Pennsylvania wanted a protective tariff in 1824, the charismatic qualities of Andrew Jackson eliminated the necessity of his committing himself on this or any other question. George Dallas and William Darlington of the Keystone State, who had originally supported Calhoun, sadly concluded that the Tennessean's military exploits spread an aura of glamour about him that cancelled all rational examination of his desirability as a presidential candidate. Dallas later added that Jackson's image was so overpowering that he appeared to possess "every qualification that can be desired in an American pilot" and the ability to lead the nation "through the storm."[89]

In New Jersey, also, the catalogue of reasons for which people voted the Jackson ticket did not include his being a "great democrat." Old Hickory was honored, in the first place, for his outstanding military achievements. These exploits would evoke the respect of other countries who would think twice before picking a quarrel with the United States. He was also esteemed as a great statesman whose "ability . . . mental faculties . . . honesty, honor, and attachment to the rights of man" would make him a splendid candidate for the presidency. It was necessary, finally, to break the precedent that insisted that the president be chosen from the ranks of cabinet members.[90]

The public image of Jackson was not much different in the South and West from what it was in the North. His magnetic personality and his brilliant achievements in war were the primary focuses of the campaign propaganda. Almost everyone was aware of the battles he waged against the British, Spanish, and Indians. His numerous nicknames such as "Old Hickory," "the last of the Revolutionary patriots," "the pillar of the Republic," and the "second Washington" suggest the awe and respect the people felt toward him. One broadside declared: "His history is . . . the record of his country's glory." P. H. Mangum, a Jacksonian leader in North Carolina, expressed the view that "The people were fascinated and interested by the splendor of his military fame *alone*. It is not that they think or care about his being an able statesman that they will vote for him. . . . He has slain Indians & flogged the British & spilled his blood in defense of his country's rights —therefore he is the bravest, wisest, and greatest man in the nation—even the memory of Washington is lost in the blaze of his bloody laurels."[91] The literature of the Jackson corresponding committee of Ohio discloses in similar fashion that it was Jackson's popularity, personality, military attainments, and unimpeachable character that were uppermost in the minds of his supporters.[92]

The lack of connection between Jackson and the cause of democracy is suggested also by the numerous Federalists all over the country who flocked to his banner in 1824 and 1828. In Pennsylvania, for example, outstanding Federalist leaders such as Andrew Gregg enthusiastically supported Andrew Jackson. Moreover, when Pennsylvania Republicans asked Jackson to renounce the backing of Federalists, he refused to do so. Old Hickory's Federalist supporters in the Keystone State felt that they could enhance their political fortunes by capitalizing on Jackson's charisma.[93] In Ohio, the General's opponents also vituperated against him because of the aid offered by Federalists; in Tennessee, he was condemned as an aristocrat and as an enemy of universal suffrage. Incidentally, the nominating convention in Ohio that named Jackson as its candidate for the presidency in 1824 was less democratic than the conventions that chose Adams and Clay, and it contained fewer delegates and represented fewer counties.[94]

There were so many Federalists in the forefront of the Jacksonian ranks in New Jersey that the supporters of Adams were highly incensed that the Jackson men should use the Republican name. It was argued that the Jacksonian ranks consisted principally of Federalists in disguise who were using the

Tennessean's military reputation as a "stalking horse upon which to ride into power."[95] The foremost members of the Jacksonian party in New Jersey included names like the Ogdens, the Stocktons, the Scots, the De Vrooms, the Parkers, and the Chetwoods. Indeed, the head of the Jackson Central Committee in the Garden State was a venerable Federalist by the name of Wall. In addition, three Federalists were included on the Jacksonian congressional ticket from New Jersey. It was not far from the truth to say that "without those once called *Federalists*, the Jackson Cause in New Jersey would be utterly a hopeless cause."[96] Thus, in many different ways, it is clear that the development of political democracy in the United States owes no special debt of gratitude to Andrew Jackson.

X

CONCLUSIONS

Allan Nevins has observed that there is presently a greater interest in history than ever before: "In the large view, this is so, no doubt, mainly because the unprecedented events in the last generation have stimulated an appetite for parallels, contrasts and interpretations."[1] Certainly, the student of contemporary politics would find it highly illuminating to examine the political life of the Empire State during the early nineteenth century, for the outlines of our political system today are deeply imbedded in the practices that emerged during that era.

New York's political parties in the period between Jefferson and Jackson did not embody distinct ideological positions; they consisted rather of opportunistic conglomerations of men from all walks of life who organized their energies and talents in order to elect certain candidates to public office. Since this was the main reason for the existence of political organizations, party activity was seasonal, and its pace was regulated by the rhythm of the elections. The parties also performed a number of secondary functions such as providing unity in a government with numerous elective posts and multiple foci of power; maintaining continuity amidst the perennial changes of administration; and mobilizing the populace to vote at election time. These political organizations were highly personalized machines, revolving about certain notable political figures; indeed, a political party rarely survived the death of its leader. As a result, factions constantly formed and re-formed in seemingly endless succession. The rapid and often unpredictable passage of the electors from one party to another was made easier by the fact that the elections rarely turned on matters of principle, and a large percentage of New York's population consisted of recent migrants who had no deeply rooted habits of party loyalty. The factionalism that emerged in the Republican Party of New York during the pre-Jacksonian era also shows how strong leadership in a predominantly one-party system forces rival elements to organize their own political factions.

Although New York's political parties were animated primarily by the pursuit of political office rather than the desire to promote specific programs, they did enact many notable and useful reforms. These improvements resulted from the necessity of favoring legislation that would win the support of the electorate. In truth, most of the changes that transformed the Empire State into an equal-rights democracy, such as the expansion of the suffrage and the substitution of the nominating convention for the legislative caucus, came about via this route. New York's political structure, as it finally emerged, was deeply affected by British and colonial precedent; a fluid and mobile social structure; the absence of deeply rooted ideological conflict; and the existence of such technical electoral procedures as the simple majority and single ballot system. The idea of party membership remained nebulous, although there were essentially three levels of participation in party activities that differed in intensity of involvement: the voters, the backers, and the zealots. Party members belonged to no particular social or economic groupings, although most of the leaders were lawyers by profession.

The effective operation of the highly developed political machines that evolved in New York state at this time required the members to adhere to strict discipline. The granting or withholding of patronage provided a useful tool for the maintenance of this discipline. The party's power to name its candidates for public office also enabled the organization to reward the faithful and advance their careers in public life. In its effort to secure electoral victories, the machine relied upon several techniques. Among the most important of these was the party press, which involved the control of one or more newspapers whose leadership tailored and interpreted the news in accordance with the organization's dictates. Committees of correspondence, which helped to coordinate the activities of local units with the state party's overall electoral strategy, played a significant role in making the candidates known, publicizing their point of view, and arousing the enthusiasm of the citizenry. Committees of vigilance were also essential in order to combat the chicanery and deception too often associated with electioneering. The machine's influence over public policy was aided by a number of governmental institutions such as the Council of Revision and the Council of Appointment. The veto power of the Council of Revision, which consisted of the governor, the chancellor, and the justices of the state supreme court, sharply limited the legislature's ability to pass laws during the forty-four years of its operation from 1777 to 1821. The Council of Appointment, made up of the governor and one senator chosen annually by the Assembly from each of the four senatorial districts, controlled over fifteen thousand state jobs at the height of its power, before it too was abolished in 1821. Further, the ability of the party to guide the proceedings of the legislative caucus, and the indirect selection of presidential electors by the legislature empowered the party organization to scrutinize closely the various aspirants to public office. Social and benevolent organizations such as the Tammany Society and the Washington Benevolent Society, which were deeply tinged with political coloration, enabled the party machines to exert their influence even further into the private lives of the people.

The effective operation of a party organization in a federal system such as ours necessitates the existence of regular means of communication between the various centers of government. The state machines utilized many different methods to control political activity on the local level throughout New York. For a long while, for example, key community officials such as mayors, justices of the peace, and sheriffs were chosen in Albany. Party managers also utilized tavern owners to manipulate public opinion because of the latter's ability to reach people in an environment where they were more psychologically susceptible to political propaganda. Similarly, prominent officials of the large land companies were induced to employ their powers to propound a particular point of view among those who inhabited their territories. In order to insure electoral victory, local units of the state machine transported prospective voters to and from the polls on election day; they compiled lists of citizens who would be most likely to vote in the "right" way; they persuaded landlords to pressure their tenants into choosing certain officials; and they even fraudulently registered voters who were not authorized to cast ballots in a particular locality. State leaders also maintained intimate relationships with members of the party who served in the national government. Indeed, De Witt Clinton's famous Green Bag Message of 1821 showed that Martin Van Buren at the behest of Bucktail officials in Albany used his position as a United States senator to pressure the government into discharging certain postal officials in the Empire State. Van Buren also travelled to many other states in order to solidify the connections that linked the Democratic machine in New York state to its counterparts throughout the Union.

Despite the interrelationships of state and national politics, New Yorkers were much more concerned with political life in the state than with the governmental activities at Washington. The Missouri Compromise of 1820, for example, interested the people much less than the Bucktail-Clintonian wrangling. The Monroe Doctrine hardly received passing notice in 1823. In addition, the state election of 1824 was fought far more seriously and ardently than the national aspects of that contest. Most New Yorkers in public life, furthermore, preferred to serve in state rather than national positions. Indeed, many resigned from important posts in the federal government in order to accept what would today be regarded as minor positions within the state. The political factions in New York also subordinated the needs of the national party to local requirements. The preference of the public for state over national politics was probably enhanced, in part, by rising sectional rivalries that impeded the development of a national consciousness.

The most important consequence of the political warfare

that was waged in New York during the first three decades of the nineteenth century was the expansion of democracy. The various political factions in an effort to attain electoral victory competed with each other in trying to persuade the voter that they were the "real" guardians of his rights. The results of this rivalry were numerous governmental innovations that increased the voice of the people in public affairs. This process, which brought about the emergence of the Empire State as an equal-rights democracy, differs from Dixon Ryan Fox's interpretation of the phenomenon. Fox believed that democracy evolved in New York as a result of an ideological conflict between two groups, one of which was liberal and democratic while the other was aristocratic and conservative. The conservative point of view was expressed first by the Federalists and then by the Clintonians who absorbed the remains of the Federalist Party after it became defunct; the democratic position was upheld by the Bucktails who later merged with the Jacksonian forces in the state. The incorrectness of Fox's explanation is evident on a number of grounds. First of all, the Clintonians were not the sole heirs of the Federalists. Although many Federalists did become followers of De Witt Clinton, there were also many who joined the Bucktails. An analysis of the party leadership of both the Clintonian and Bucktail parties during the 1820's shows that about twenty-five per cent of the leadership of each group consisted of former Federalists while the rest were Jeffersonians. Moreover, the Clintonians were often in the vanguard of democratic reform. Their position on negro suffrage was much more liberal than the Bucktails'. In 1817, they supported the use of a nominating convention to choose candidates for public office rather than the legislative caucus. During the election of 1824 they made the battle against the legislative caucus and the struggle in behalf of the direct selection of presidential electors by the people their main issues. The Clintonian attitude toward the Irish also shows that they tried to stand up in behalf of the underdog. In contrast, the Bucktails who were usually looked upon as the staunch defenders of the people against the aristocrats often resisted certain democratic innovations. For example, at the Constitutional Convention of 1821, they opposed popular election of justices of the peace, county clerks, sheriffs, as well as negro suffrage. The fact is that neither side consistently supported or opposed the cause of democracy; instead they supported reform when they felt it would strengthen their control of public life and opposed change when they felt it would weaken their position.

Just as New York's political parties did not embody any consistent or coherent ideological positions, they also did not represent particular economic groups. All of the parties contained a large number of adherents from every level of economic well-being in society. This helps to explain the absence of any clear-cut party differences on the major economic issues of the time such as the chartering of banks, the protective tariff, internal improvements, the development of manufacturing, and the promotion of superior agricultural techniques. Each political faction had segments both pro and con on most of these questions, and, in all cases, it was opportunism, the desire for profits, which was decisive in determining one's political position on these economic issues. Legislation pertaining to these matters usually came about through interparty coalitions of men whose interests coincided. In view of the widespread belief that the Clintonians represented the upper classes while the Bucktails upheld the interests of the common man, it is noteworthy that on at least one significant economic issue, land policy, the Clintonians supported the poor tenants against the encroachments of the powerful land companies that were aligned with the Bucktails. In general, however, sectionalism within the state was much more important than partisan affiliation in establishing divisions within the legislature on economic problems.

Sharp ideological conflict played an extremely minor role in the political life of the Empire State. This is evident, first of all, in the use of the term "Republican" by all the factions in the state, reflecting the universal veneration felt by all groups for Thomas Jefferson and the principles for which he stood. It is also apparent in the ease with which the Federalists moved in and out of the various Republican factions within the state after 1800, as well as the zeal with which they were recruited by all of New York's major political organizations. Moreover, party leaders were often inconsistent in their stand on current issues, and frequently reversed previously held positions because of public pressure. Hence the Bucktails, dismayed by public opposition, late in 1824 altered their negative position on the direct selection of presidential electors by the people into an affirmative one. In addition, the Bucktail choice of Samuel Young as their gubernatorial candidate in 1824 despite his opposition to important planks in the party platform, the initial choice and subsequent rejection of Albert Gallatin as its vice-presidential candidate in 1824 by the Van Buren wing of the Democratic party, and the projected political union of De Witt Clinton and Martin Van Buren during 1825/26 all show the dominance of opportunism over ideology in the formulation of strategic policy. Further, if there had been deep ideological cleavages within New York's electorate, it is unlikely that the Jacksonians in 1828 could have elicited the support of so many disparate groups within the state: the Bucktails, the Clintonians, the Federalists, the working class, and the Irish. The Antimasonic controversy that erupted in 1827 indicates, however, that a serious concern for issues was not totally absent from New York politics. Some would also argue that Martin Van Buren dedicated his early public career to the revival of a national party firmly committed to the ideals of Thomas Jefferson. Nevertheless, a fair assessment of Van Buren, in my opinion, yields the conclusion that he constantly oscillated between considerations of principle and expediency; and when the two were in conflict, he always subordinated the former to the latter. Indeed, the subservience of principles to expediency is an accurate description of the political process as a whole in New York during the period between Jefferson and Jackson.

Politics occupied a major segment in the life of New Yorkers. It was somewhat like a highly popular sport that was played earnestly and seriously. The violent rhetoric of electoral campaigns shows the extent to which people got aroused over the competition. The absence of substantial issues in the elections makes the crusading atmosphere that pervaded the battle for votes all the more remarkable. The heated proceedings produced defamation of character, bloody duels, and enduring personal animosities that outlasted the political conflicts. One's attitude on political matters frequently found expression in other areas of life. Indeed, avid partisans of one faction would not join social clubs that admitted partisans of an opposing faction. Each group had its own songs, banks, and business ventures in which participation was denied to the foe. Despite the widespread interest in politics, it is noteworthy that even in the most hotly contested elections of this era, no more than two-thirds of the eligible voters ever cast ballots. The apparent apathy of one-third of the electorate at a time when politics awakened deep-seated emotions in so many confirms the unfortunate truth, evident to contemporary observers as well, that there is a large percentage of the population upon whom public affairs make little impression. The extensive involvement of large numbers of people in electoral campaigns was paralleled by the eagerness of many young men to seek public office. Public service was an effective avenue to success no matter what one's prior social or economic class. In fact, in a community growing rapidly more democratic, where the privileges formerly conferred by family background came under attack and old distinctions were blurred, the pursuit of public office became even more intense as people desperately searched out objective indicia of status. Public zeal for politics also resulted from a paucity of other outlets for people's energies, which sought release from the tedium of daily labor. The acrid expression of political conflict in the pre-Jacksonian era is also partially explicable by the fact that the legitimacy of an opposition party had not yet been accepted as an integral element in the framework of American democracy.

Political life in New York during the early nineteenth century had much in common with events throughout the country. In most states, parties were coalitions based on opportunism rather than principle, and the expansion of democracy was rarely a party question. In contrast to the popular stereotypes, there are several instances on record of the Federalists supporting the expansion of democracy and the Republicans obstructing such developments. It is noteworthy also that political factions friendly to De Witt Clinton in Pennsylvania and Ohio during 1824 were as opposed to the legislative caucus as a method of nominating candidates as the Clintonian Party in New York. Sectionalism was often a more important factor than partisan affiliation in determining positions on public questions. Throughout the Union, party alignments were ephemeral at this time. The emergence of an equal-rights democracy occurred everywhere prior to and completely apart from Andrew Jackson's presidency. The primacy of state over national politics was also a widespread phenomenon. Finally, sectional consciousness was manifesting itself all over the United States, although intrasectional jealousy occasionally softened the intersectional rivalry.

NOTES

PREFACE

1. Although the origin of this concept cannot be definitely ascertained, it is used, with varying shades of meaning, by the following impressive list of historians: John Spencer Bassett, *The Life of Andrew Jackson* (New York: The Macmillan Company, 1931); Charles A. & Mary R. Beard, *The Rise of American Civilization* (2 vols., New York: The Macmillan Company, 1927); W. E. Binkley, *American Political Parties; Their Natural History* (2nd ed., New York: A. A. Knopf, 1945); Claude Bowers, *The Party Battles of the Jackson Period* (Boston: Houghton Mifflin Company, 1922); Carl Russell Fish, *The Rise of the Common Man, 1830-1850* (New York: American Book Company, 1937); Marquis James, *The Life of Andrew Jackson* (2 vols. in 1, Indianapolis: Grosset & Dunlap, 1938); Vernon L. Parrington, *Main Currents in American Thought* (3 vols., New York: Harcourt, Brace & Company, 1927-30); Arthur Schlesinger, Jr., *The Age of Jackson* (Boston: Little, Brown & Company, 1945); Frederick Jackson Turner, "Contributions of the West to American Democracy," *The Frontier in American History* (New York: Henry Holt & Company, 1950 printing), pp. 243-68; Leonard D. White, *The Jacksonians: A Study in Administrative History, 1829-1861* (New York: The Macmillan Company, 1954).

I

INTRODUCTION

1. *Webster's Third New International Dictionary,* Philip Babcock Gove, editor-in-chief (Springfield: G. & C. Merriam Company, 1961), p. 1775.
2. John Franklin Carter, *Power and Persuasion* (New York: Duell, Sloan and Pearce, 1960), p. x.

3. V. O. Key, *Politics, Parties, and Pressure Groups* (New York: Thomas Y. Crowell Company, 1958), p. 4.

4. *Ibid.*, pp. 12-14.

5. J. A. Schlesinger, "A Two-Dimensional Scheme for Classifying States According to Degree of Inter-Party Competition," *American Political Science Review*, XLIX (1955), 1120-28.

6. Chilton Williamson, *American Suffrage from Property to Democracy, 1760-1860* (Princeton: Princeton University Press, 1960), p. 111.

7. Van Buren to Charles E. Dudley, January 10, 1822, Charles R. King, ed., *The Life and Correspondence of Rufus King* (New York: G. P. Putnam's Sons, 1878), VI, 438.

8. Michael Ulshoeffer to Martin Van Buren, January 27, 31, 1822, Van Buren Papers.

9. Van Buren to Andrew Jackson, September 14, 1827, Van Buren Papers.

10. Circular of the Central Committee for De Witt Clinton, October 30, 1824, New York Public Library.

11. Dixon Ryan Fox, *The Decline of Aristocracy in the Politics of New York* (New York: Columbia University Press, 1919).

12. Lee Benson, *The Concept of Jacksonian Democracy* (Princeton: Princeton University Press, 1961).

13. Dorothy Bobbe, *De Witt Clinton* (New York: Minton, Balch, & Company, 1933), p. 201.

14. Lee Benson, *op. cit.*, pp. 163-65.

15. Angus Campbell, *et al., The Voter Decides* (Evanston: Row, Peterson, 1954), *passim.*

16. Martin Van Buren, "The Autobiography of Martin Van Buren," American Historical Association, *Annual Report for the Year 1918* (Washington: Government Printing Office, 1920), II, 169-71.

17. Roy F. Nichols, *The Disruption of American Democracy* (New York: The Macmillan Company, 1948).

II

THE NEW YORK POLITICAL SYSTEM

1. Marcy to Azariah C. Flagg, January 28, 1826, Flagg Papers.
2. Croswell to Flagg, December 9, 1825, Flagg Papers.

3. Martin Van Buren, "The Autobiography of Martin Van Buren," John C. Fitzpatrick, ed., American Historical Association, *Annual Report for the Year 1918* (Washington: Government Printing Office, 1920), II, 81.

4. Martin Van Buren to Croswell, January 11, 1827, Van Buren Papers.

5. Van Buren to Charles E. Dudley, January 10, 1822, Mrs. Catherine V. R. Bonney, *A Legacy of Historical Gleanings* (Albany: J. Munsell, 1875), pp. 352-84.

6. Bunner to Gulian C. Verplanck, January 18, 1822, Verplanck Papers.

7. Plumer, Jr., to Plumer, January 3, 1822, Everett S. Brown, ed., *The Missouri Compromise and Presidential Politics, 1820-1825* (St. Louis: Missouri Historical Society, 1926), p. 74.

8. Van Buren to Gulian C. Verplanck, December 22, 1822, Van Buren Papers.

9. Memorandum to Rufus King, Charles R. King, ed., *The Life and Correspondence of Rufus King* (New York: G. P. Putnam's Sons, 1898), VI, 521; De Witt Clinton to C. G. Haines, December 9, 1823, Clinton Papers, Columbia University Library; Clinton to Henry Post, August 6, 1823, John Bigelow, ed., "De Witt Clinton as a Politician," *Harper's Magazine* L (December, 1874, to May, 1875), 568.

10. Marcy to Van Buren, January 11, 1824, Van Buren Papers.

11. John A. King to Rufus King, January 9, 1824, King, *op. cit.*, p. 546.

12. Charles Z. Lincoln, ed., *Messages from the Governors* (Albany: J. B. Lyon Company, 1909), III, 30.

13. *New York American,* March 11, 1824; *Albany Daily Advertiser,* April 8, 1824; *New York Statesman,* April 13, 1824.

14. John Jay to Robert R. Livingston and Gouverneur Morris, April 29, 1777, H. P. Johnston, ed., *The Correspondence and Public Papers of John Jay* (New York: G. P. Putnam and Sons, 1890-93), I, 128.

15. Charles Z. Lincoln, *The Constitutional History of New York* (Rochester: The Lawyers Cooperative Publishing Company, 1906), I, 56, 178, 191, 531, 600-02, 610-11.

16. R. Troup to Rufus King, April 9, 1802, Charles R. King, ed., *op. cit.,* IV, 102-04.

17. H. L. McBain, *De Witt Clinton and the Origin of the Spoils System* (New York: Columbia University Press, 1907), *passim.*

18. Peter B. Porter to Van Buren, November 1, 1820, Van Buren Papers.

19. D. S. Alexander, *A Political History of the State of New York* (New York: Henry Holt and Company, 1906-23), I, 288.

20. Jabez D. Hammond, *The History of Political Parties in the State of New York* (Cooperstown: H. & E. Phinney, 1845), I, 569.

21. The power of appointment of the mayor of New York City was transferred in 1821 from the Council of Appointment at Albany and given to the city corporation. Formerly, the mayoralty occupant varied with every change of power at Albany.

22. Hammond, *op. cit.,* II, 77.

23. November 4, 1828.

24. *Ibid.*

25. Florence Weston, *The Presidential Election of 1828* (Washington: The Ruddick Press, 1938), p. 67; *Albany Argus,* September 26, 1828.

26. July 15, 1828, Van Buren Papers.

27. *Albany Argus,* July 8, September 30, 1828; *New York Enquirer,* November 15, 1827.

28. R. M. Livingston to J. W. Taylor, September 12, 1828, Taylor Papers; F. Granger to Weed, September 28, 1828, October 26, 1828, Granger Papers, Library of Congress.

29. August 24, 1802, Rufus King Papers, New York Historical Society.

30. See Hammond, *op. cit.,* I, 164-429, for a more detailed presentation of these political events.

31. U.S. Bureau of the Census, *A Century of Population Growth: Population in the Colonial and Continental Periods* (Washington: Government Printing Office, 1909), p. 6.

32. U.S. Bureau of the Census, *Twelfth Census of the United States* (Washington: Government Printing Office, 1900), I, 22-23.

33. James Macauley, *Natural Statistical and Civil History of the State of New York* (New York: Gould and Banks, 1829), III, 416-29.

34. Hammond, *op. cit.,* p. 104.

35. V. O. Key, *Southern Politics In State and Nation* (New York: A. A. Knopf, 1949), p. 124.

36. Alexander, *op. cit.,* I, 162-65.

37. Hammond, *op. cit.,* I, 291-94.

38. Henry Jones Ford, *The Rise and Growth of American Politics* (New York: The Macmillan Company, 1898), p. 201.

39. Maurice Duverger, *Political Parties* (London and New York: J. Wiley, 1954), pp. 203-05.

40. *Journal of the Legislative Council of the Colony of New York* (Albany: Weed, Parsons & Company, 1861), pp. x-xiii.

41. H. L. Osgood, *American Colonies in the Seventeenth Century* (New York: The Macmillan Company, 1904-07), chapters 12, 15; Edward Channing, *History of the United States* (New York: The Macmillan Company, 1909), II, chapter 2. See pp. 208-66 of A. E. McKinley, *The Suffrage Franchise in the Thirteen English Colonies in America* (Philadelphia: University of Pennsylvania, 1905), for a discussion of the franchise in colonial New York.

42. David M. Ellis, *et al.*, *A Short History of New York State* (Ithaca: Cornell University Press, 1957), pp. 29-49.

43. Dixon Ryan Fox, *The Decline of Aristocracy in the Politics of New York* (New York: Columbia University Press, 1919), *passim*.

44. Alexis de Tocqueville, *Democracy in America* (New York: Vintage Books, 1955), I, 282-90.

III

THE STRUCTURE OF THE POLITICAL MACHINE

1. Azariah C. Flagg to Silas Wright, October 28, 1823, Flagg Papers; Flagg to Van Buren, November 12, 1823, Van Buren Papers.

2. Azariah C. Flagg to Silas Wright, October 28, 1823, Flagg to Van Buren, November 12, 1823, Flagg Papers.

3. Hoffman to Flagg, December 20, 1827, Flagg Papers.

4. William L. Marcy to Flagg, February 6, 1830, Flagg Papers.

5. D. S. Alexander, *A Political History of the State of New York* (New York: Henry Holt & Company, 1906), I, 62.

6. Jabez D. Hammond, *The History of Political Parties in the State of New York* (Cooperstown: H. & E. Phinney, 1845), I, 181-82.

7. Hammond, *op. cit.*, pp. 214-15.

8. Nathaniel H. Carter and William L. Stone, *Reports of the Proceedings and Debates of the Convention of 1821* (New York: E. & E. Hosford, 1821), pp. 321-22, 340.

9. *Ibid.*, p. 341.

10. Butler to Van Buren, March 27, 1824, Van Buren Papers.

11. John S. Jenkins, *History of Political Parties in the State of New York* (Auburn: Alden & Markham, 1849), p. 290.

12. William M. Holland, *The Life and Political Opinions of Martin Van Buren* (Hartford: Belknap & Hamersley, 1836), pp. 38-43.

13. John Arthur Garraty, *Silas Wright* (New York: Columbia University Press, 1949), p. 32.

14. Wright to Flagg, August 29, 1827, December 20, 1827, Flagg Papers.

15. Marcy to Van Buren, February 15, 1824, Van Buren Papers.

16. Van Buren to G. A. Worth, February 22, 1824, Van Buren Papers.

17. October 12, 1824, *Orange County Farmer*; reprinted in proceedings of a meeting of Democratic-Republican young men held in the town of Delhi on October 22, 1824, New York Public Library.

18. *Albany Daily Advertiser, Albany Gazette,* 1824; from a circular in which both papers were requesting additional subscriptions, New York Public Library.

19. Address to the Electors of Montgomery County on behalf of the People's Ticket, New York Public Library.

20. October 28, 1824, *Albany Daily Advertiser, Extra.* "One Million of Money Lost."

21. October 10, 1824, Charles G. Haines, circular letter in support of De Witt Clinton.

22. All these ideas repeat themselves frequently in the rich collection of broadsides on the election of 1824, which is found at the New York Public Library.

23. Circular of the General Corresponding Committee, October 22, 1824, New York Public Library.

24. *Albany Argus, Extra,* October 8, 1824.

25. "People's Right. Beware of wolves in Sheep's Clothing," anti-Clintonian handbill, October 1824; "Caucus Calumny Refuted," Clintonian handbill, October 1824.

26. "Plain Truth Republicans, be on your guard," anti-Clintonian handbill.

27. "Political Consistency. Look ere you leap," anti-Clintonian handbill.

28. *Albany Argus, Extra,* October 18, 1824.

29. *Albany Argus,* August 23, 1824; *Albany Daily Advertiser,* August 24, 1824; *New York American,* August 26, 1824.

30. July 3, 1792.

31. Quoted in William Jay, *Life of John Jay* (New York: J. S. Taylor, 1833), I, 290.

32. Hamilton to Jay, May 7, 1800, Henry Cabot Lodge, ed., *The Works of Alexander Hamilton* (New York: Houghton Mifflin & Company, 1886), VIII, 549.

33. Philip Schuyler to Jay, May 7, 1800, H. P. Johnston, ed., *The Correspondence and Public Papers of John Jay* (New York: G. P. Putnam & Sons, 1890-93), IV, 273.

34. *Ibid.*, p. 272.

35. A. B. Street, *The Council of Revision* (Albany, 1859), p. 9.

36. *Ibid.*, pp. 481-547.

37. Clinton to Henry Post, November 19, 1820, John Bigelow, ed., "De Witt Clinton as a Politician," *Harper's New Monthly Magazine*, I (December, 1874, to May, 1875), 413.

38. John T. Horton, *James Kent, A Study in Conservatism* (New York: D. Appleton-Century Company, 1939), p. 244.

39. Clinton to Henry Post, November 27, 1820, Bigelow, *op. cit.*, p. 414.

40. Jenkins, *op. cit.*, p. 231.

41. Clinton to Henry Post, November 27, 1820, Bigelow, *op. cit.*, p. 414.

42. Alexander C. Flick, ed., *History of the State of New York* (New York: Columbia University Press, 1934), VI, 13-16.

43. Carter and Stone, *op. cit.*, pp. 45, 75.

44. See Chapter II, pp. 13-15.

45. Frederick W. Dallinger, *Nominations for Elective Office in the United States* (New York: Longmans, Green & Company, 1897), pp. 13-21. The evidence for this contention is found in Dallinger's volume.

46. Leonard D. White, *The Jeffersonians, A Study in Administrative History, 1801-1802* (New York: The Macmillan Company, 1951), p. 53.

47. From a draft of Van Buren's reply against a resolution against a congressional nomination passed by the Tennessee legislature in January 1824.

48. Benjamin F. Butler to Jesse Hoyt, January 29, 1824, William L. Mackenzie, *The Lives and Opinions of Benjamin Franklin Butler and Jesse Hoyt* (Boston: Cook & Company, 1832), pp. 168-69.

49. Marcy to Van Buren, December 14, 1823, Van Buren Papers.

50. Croswell to Flagg, December 9, 1823, Flagg Papers; Croswell to Jesse Hoyt, January 31, 1824, Mackenzie, *op. cit.*, p. 194.

51. *New York Statesman*, August 13, 1824, handbill announcing meeting at the Tontine Coffee House, New York Public Library.

52. *Ibid.*

53. *New York American,* July 28, 1823.

54. For the arguments used by the friends of repeal see *New York American,* July 28, October 8; *New York Patriot,* June 19, 21, 27, July 3, 14, August 6, September 17, 18, 22, October 1; *Albany Daily Advertiser,* September 16, 18, 26; *New York Statesman,* June 27, 30, 1823.

55. *Albany Argus,* December 23, 1823.

56. *Ibid.,* July 8, 1823.

57. *Ibid.*

58. Croswell to Flagg, December 9, 1825, Flagg Papers.

59. Plumer, Jr., to Plumer, February 29, 1824, Everett S. Brown, ed., *The Missouri Compromise and Presidential Politics, 1820-1825* (St. Louis: Missouri Historical Society, 1926), pp. 103-04.

60. Van Buren to Benjamin F. Butler, February 17, 1824, Van Buren Papers.

61. Gustavus Myers, *The History of Tammany Hall* (New York: Boni & Liveright, 1917), pp. 1-2.

62. *Ibid.,* pp. 11-12.

63. Dixon Ryan Fox, *The Decline of Aristocracy in the Politics of New York* (New York: Columbia University Press, 1919), pp. 89-90.

64. T. E. V. Smith, *Political Parties* (New York, 1889), p. 11. The New York Public Library has an excellent collection of the society's publications including poems and orations.

IV

LOCAL, STATE, AND NATIONAL POLITICS

1. Silas Wright to Azariah C. Flagg, July 26, 1830, Flagg Papers.

2. Jabez D. Hammond, *The History of Political Parties in the State of New York* (Cooperstown, New York: H. & E. Phinney, 1845), II, 76-79, 479.

3. Nathaniel H. Carter and William L. Stone, *Reports of the Proceedings and Debates of the Convention of 1821* (Albany: E. & E. Hasford, 1822), p. 315.

4. *Ibid.,* p. 383.

5. Rufus King to Charles King, October 20, 1821, Charles King,

ed., *The Life and Correspondence of Rufus King* (New York: G. P. Putnam & Sons, 1898), VI, 414.

6. Peter A. Jay to John Jay, October 10, 1821, H. P. Johnston, ed., *The Correspondence and Public Papers of John Jay* (New York: G. P. Putnam & Sons, 1890-93), IV, 453.

7. Carter and Stone, *op. cit.,* pp. 338-40.

8. W. H. Bayles, *Old Taverns of New York* (New York, 1915), p. XVI.

9. Paul Evans, *The Holland Land Company* (Buffalo: Buffalo Historical Society, 1924), pp. 338-39.

10. Chilton Williamson, *American Suffrage from Property to Democracy* (Princeton: Princeton University Press, 1960), p. 159.

11. Samuel A. Law Papers, New York State Library, as quoted in Williamson, *op. cit.,* p. 159.

12. *Journals of the House and Assembly of the State of New York, 1792,* pp. 64-98, 183-207.

13. *Albany Argus,* September 18, 1820; *New York American,* July 8, 1819.

14. Charles Z. Lincoln, ed., *Messages from the Governors* (Albany: J. B. Lyon Co., 1909), II, 1042.

15. De Witt Clinton to Henry Post, November 19, 1820, John Bigelow, ed., "De Witt Clinton as a Politician," *Harper's New Monthly Magazine,* L (December, 1874), 413.

16. Clinton to Henry Post, November 27, 1820, *ibid.,* p. 414.

17. William W. Van Ness to Solomon Van Rensselaer, January 24, 1821, Catherine V. R. Bonney, *A Legacy of Historical Gleanings* (Albany: J. Munsell, 1875), p. 361.

18. Clinton to C. G. Haines, December 9, 1823, Clinton Papers, Columbia University Library.

19. John Calhoun to Samuel Gouverneur, November 9, 1823, Gouverneur Papers.

20. Van Buren to Flagg, April 2, 1827, Flagg Papers, Columbia University Library.

21. E.g., *New York American,* March 15, 1823.

22. In the second volume of his *History of Political Parties in the State of New York,* Hammond cites the names of the leaders of the People's Party—men such as Thurlow Weed, Henry Wheaton, John Taylor, and James Tallmadge—who were ardent supporters of John Quincy Adams.

23. In a poster announcing the slate of the People's Party in Albany County, John Crary, a candidate for the State Assembly,

received a higher billing than Henry Marshall, the candidate for Congress. Moreover, in an address to the electors found on the poster, a short biography of Crary was given, while no facts about the life of Marshall were offered. Another example is found in a poster published by the campaign committee of the People's Party for Onondaga County where the name of the candidate for State Assembly, John C. Spencer, received greater prominence than the name of the candidate for Congress, Luther Badger.

24. John Quincy Adams, *Memoirs of John Quincy Adams*, Charles Francis Adams, ed. (12 vols.; Philadelphia: J. B. Lippincott Company, 1874-77), VI, 316.

25. Martin Van Buren to Silas Wright, September 24, 1824, Van Buren Papers.

26. *Albany Argus*, July 7, September 5, 1825.

27. William L. Marcy to Martin Van Buren, December 17, 1825, Van Buren Papers.

28. Wright to Flagg, December 23, 1827, Flagg Papers.

29. Wright to Flagg, December 20, 1827, Flagg Papers.

30. D. S. Alexander, *A Political History of the State of New York* (New York: Henry Holt & Company, 1906), I, 162-73.

31. Harriet A. Weed, ed., *Autobiography of Thurlow Weed* (Boston: Houghton Mifflin & Company, 1853), pp. 120-30.

32. J. C. Fitzpatrick, ed., "The Autobiography of Martin Van Buren," American Historical Association, *Annual Report for the Year 1918* (Washington: Government Printing Office, 1920), II, 151-52.

33. Charles McCarthy, "The Anti-Masonic Party: A Study of Political Anti-Masonry in the United States, 1827-1840," American Historical Association, *Annual Report for the Year 1902* (Washington: Government Printing Office, 1903), pp. 371-420.

34. Robert V. Remini, *Martin Van Buren and the Making of the Democratic Party* (New York: Columbia University Press, 1959), *passim.*

35. *The National Democrat, Extra,* January 8, 1824; "Republican Fellow-Citizens of The City of Albany"—Announcement at the refusal of the Republican Committee to call a meeting for the promotion of an electoral law, appeal from their decision to the people, and notice of a meeting to be held at the Capitol, February 14, 1824.

36. *Independent Whig,* January 13, 1824.

37. Address to the Electors of Montgomery County on behalf of the People's ticket, New York Public Library.

38. Van Buren to Cambreleng, July 4, 1827, Van Buren Papers.

39. Van Buren, *Autobiography,* pp. 169-71.

40. Silas Wright to Azariah Flagg, December 20, 1827, Flagg Papers.

41. William L. Marcy to Van Buren, January 29, 1828, Van Buren Papers.

42. Remini, *op. cit.,* pp. 170-85.

43. Silas Wright to Azariah Flagg, December 23, 1827, Flagg Papers.

44. Martin Van Buren to Andrew Jackson, November 4, 1827, John Spencer Bassett, *Correspondence of Andrew Jackson* (Washington: Carnegie Institute of Washington, 1928), III, 384.

45. Silas Wright to William L. Marcy, February 18, 1828, Flagg Papers.

46. Silas Wright to Azariah Flagg, December 23, 1827, Flagg Papers.

V

THE DEMOCRATIC TRANSFORMATION

1. James Madison to James Monroe, June 4, 1806, James Madison, *Letters and Other Writings of James Madison* (Philadelphia: J. B. Lippincott & Co., 1865), II, 225; see also Madison to John Nicholas, May 30, 1816, *ibid.,* III, 5.

2. Dixon Ryan Fox, "New York Becomes a Democracy," Chapter 1 of Alexander Flick, ed., *History of the State of New York* (New York: Columbia University Press, 1934), VI, 4-5. Fox's famous book, *The Decline of Aristocracy in the Politics of New York* (New York: Columbia University Press, 1919), is an elaboration of these fundamental contentions.

3. David M. Ellis *et al., A Short History of New York State* (Ithaca: Cornell University Press, 1957), p. 137.

4. James A. Hamilton, *Reminiscences of James Alexander Hamilton* (New York: C. Scribner, 1869), p. 44; Charles R. King, ed., *The Life and Correspondence of Rufus King* (New York: G. P. Putnam's Sons, 1898), V, 270-71.

5. Jabez D. Hammond, *The History of Political Parties in the State of New York* (Cooperstown: H. & E. Phinney, 1845), I, 343-44.

6. Ambrose Spencer to De Witt Clinton, September 23, 1811, Clinton Papers.

7. W. C. Bryant, *A Discourse on the Life and Writings of Gulian Crommelin Verplanck* (New York: G. P. Putnam, 1870), pp. 4-14, 18.

8. Hammond, *op. cit.,* p. 399.

9. *A Fable for Statesmen and Politicians of all Parties and Descriptions, by Abimelech Coody, Esq., Formerly Ladies Shoemaker* (New York, 1815), p. 8, quoted in Fox, *Decline of Aristocracy,* p. 204. Despite Fox's awareness of many of these facts relating to anti-Clintonian feeling among the Federalists, his conclusions seem to ignore them.

10. Gulian C. Verplanck, *Bucktail Bards* (New York: Printed for the author, 1819), p. 134.

11. De Witt Clinton, *An Account of Abimelech Coody and other celebrated writers of New York; in a letter from a travellor to his friend in South Carolina* (New York, 1815).

12. *Ibid.,* pp. 12, 14-15, also quoted in Fox, *op. cit.,* pp. 204-05.

13. *New York American,* March 3, 1819.

14. Rufus King to Charles King, February 11, 1819, Charles R. King, *op. cit.,* VI, 213.

15. Shaw Livermore, *The Twilight of Federalism* (Princeton: Princeton University Press, 1962), p. 70.

16. *New York American,* April 14, 1819.

17. Rufus King to John A. King, January 14, 1820, King Papers, New York Historical Society.

18. Rufus King to John A. King, March 18, 1920, King, *op. cit.,* VI, pp. 317-18.

19. Rufus King to John A. King, January 14, 1820, King Papers, New York Historical Society; Van Buren to Rufus King, February 26 and March 12, King, *op. cit.,* VI, 291, 322.

20. Martin Van Buren, "The Autobiography of Martin Van Buren," John C. Fitzpatrick, ed., American Historical Association, *Annual Report for the Year 1918* (Washington: Government Printing Office, 1920), II, 89-92.

21. Samuel Talcott to Van Buren, April 15, 1820, Van Buren Papers.

22. Van Buren, *op. cit.,* pp. 173-75.

23. *New York American,* July 3, 21, August 14, 1819.

24. The pamphlet, which consisted of a series of letters, appeared first in the *New York Columbian* during the spring of 1819.

25. Barent Gardenier to Van Buren, January 20, 1821, Van Buren Papers.

26. John A. King to Charles King, January 6, 1820, King, *op. cit.,* VI, pp. 243-45.

27. *An Address to the Independent Electors of the State of New York* (Albany, 1820), *passim*.

28. Hammond, *op. cit.,* p. 259.

29. *Albany Advertiser,* April 21, 1820.

30. W. W. Van Ness to Solomon Van Rensselaer, February 7, 1821, Mrs. Catherine V. R. Bonney, *A Legacy of Historical Gleanings* (Albany: J. Munsell, 1875), p. 363.

31. Coleman to J. A. King, February 1, 1820, King Papers, New York Historical Society.

32. Hammond, *op. cit.,* p. 128.

33. *Journal of the Assembly of the State of New York* (Albany, 1817), pp. 126, 563; *Journal of the Senate of the State of New York* (Albany, 1817), p. 251.

34. Alexander Hamilton to John Jay, May 7, 1800, *The Works of Alexander Hamilton,* edited by Henry Cabot Lodge (New York: Houghton Mifflin & Co., 1886), VIII, 549.

35. Charles Z. Lincoln, ed., *Messages from the Governors* (Albany: J. B. Lyon Company, 1909), II, 1022-23.

36. *Niles Register,* III, 18.

37. *New York Evening Post,* March 6, 1817.

38. *Civil List, State of New York* (1887), p. 166; Alexander C. Flick, ed., *History of the State of New York* (New York: Columbia University Press, 1934), VI, 50-51. The total number of votes cast in this election was only about 55 per cent of the potential electorate. The small turnout can be explained in part by the absence of a genuine contest since only a few Tammanyite fanatics and "Coodies" supported Peter B. Porter for the governorship, and by the fact that this was not a regularly scheduled election.

39. Dixon Ryan Fox, *op. cit.*

40. Peter B. Porter to Van Buren, November 1, 1820, Van Buren Papers.

41. Nathaniel H. Carter and William L. Stone, *Reports of the Proceedings and Debates of the Convention of 1821* (Albany: E. & E. Hosford, 1821), pp. 41-48, 338-40, 383.

42. Benjamin Romaine, *A Comparative View and Exhibition of*

*Reasons Opposed to the Adoption of the New Constitution etc.,
by An Old Citizen* (New York, 1822), pp. 5-17.

43. Carter and Stone, *op. cit.,* pp. 338-40; Peter A. Jay to John
Jay, October 10, 1821, H. P. Johnston, ed., *The Correspondence and
Public Papers of John Jay* (New York: G. P. Putnam & Sons, 1890-
93), IV, 453.

44. Carter and Stone, *op. cit.,* pp. 361-72, 181-88.

45. Hammond, *op. cit.,* p. 20.

46. Carter and Stone, *op. cit.,* pp. 137-48, 590-610.

47. The nativism that characterized Tammany Hall in the first
quarter of the nineteenth century is stressed by Gustavus Myers in
The History of Tammany Hall (New York: Boni & Liveright,
1901), pp. 36-37.

48. March 16, 1816, De Witt Clinton Papers.

49. J. G. Shea, *History of the Catholic Church in the United
States* (New York: J. G. Shea, 1888), II, 165-67.

50. *New York Evening Post,* March 24, 1817.

51. Quoted in Hammond, *op. cit.,* p. 400.

52. Broadsides, "An Elector," "To All Independent Electors."

53. "Fagot holding" was a device to enable unqualified citizens
to vote by giving them deeds to land just before election time.
Immediately after the election, the deeds were taken back.

54. Martin Van Buren to De Witt Clinton, April 28, 1812, Clinton
Papers.

55. Hammond, *op. cit.,* pp. 413-18.

56. Gustavus Myers, *op. cit.,* pp. 50-60.

57. *Ibid.,* pp. 56-57.

58. William Plumer, Jr., to William Plumer, Sr., April 7, 1820,
and February 2, 1821, Everett S. Brown, ed., *The Missouri Compromise and Presidential Politics, 1820-1825* (St. Louis: Missouri
Historical Society, 1926), pp. 16-33.

59. Rufus King to John A. King and Charles King, March 5,
1820, King, *op. cit.,* VI, 291.

60. Van Buren, *op. cit.,* p. 100.

61. C. G. Haines to Clinton, May 29, 1820, Clinton Papers,
Columbia University Library.

62. Rufus King to Charles King, October 20, 1821, Charles King,
ed., *op. cit.,* VI, 414.

63. Hammond, *op. cit.,* pp. 60-61.

64. Under the new law, all adult males who had lived a year in
the state and six months in the county could vote. It is revealing

that De Witt Clinton was the sponsor of this new law. (*Albany Argus,* January 21, 1825)

65. Wright to Flagg, December 20, 23, 1827, Hoffman to Flagg, December 27, 1827, Flagg Papers; Van Buren to Butler, January 13, 1828, Marcy to Van Buren, January 29, 1828, Van Buren Papers.

66. Wright to Flagg, December 20, 1827, Flagg Papers.

67. *Albany Argus,* November 4, 1828.

68. Richard McCormick, "New Perspectives in Jacksonian Politics," *American Historical Review,* LXV (January, 1960), 287-301.

VI

ECONOMICS AND POLITICS

1. Oben Edson, *History of Chautuqua County, New York* (Boston, 1894), p. 328.

2. George Dangerfield, *Chancellor Robert R. Livingston* (New York: Harcourt, Brace, & Company, 1960), pp. 222-24.

3. Richard P. McCormick, "Suffrage Classes and Party Alignments," *Mississippi Valley Historical Review,* XLVI (December, 1959), 398-410.

4. It will be remembered that the governor was elected at this time by 1,100 freeholders alone while the total electorate voted for members of Congress.

5. Reprinted with permission from McCormick, *op. cit.,* p. 406.

6. D. C. Sowers, *Financial History of New York* (New York: Columbia University Press, 1914), p. 49.

7. Beatrice G. Reubens, "Burr, Hamilton, and the Manhattan Company," *Political Science Quarterly,* LXXII (December, 1957), 578-607, and LXXIII (March, 1958), 100-25.

8. Shaw Livermore, *The Twilight of Federalism* (Princeton: Princeton University Press, 1962), pp. 14-15.

9. Jabez D. Hammond, *The History of Political Parties in the State of New York* (Cooperstown: H. & E. Phinney, 1849), I, 329-39.

10. Robert Chaddock, *History of the Safety Fund Banking System of New York* (Washington: Government Printing Office, 1910), pp. 241-49.

11. Paul Evans, *The Holland Land Company* (Buffalo: Buffalo Historical Society, 1924), p. 336.

12. William James, Jr., to A. C. Flagg, 1 May 1830, GCC, quoted in Nathan Miller, *The Enterprise of a Free People* (Ithaca: Cornell University Press, 1962), pp. 156-57.

13. Hammond, *op. cit.,* II, 350.

14. Gabriel Mead to Martin Van Buren, February 13, 1827. Robert Remini points out that the Tariff of Abominations, which Van Buren supported in 1827, advocated higher duties on raw materials but not on manufactured goods. (Robert V. Remini, *Martin Van Buren and the Making of the Democratic Party* [New York: Columbia University Press, 1959], pp. 170-85.)

15. Wright to Flagg, January 16, 1828, Hoffman to Flagg, February 3, 1828, Flagg Papers.

16. Benjamin Knower to Martin Van Buren, January 27, 1828, Van Buren Papers.

17. Hammond, *op. cit.,* II, 323-24.

18. *Albany Daily Advertiser,* June 27, 1827; *Albany Argus,* June 23, 30, July 4, 21, 1827.

19. *Albany Argus,* March 20, 27, 1828.

20. *Ibid.,* April 9, 1824.

21. *New York American,* January 27, 1823.

22. *Ibid.,* February 17, 18, 23, March 5, 1824.

23. W. F. Gephart, *Transportation and Industrial Development in the Middle West* ("Columbia University Studies in History, Economics, and Public Law," Vol. XXXIV [New York: Columbia University Press, 1909]), pp. 110-11.

24. Charles Z. Lincoln, ed., *Messages from the Governors* (Albany: J. B. Lyon Company, 1909), II, 973-77.

25. T. A. Emmett to Clinton, March 22, 1824, Clinton Papers.

26. Miller, *op. cit.,* p. 41.

27. *Albany Daily Advertiser,* August 12, 1816.

28. J. C. Fitzpatrick, ed., "The Autobiography of Martin Van Buren," American Historical Association, *Annual Report for the Year 1918* (Washington: Government Printing Office, 1920), II, 84-85.

29. Miller, *op. cit.,* p. 45.

30. Silas Wright to A. C. Flagg, November 18, 1826, Flagg Papers; Hammond, *op. cit.,* II, 232.

31. Robert R. Livingston to De Witt Clinton, September 4, 1811, Samuel Young to De Witt Clinton, December 14, 1816, De Witt Clinton Papers.

32. Quoted in Miller, *op. cit.,* pp. 33, 55.

33. *Albany Argus,* January 5, 1825, January 2, 1827.

34. *New York Senate Journal,* 1826, p. 170.

35. Michael Hoffman to A. C. Flagg, January 8, 1827, Flagg Papers.

36. *New York Senate Journal,* 1826, pp. 150-68.

37. *Congressional Debates,* 1825-26, II, 618-38, 715-18.

38. G. A. Worth, *Random Recollections of Albany* (Albany: J. Munsell, 1866), pp. 51-53.

39. *Albany Argus,* March 8, April 2, June 5, 1825.

40. *Ibid.,* March 4, 1825.

41. *New York American,* February 23, 1824.

42. David M. Ellis, *Landlords and Farmers in the Hudson-Mohawk Region, 1790-1850* (Ithaca: Cornell University Press, 1946), pp. 128-29.

43. *Albany Argus,* April 9, 1824.

44. Nathaniel H. Carter and William L. Stone, *Reports of the Proceedings and Debates of the Convention of 1821* (Albany: E. & E. Hosford, 1821), pp. 253-344.

45. *Albany Argus,* October 7, 8, 9, December 1, 2, 3, 28, 30, 1817; May 4, June 6, 9, 1818.

46. Lincoln, *op. cit.,* II, 898.

47. *New York Assembly Journal,* 1818, pp. 407-11.

48. Ellis, *op. cit.,* pp. 98-99.

49. Fox, *The Decline of Aristocracy in the Politics of New York* (New York: Columbia University Press, 1919), pp. 317-18, 355.

50. Ellis, *op. cit.,* pp. 2, 154.

51. *New York Assembly Journal,* 1812, pp. 110-11.

52. The series began on September 28, 1819.

53. Paul Evans, *The Holland Land Company* (Buffalo: Buffalo Historical Society, 1824), pp. 340-41.

54. Lincoln, *op. cit.,* II, 103 ff.

55. April 13, 1820, Charles R. King, ed., *The Life and Correspondence of Rufus King* (New York: G. P. Putnam's Sons, 1898), IV, 331.

56. Evans, *op. cit.,* pp. 271-73.

57. *Journal of the Assembly,* 1820, p. 983.

58. Evans, *op. cit.,* pp. 344-47.

59. *Ibid.,* pp. 355-56.

60. *Journal of the Assembly,* 1829, pp. 417 ff.

61. Evans, *op. cit.,* pp. 386-87.

62. H. N. Butler to De Witt Clinton, March 12, 1809, Clinton Papers.

63. D. Hosack, *Memoir of Clinton* (New York: J. Seymour, 1829), pp. 488-91.

64. De Witt Clinton to Joseph Ellicott, 20 September, 1816, quoted in Severance, ed., *The Holland Land Company* (Buffalo: Buffalo Historical Society, 1910), p. 71.

65. *Albany Daily Advertiser,* May 26, 1826.

66. *Albany Argus,* January 20, 1827; *Albany Daily Advertiser,* January 22, 26, 27, 31, February 1, 2, 4, 1827.

67. Hammond, *op. cit.,* II, 245.

68. Miller, *op. cit.,* p. 140.

69. *Ibid.,* pp. 172-73.

70. *Ibid.,* pp. 140-41.

VII

THE ROLE OF IDEOLOGY IN POLITICS

1. Henry Adams, *History of the United States* (New York: C. Scribner's Sons, 1889-98), I, 230.

2. Fox, *The Decline of Aristocracy in the Politics of New York* (New York: Columbia University Press, 1919), *passim.*

3. Robert V. Remini, *Martin Van Buren and the Making of the Democratic Party* (New York: Columbia University Press, 1959), *passim.*

4. September, 1824, circular announcing the State Convention at Utica and urging the nomination of Clinton and Tallmadge, New York Public Library.

5. Fox, *op. cit.,* p. 199.

6. Martin Van Buren, "The Autobiography of Martin Van Buren," John C. Fitzpatrick, ed., American Historical Association, *Annual Report for the Year 1918* (Washington: Government Printing Office, 1920) II, 124-26.

7. The name "Keepers of the Jeffersonian Conscience" is the title of Chapter Three of Arthur M. Schlesinger, Jr.'s *The Age of Jackson* (Boston: Little, Brown, and Company, 1945). It is used to describe such men as John Taylor of Carolina and John Randolph of Roanoke who remained true to the Jeffersonian heritage

when the Virginian dynasty of Madison and Monroe deviated from it.

8. For a detailed elaboration of this idea see Merrill D. Peterson, *The Jefferson Image in the American Mind* (New York: Oxford University Press, 1960), pp. 17-29.

9. Erastus Root to John Taylor, July 16, 1840, John Taylor Papers, New York Historical Society.

10. Clinton to Henry Post, October 21, 1822, John Bigelow, ed., "De Witt Clinton as a Politician," *Harper's New Monthly Magazine*, L (December, 1874, to May, 1875), 567.

11. *Albany Argus*, October 8, 1824; *Albany Argus, Extra*, October 15, 1824.

12. See pp. 80-81.

13. Shaw Livermore, *The Twilight of Federalism* (Princeton: Princeton University Press, 1961), p. 126.

14. *New York American*, March 3, 1819.

15. *Ibid.*

16. *New York Evening Post*, April 20, 1816.

17. Rufus King to Christopher Gore, November 5, 1816, Charles R. King, ed., *The Life and Correspondence of Rufus King* (New York: G. P. Putnam's Sons, 1898), VI, 34.

18. Livermore, *op. cit.*, p. 265.

19. *Philadelphia National Gazette*, January 31, 1824, quoted in *ibid.*, p. 136.

20. John Quincy Adams, *Memoirs of John Quincy Adams*, Charles Francis Adams, ed. (Philadelphia: J. B. Lippincott & Co., 1874-77), VII, 396.

21. Smith Thompson to Martin Van Buren, January 30, 1821, Van Buren Papers.

22. *New York Enquirer*, October 16, 1827.

23. *National Advocate*, November 14, 1820.

24. Mordecai M. Noah to Martin Van Buren, July 13, 1819, Van Buren Papers.

25. J. J. Crittenden was appointed a justice of the Supreme Court; John Duer, United States attorney in New York; Joseph Hopkinson, district judge in Pennsylvania; Rufus King, minister to England; John Sergeant, delegate to the Panama Congress; Nathan Smith, United States attorney in Connecticut.

26. Daniel Webster to E. Webster, November 30, 1823, *The Works of Daniel Webster* (Boston: Little, Brown & Company, 1903), XVII, 329.

27. James A. Hamilton, *Reminiscences of James Alexander Hamilton* (New York: C. Scribner & Co., 1869), p. 62.

28. John Calhoun to J. C. Swift, April 29, 1823, T. R. Hay, ed., "John C. Calhoun and the Presidential Election of 1824, Some Unpublished Calhoun Letters," *American Historical Review*, XL (October, 1930, to January, 1936), 84.

29. Adams, *Memoirs*, VI, 389-92.

30. Jackson to Monroe, November 12, 1816, J. S. Bassett, ed., *Correspondence of Andrew Jackson* (Washington: Carnegie Institute of Washington, 1928), II, 265.

31. *New York Post*, April 4, 1828.

32. Denis T. Lynch, *An Epoch and a Man: Martin Van Buren and His Times* (New York: H. Liveright, 1929), p. 270.

33. Claiborne Gooch to Van Buren, September 14, 1824, Van Buren Papers.

34. Gallatin to Van Buren, October 2, 1824, Van Buren Papers.

35. Josiah Johnston to Henry Clay, September 4, 1824, Calvin Colton, ed., *The Private Correspondence of Henry Clay* (Cincinnati: A. S. Barnes and Co., 1856), pp. 100-01.

36. Clay to Johnston, September 10, 1824, *ibid.*, p. 103.

37. Livingston to Van Buren, November 30, 1825, Van Buren Papers.

38. Jabez D. Hammond, *The History of Political Parties in the State of New York* (Cooperstown: H. & E. Phinney, 1845), II, 212.

39. Van Buren, *Autobiography*, pp. 159, 376-78.

40. Martin Van Buren to William Coleman, 1827, Van Buren Papers.

41. Broadside Collection, New York Public Library.

42. *New York American*, November 6, 1827, November 21, 1827; *New York Advocate*, November 12, 1827.

43. D. S. Alexander, *A Political History of the State of New York* (New York: Henry Holt and Company, 1906-23), I, 336.

44. "De Witt Clinton's Letters to Henry Post," *Harper's Magazine*, L (August, 1824), 563.

45. *Proceedings of the New York State Convention Held at Albany on June 10 and 11, 1828, by Friends of the Present Administration of our National Government* (Albany, 1828), p. 31.

46. Shaw Livermore, *op. cit.*, p. 220.

47. *Ibid.*, p. 241.

48. Alexander Flick, ed., *History of the State of New York* (New York: Columbia University Press, 1934), VII, 40-43.

49. Charles McCarthy, "The Anti-Masonic Party: A Study of Political Anti-Masonry in the United States, 1827-1840," American Historical Association, *Annual Report for the Year 1920,* pp. 371-420.

50. Van Buren to Cambreleng, October 23, 1827, Van Buren Papers.

51. McCarthy, *op. cit.,* pp. 380-93.

52. Van Buren to James A. Hamilton, August 25, 1828, James A. Hamilton, *op. cit.,* pp. 78-79.

53. Harriet A. Weed, ed., *Autobiography of Thurlow Weed* (Boston: Houghton, Mifflin & Company, 1883), pp. 210-98.

54. Butler to Azariah C. Flagg, September 5, 1828, Flagg Papers.

55. Griffin to Flagg, July 30, 1828, Flagg Papers.

56. II Samuel, 16:7. Translation is taken from Harkovy edition (New York: Hebrew Publishing Company, 1916), I, 469.

57. Among his detractors are Holmes Alexander, *The American Talleyrand* (New York: Harper & Brothers, 1935); Denis T. Lynch, *An Epoch and a Man: Martin Van Buren and His Times* (New York: H. Liveright, 1929) ; and most recently, Lee Benson, *The Concept of Jacksonian Democracy* (Princeton: Princeton University Press, 1961). His foremost defenders are Dixon Ryan Fox, *The Decline of Aristocracy in the Politics of New York* (New York: Columbia University Press, 1919) ; and Robert V. Remini, *Martin Van Buren and the Making of the Democratic Party* (New York: Columbia University Press, 1959).

58. *Albany Argus, Extra,* October 15, 1824.

59. Rufus King to John A. King, January 14, 1820, King Papers, New York Historical Society.

60. Van Buren, *op. cit.,* pp. 172-76.

61. Martin Van Buren to Charles Dudley, January 10, 1822, Mrs. Catherine V. R. Bonney, *A Legacy of Historical Gleanings* (Albany: J. Munsell, 1875), I, 382-83.

62. Martin Van Buren to Rufus King, May 31, 1822, King, *op. cit.,* p. 472.

63. Charles King to Henry Clay, March 21, 1825, Clay Papers, Library of Congress.

64. New York State, *Senate Journal,* 39th Session, p. 299.

65. Alexander, *op. cit.,* pp. 261-62.

66. Van Buren, *op. cit.,* pp. 124-26.

67. Martin Van Buren to Charles E. Dudley, January 10, 1822, Van Buren Papers.

68. Van Buren, *op. cit.*, pp. 193-96.

69. Van Buren to Coleman, April 4, 1828, Van Buren Papers.

70. Van Buren to Nicholas, November 29, 1826, Van Buren Papers.

71. Van Buren to Thomas Ritchie of Virginia, January 13, 1827, Van Buren Papers. The best account of Martin Van Buren's role in the formation of a new national political alignment can be found in Robert V. Remini, *Martin Van Buren and the Making of the Democratic Party* (New York: Columbia University Press, 1959).

72. Wright to Flagg, December 20, 1827, Flagg Papers.

73. Van Buren to Benjamin Ruggles, August 26, 1824, Van Buren Papers.

74. George F. Dangerfield, *Era of Good Feelings* (New York: Harcourt, Brace, 1952), pp. 348-53.

VIII

POLITICS IN THE LIFE OF THE COMMUNITY

1. D. S. Alexander, *A Political History of the State of New York* (New York: Henry Holt and Company, 1906-23), I, 280.

2. Van Buren to Rufus King, January 19, 1820, King Papers.

3. Van Buren to Gorham Worth, June 1, 1820, Van Buren Papers.

4. Charles G. Haines to Clinton, May 29, 1820, Clinton Papers, Columbia University Library.

5. April 24, 1824.

6. *Albany Argus, Extra,* October 18, 1824.

7. *New York Statesman,* April 6, 1824.

8. October 10, 1824, Charles G. Haines, circular letter in support of De Witt Clinton.

9. Circular of the General Corresponding Committee, October 22, 1824, New York Public Library.

10. Henry Adams, *History of the United States* (New York: C. Scribner's Sons, 1889-91), I, 331-33.

11. Jabez D. Hammond, *The History of Political Parties in the State of New York* (Cooperstown: H. & E. Phinney, New York, 1845), I, 225-30.

12. Van Buren to John V. N. Yates, November 6, 1821, Miscellaneous Papers, New York State Library.

13. Quoted in Hammond, *op. cit.*, p. 87.

14. *Ibid.*, pp. 325, 332-33; M. M. Bagg, *The Pioneers of Utica* (Utica: Curtiss and Childs, 1877), pp. 158-60.

15. J. F. Seymour, *Centennial Address Delivered at Trenton, New York* (Utica: White and Floyd, 1877), pp. 27-29.

16. H. M. Morse, *Historic Old Rhinebeck* (Rhinebeck, 1908), pp. 239-45.

17. Storrs to Clay, September 23, 1824, Clay Papers, quoted in Robert V. Remini, "The Early Career of Martin Van Buren," (doctoral dissertation, Columbia University, 1951), pp. 451-52.

18. Richard P. McCormick, "Suffrage Classes and Party Alignments: A Study in Voter Behavior," *Mississippi Valley Historical Review*, XLVI (December, 1959), 404-08.

19. Everett to J. McLean, August 18, 1828, McLean Letters, LC, quoted in Shaw Livermore, *The Twilight of Federalism* (Princeton: Princeton University Press, 1962), pp. 266-67.

20. Livermore, *op. cit.*, p. 291.

21. Henry Adams, *op. cit.*, I, 112-13.

22. George Dangerfield, *Chancellor Robert R. Livingston of New York, 1746-1813* (New York: Harcourt, Brace, & Company, 1960), p. 6.

23. *Ibid.*, p. 300.

24. *Ibid.*, pp. 39, 249-54.

25. E. W. Spaulding, *New York in the Critical Period* (New York: Columbia University Press, 1932), pp. 192-231.

26. Rufus King to Christopher Gore, November 9, 1821, Charles R. King, ed., *The Life and Correspondence of Rufus King* (New York: G. P. Putnam's Sons, 1898), VI, 423-24; Peter A. Jay to John Jay, November 15, 1821, H. P. Johnston, ed., *The Correspondence and Public Papers of John Jay* (New York: G. P. Putnam's Sons, 1890-93), IV, 455.

27. Rufus King to Christopher Gore, February 9, 1823, King, *op. cit.*, VI, 500.

28. Livermore, *op. cit.*, pp. 177-79, 180-82.

29. Philip Schuyler to John Jay, July 3, 1777, Johnston, *op. cit.*, I, 146.

30. Walter Livingston, to John Carter Teviotdale, August 11, 1777, Walter Livingston Letter Books, RRLP, as quoted in Dangerfield, *op. cit.*, pp. 97-98.

31. John Woodworth, *Reminiscences of Troy, 1790-1807* (Albany: J. Munsell, 1807), p. 44.

IX

NEW YORK AND THE REST OF THE UNION

1. Walter R. Fee, *The Transition from Aristocracy to Democracy in New Jersey* (Somerville: Somerset Press, 1933), p. 114.

2. *Ibid.,* p. 115.

3. Phillip S. Klein, *Pennsylvania Politics, A Game without Rules, 1812-1832* (Philadelphia: Historical Society of Pennsylvania, 1940), p. 195.

4. Chilton Williamson, *American Suffrage from Property to Democracy* (Princeton: Princeton University Press, 1960), pp. 188-90.

5. Henry J. Ford, *The Rise and Growth of American Politics* (New York: The Macmillan Company, 1898), p. 152.

6. Arthur B. Darling, *Political Changes in Massachusetts, 1824-1828* (New Haven: Yale University Press, 1925), pp. 24-29.

7. Quoted in Richard P. McCormick, *The History of Voting in New Jersey* (New Brunswick: Rutgers University Press, 1953), p. 98; Albert Ray Newsome, *The Presidential Election of 1824 in North Carolina* (Chapel Hill: University of North Carolina Press, 1939), pp. 65-71; Williamson, *op. cit.,* p. 146.

8. Klein, *op. cit.,* pp. 48-51, 110-11.

9. Fee, *op. cit.,* pp. 100-21.

10. McCormick, *op. cit.,* pp. 100-01; Fee, *op. cit.,* pp. 215-18.

11. Williamson, *op. cit.,* pp. 172, 175, 179.

12. Charles G. Sellers, "Banking and Politics in Jackson's Tennessee," *Mississippi Valley Historical Review,* XLI (June, 1954), 63; Williamson, *op. cit.,* pp. 145, 152.

13. Klein, *op. cit.,* p. 195; Newsome, *op. cit.,* p. 34; McCormick, *op. cit.,* pp. 101-04, 107-09.

14. Fee, *op. cit.,* pp. 17, 39.

15. Alex Hayes to George Wolf, November 9, 1829, Wolf Papers, as quoted in Klein, *op. cit.,* p. 70.

16. *Democratic Press,* October 18, 1816, *Lancaster Weekly Journal,* May 12, 1817, as quoted in *ibid.,* p. 70.

17. Quoted in *ibid.,* p. 101, from William Rawle's Journal, I, p. 26.

18. Fee, *op. cit.,* pp. 114-15.

19. The law was repealed by the Republicans in 1813. (Fee, pp. 93-96, 120, 183-85.)

20. *Lancaster Weekly Journal,* June 6, 1820, as quoted in Klein, *op. cit.,* p. 107. See also Klein, pp. 79-82.

21. *Ibid.,* pp. 194-95.

22. Ford, *op. cit.*, p. 152.

23. Newsome, *op. cit.*, pp. 63-64, 137.

24. C. J. Ingersoll to Richard Rush, February 23, 1817, W. M. Meigs, *Life of Charles J. Ingersoll* (Philadelphia: J. B. Lippincott & Company, 1897), p. 106, as quoted in Klein, *op. cit.*, p. 94.

25. William H. Crawford to Albert Gallatin, April 23, 1817, Henry Adams, *Writings of Gallatin* (Philadelphia: J. B. Lippincott & Company, 1897), II, 37.

26. Eugene H. Roseboom, "Ohio in the Presidential Election of 1824," *Ohio Archeological and Historical Quarterly*, XXVI (April, 1917), 168, 170-77.

27. Fee, *op. cit.*, pp. 238-39.

28. *Ibid.*, pp. 164, 167-68.

29. *Centinel of Freedom*, February 11, 1806, as quoted in Fee, *op. cit.*, pp. 144-46.

30. *Ibid.*, pp. 238-39.

31. *Ibid.*, pp. 146-48, 228, 242.

32. Darling, *op. cit.*, pp. 3, 12-13, 21-22, 34-35.

33. *Ibid.*, pp. 3, 13-14, 42-43.

34. Richard McCormick, "Suffrage Classes and Party Alignments," *Mississippi Valley Historical Review*, XLVI (December, 1959), 401-03.

35. Newsome, *op. cit.*, pp. 10-15, 32-33, 42.

36. Darling, *op. cit.*, pp. 38-46.

37. *Ibid.*, pp. 51-53.

38. *Ibid.*, pp. 62-64.

39. Fee, *op. cit.*, pp. 89-90.

40. *Ibid.*, pp. 223-25, 244-46.

41. *Ibid.*, pp. 249-59, 263-67.

42. Charles G. Sellers, "Banking and Politics in Jackson's Tennessee; *Mississippi Valley Historical Review*, XLI (June, 1954), 62, 84.

43. Newsome, *op. cit.*, pp. 147-48.

44. Roseboom, *op. cit.*, pp. 157-62, 179, 182-83, 194, 206-07.

45. Klein, *op. cit.*, pp. 34-38.

46. J. R. Pole, "Suffrage and Representation in Maryland from 1776 to 1810: A Statistical Note and Some Reflections," *Journal of Southern History*, XXIV (May, 1958), 218-24.

47. McCormick, *The History of Voting in New Jersey*, pp. 100-01; J. R. Pole, "Suffrage in New Jersey, 1790-1807," *Proceedings of the New Jersey Historical Society*, LXXI (January, 1953), 39-61.

48. Ford, *op. cit.*, p. 167.

49. Pole, "Suffrage and Representation in Maryland," p. 222.

50. Pole, "Suffrage in New Jersey, 1790-1807," pp. 40-48.

51. Robert Brown, *Middle-Class Democracy and the Revolution in Massachusetts* (Ithaca: Cornell University Press, 1955), *passim;* J. R. Pole, "Suffrage and Representation in Massachusetts: A Statistical Note," *William and Mary Quarterly,* 3rd Series, XIV (October, 1957), 560-92.

52. John S. Bassett, "Suffrage in the State of North Carolina (1776-1861)," *Annual Report of the American Historical Association, 1895* (Washington, 1896), pp. 271-85; John W. Corr, "The Manhood Suffrage Movement in North Carolina," *Historical Papers of the Trinity College Historical Society* (Durham, 1915) XI, 47-78; J. G. de Roulbac Hamilton, *Party Politics in North Carolina, 1835-1860* (Chapel Hill: The Seeman Printery, 1916), pp. 77, 84, 117-21.

53. Neil Andrews, *The Development of the Nominating Convention in Rhode Island* (Providence: Rhode Island Historical Society Publications, 1893), *passim;* M. Ostrogorski, "The Rise and Fall of the Nominating Caucus," *American Historical Review,* V (January, 1900), 253-83.

54. *Lancaster Weekly Journal,* July 15, 1818, quoted in Klein, *op. cit.,* p. 57.

55. *Lancaster Weekly Journal,* May 21, 1817, quoted in *ibid.,* p. 91.

56. Williamson, *op. cit.,* pp. 183-84.

57. Ostrogorski, *op. cit.,* pp. 273, 278, 280.

58. Herman Hailperin, "Pro-Jackson Sentiment in Pennsylvania, 1820-1828," *Pennsylvania Magazine of History and Biography,* I (July, 1926), 198.

59. Quoted in Klein, *op. cit.,* p. 150.

60. *Delaware Patron,* March 4, 1824, as quoted in Roseboom, *op. cit.,* pp. 179-80.

61. *Columbus Gazette,* February 26, 1824, as quoted in *ibid.,* p. 180; Newsome, *op. cit.,* p. 197.

62. Hailperin, *op. cit.,* p. 197.

63. *Stuebenville Gazette,* August 2, 1823, as quoted in Roseboom, *op. cit.,* p. 166.

64. Newsome, *op. cit.,* pp. 10-15, 32-33, 42.

65. Fee, *op. cit.,* pp. 160, 230-32, 236-39.

66. Hailperin, *op. cit.,* p. 198.

67. Darling, *op. cit.,* pp. 2-3.

68. Newsome, *op. cit.,* p. v.

69. J. R. Pole, "Election Statistics in North Carolina to 1861," *Journal of Southern History,* XXIV (May, 1958), 225-28.

70. Richard McCormick, "New Perspectives in Jacksonian Politics," *American Historical Review*, LXI (January, 1960), 280-301.

71. Newsome, *op. cit.*, p. 57.

72. *Ibid.*, p. 155.

73. November 30, 1824, as quoted in Newsome, *op. cit.*, p. 158.

74. Roseboom, *op. cit.*, p. 160.

75. *Ibid.*, pp. 214-15.

76. Fee, *op. cit.*, p. 227.

77. Darling, *op. cit.*, pp. 55-64.

78. All of the conclusions of this paragraph are based on an analysis of Table I of Richard McCormick's article, "New Perspectives on Jacksonian Politics," p. 292.

79. *Ibid.*, pp. 295-96.

80. Roseboom, *op. cit.*, p. 175.

81. Quoted in Newsome, p. 104.

82. September 17, 1824, quoted in *ibid.*, p. 145.

83. *Ibid.*

84. *Ibid.*, pp. 116-18.

85. *Ibid.*, pp. 100-01.

86. Thomas R. Hay, ed., "Calhoun-Fisher Correspondence," *North Carolina Historical Review*, VII (1930), 478.

87. Richard McCormick, "New Perspectives on Jacksonian Politics," pp. 293 ff.

88. Hailperin, *op. cit.*, p. 200.

89. Quoted in Klein, *op. cit.*, p. 161; see also pp. 159-60.

90. Fee, *op. cit.*, pp. 257-58.

91. Quoted in Newsome, *op. cit.*, p. 130.

92. Roseboom, *op. cit.*, pp. 163, 168, 181-82, 186, 188.

93. Klein, pp. 168-69, 202.

94. Roseboom, *op. cit.*, pp. 188, 204.

95. *New Jersey Eagle*, July 18, 1828, quoted in Fee, *op. cit.*, p. 263.

96. *Centinel of Freedom*, September 30, 1828, quoted in *ibid.*, p. 265.

X

CONCLUSIONS

1. Allan Nevins, "The Telling of a Nation's Story," *The New York Times Book Review* (February 16, 1958), p. 1.

GLOSSARY

Albany Regency: the governing clique of the Bucktail Party during the 1820's that exercised virtually absolute control over patronage and party policy.

Bucktails: the Republicans in New York state who opposed De Witt Clinton. The name arose from a custom observed by the members of the Tammany Society, the group that formed the core of Clinton's enemies, whereby they hung the tails of deer in their hats at public meetings.

Coodies: a name coined by De Witt Clinton to describe Federalists opposed to him. The title sprang from the pseudonym "Abimelech Coody," which Gulian C. Verplanck, the leader of the Federalists, employed in pamphlets satirizing Clinton.

Council of Appointment: a body consisting of the governor and one senator chosen annually from each of New York's four senatorial districts in which the state constitution of 1777 vested the power of naming officials to fill the overwhelming majority of the Empire State's nonelective posts.

Council of Revision: a body consisting of the governor, the chancellor, and the judges of the state supreme court, which had the power under the Constitution of 1777 to veto legislation. A two-thirds majority of each house of the legislature was required to override the Council's veto.

The Hero: one of the many nicknames for Andrew Jackson that emphasize his qualities of courage and heroism.

High-minded Federalists: a sarcastic description by De Witt Clinton of Federalists who opposed him. It grew out of a public statement promulgated by these Federalists in which they accused Clinton of surrounding himself with sycophants "disgusting to the feelings of all truly high-minded and honorable men."

Lewisites: a Republican faction during the first decade of the nineteenth century whose members supported Morgan Lewis for governor.

Magnus Apollo: a nickname for De Witt Clinton that lays stress on his lordly and majestic manner.

Martling Men: a political faction of the Empire State that arose in protest over the Clintonian-Burrite union of 1806. The group, which consisted primarily of members of the Tammany Society, derived its name from Abraham Martling, a Tammany sachem, in whose tavern their meetings took place.

People's Party: a Republican political faction in New York state that came into being as a protest against the Bucktail opposition in 1824 to the selection of presidential electors by the people and to the abrogation of the legislative caucus as a method of nominating candidates for public office. This party was also the vehicle that restored De Witt Clinton to the governorship in 1824.

Quids: another name for the Lewisites, or adherents of Morgan Lewis. The term is probably short for "tertium quid," which suggests a third element, an additional political faction.

Tammany Society: a social and benevolent organization transformed by George Clinton and Aaron Burr during the late 1790's into an effective political machine. During the early nineteenth century, it became estranged from De Witt Clinton, and formed the core of his opposition in the Empire State.

Washington Benevolent Society: an organization formed by the Federalists in 1808 to compete with the Tammany Society in promoting conviviality among its members, providing financial help for those in need, and solidifying political loyalties to the Federalist Party.

NOTE ON SOURCES

Although the judgments of this volume are based for the most part on an examination of primary sources, I do not claim to have utilized documents that have been hitherto unknown or unused by other students of the period. I do maintain, however, that a careful, thorough, and complete reading of the sources yields interpretations quite different from those that have prevailed about this era until quite recently. The manuscript collections of New York's leading politicians, upon which I have relied, give an intimate portrait of the decisive political moves of the time along with the calculations of the movers. The most important of these collections are the De Witt Clinton Papers, Columbia University Library, New York Public Library; the Azariah C. Flagg Papers, Columbia University Library, New York Public Library; Rufus King Papers, New York Historical Society; John W. Taylor Papers, New York Historical Society, New York Public Library; Martin Van Buren Papers, Columbia University Library (on microfilm), New York Historical Society; Stephen Van Rensselaer Papers, New York Historical Society; Gulian C. Verplanck Papers, New York Historical Society; and Silas Wright Papers, New York Public Library. The Martin Van Buren Papers disclose the always clever, often brilliant, designs of a shrewd, wily, and dedicated political leader. The Flagg Papers and the Wright Papers are particularly useful for understanding the political problems of the time and the response of the newly emerging brand of professional politicians.

The newspapers of the period because of their frank partisan identification are also excellent records of New York's political activities and the attempted manipulation of public opinion. *The Albany Argus* with its Bucktail bias, the *Albany Daily Advertiser,* which was pro-Clinton, and the *New York American,* which supported the Anti-Bucktails who also disliked Clinton, are the most revealing periodicals for the student of this era. In addition, the *Albany Gazette* from 1819 to 1824, the *Independent Whig* for 1824, the *National Intelligencer* from 1824 to 1828, the *New York Evening Post* from 1802 to 1824, the *New York Statesman* from 1823 to 1824, *Nile's Weekly Register* from 1819 to 1824, and the *Rochester Telegraph* from 1819 to 1820 also proved quite illuminating. Other valuable sources include the New York Public Library's rich collection of political pamphlets and broadsides; the published correspondence and writings of John Quincy Adams, Albert Gallatin, De Witt Clinton, Thomas Jefferson, Andrew Jackson, Martin Van Buren, James A. Hamilton, John Jay, James Kent, Rufus King, Benjamin Franklin Butler, Jesse Hoyt, Gouverneur Morris, Gulian C. Verplanck, and Thurlow Weed; the *Annals of Congress* from 1821 to 1825; the *Journal of the Assembly and Senate of New York* from 1812 to 1828; and Nathaniel H. Carter and William L. Stone's *Reports of the Proceedings and Debates of the Convention of 1821.*

I have also attempted to utilize all of the secondary materials related to the subject of this study. Recent revival of interest in the early political development of this country has produced a number of significant monographs that I have found quite useful. The work of Lee Benson, Richard McCormick, Marvin Meyers, Robert V. Remini, and Chilton Williamson has been particularly important. I have tried in the footnotes to the manuscript to cite as fully as possible at the appropriate points the numerous sources—both primary and secondary—upon which the findings of this study rest.

I believe that our understanding of New York politics in this early period would be deepened by new biographical studies on such governmental leaders in the Empire State as Azariah C. Flagg, William L. Marcy, and Benjamin Knower, to name only a few. A definitive biography of De Witt Clinton still remains unaccomplished. Our knowledge of the emergence of political democracy in this country as a whole would be greatly broadened if systematic studies of the individual states after the pattern of this one were to be undertaken by other scholars.

INDEX

Adams, John Quincy: attitude of Bucktails toward, 67; courted Federalist support in 1824, 118; antagonism of Van Buren toward, 130-31; chosen as President by the House in 1824, 139

Agriculture, improvement of, 103-04, 175

Albany Regency: on electoral reform, 12; function of, 33-34; formed statewide machine, 56

Allen, Henry, 88

Allen, Peter, 88

Antifederalists, genesis of, 4

Antimasonic Party: supported nominating convention, 22; in election of 1828, 68; opposed to policies of Holland Land Company, 109

Antimasonry: effect on Bucktails, 125-27; genesis of, 125; consequences of, 126-27; as a political issue, 176

Armstrong, John, 115

Assembly: genesis of, 22-23; expansion of its powers, 23

Baldwin, Ebenezer: supported compulsory voting for all citizens, 124-25

Banks: incorporation of Manhattan Company, 95; nonpartisan issue, 95-97, 116, 175; struggle for control of Niagara

Bank, 96; some denied service to Republicans, 137

Bar, political role of, 58

Barbour, Philip B., 136

Barker, Jacob, 80

Barstow, Gamaliel, 110

Benson, Judge Egbert, 96

Bowne, Walter, 79

Brasher, Philip, 78, 128

Bucktails: provided unity in government, 11; conflict with Clintonians, 24; social and economic background of, 26-27; in presidential campaign of 1824, 62; support of William Crawford, 66; ignored national politics in 1825, 67; refrained from endorsing a vice-presidential candidate in 1828, 71-72; relation to Federalists, 77-78, 80-81, 114-16, 117-18, 174; opposed negro suffrage, 85; on democratic reform, 87-92, 174; at Constitutional Convention of 1821, 89-90; supported Andrew Jackson, 90-92, 122; backed charter of Chautuqua County Bank, 93, 97; "noncommittal" on tariff, 97-98; on internal improvements, 100, 102; on manufacturing, 102-03; on improvement of agriculture, 103-04; on land policy, 104-09, 175; used "Republican" caption, 112-13; venerated